The
J. Abrams
Book

THE LIFE AND WORK OF AN EXCEPTIONAL PERSONALITY

J. Abrams-Buch

Edited by
El Centro Cultural Israelita de México

Printed by
La Voz Israelita de México
Pedro Moreno 129, México D. F.
1956

English translation by Ruth Murphy
© 2016 Rebecca Nestle

TRANSLATOR'S NOTES:
Whenever possible, the following spelling conventions have been used:
1. Names of locations are given in English. When not in English, the spellings will be given in Yiddish, Russian or other languages as dictated by the text.
2. Ukrainian street names are given the modern Ukrainian spellings.
3. Jewish names with Russian pronunciation retain the Russian transliteration.
4. Yiddish names are given the YIVO[1] transliteration spelling.
5. If the non-Yiddish spelling of a name is unknown, the name is spelled per the Yiddish using YIVO transliteration spelling.
6. Historical dates are given per the Gregorian calendar.

---

1 The YIVO (Yiddish: Yidisher Visnshaftlekher Institut) Institute for Jewish Research.

*This translation is dedicated to
Jack Abrams' cousins, particularly
Ron Radosh, Ida Abrams,
her grandchildren
Charles and Rebecca Nestle,
and her son Manuel Nestle on
the occasion of his 87th birthday.*

1 May 2016

FOR THE THIRD ANNIVERSARY OF HIS DEATH

J. Abrams 1886—1953

Contents

From the Publisher 1
   Joseph Spivak: *The Life's Journey of Jacob Abrams* 3
   M. Rubinstein: *J. Abrams and His Role in Jewish Mexico* 13
   The Last Words of J. Abrams 25
   The Funeral of Jacob Abrams 27
   Mary Abrams: *An Interesting Episode During Jack's First Years in Mexico* 29
   Joseph Paul: *Jacob Abrams in Temple University Hospital* 32
   Mollie Steimer: *To Twenty Years in Prison* 35
   Courageous and Brave 40

J. Abrams—The Person, Friend, and Fighter 48
   Isaac Berliner: *J. Abrams A"H* 49
   Salomon Kahan: *1. His Faith Was Mankind* 52
   Salomon Kahan: *2. J. Abrams—The Oppositionist* 54
   Augustin Zukhi: *J. Abrams—The Idealist* 56
   M. Rubinstein: *A Human Being* 58
   J. Pat: *Friend Abrams* 61
   Julian Gorkin: *The Perfect Human Being* 65
   Sh. Tsfas: *One Who Storms, One Who Fights* 68
   Dr. Yehoshua Ustri-Din: *Like a Hero from a Romance Novel* 71

The Writings of Jacob Abrams—Autobiographical Fragments 73
   Chapter 1: *Without a Childhood* 74
   Chapter 2: *My First Contact with the Underground Movement* 102
   Chapter 3: *Odessa* 111
   Chapter 4: *Back in Uman* 128

Five Years in Soviet Russia *(Deep Conviction and Bitter Disappointment)* ...135

Portraits 278
   The Rebel Berkman 279
   Vera Figner 282
   Otto and Alice Rühle 287
   Carlo Tresca 291
   Clara Green 293
   Last Words and Thoughts 295

From the Publisher

... He was a man and is no more—may his memory live on and serve as a good example.

The Jewish Cultural Center in Mexico considers it a great honor and as an especially pleasant duty to publish the *J. Abrams Book*—in order to immortalize the memory of one of their enthusiastic activists, one of the pioneers and shapers of the Jewish community in Mexico, one of the builders of its culture and one of its public educators, and who with his performance during more than a quarter century affected and influenced for the good his society—one of those who left his mark on society as a whole and strove to give it an ideal shape:

JACOB ABRAMS

J. Abrams[2] was one of the popular, if not the more well known, community leaders in Jewish Mexico from the beginning years of the formation of the Jewish community until its complete evolution as a community. He arrived in the new land already ripe in years and although here he had to conduct a completely different genre of social-political activity than in Europe and North America; he nevertheless inserted in his public activities the belief in a better society and the aspiration to justice, which was a part of his character.

Published in the *J. Abrams Book* are commentarial pieces by J. Abrams himself assembled from his published materials and writings he left behind, memoirs from friends and comrades, and testimonials to his personality by writers and colleagues.

To all authors who have taken part in this book and all friends in Mexico and abroad who made possible its publication—we express our thanks. May their and our reward be that this work serves as a living monument to the beautiful image of the unforgettable ABRAMS—whose entire life was permeated by the belief in the struggle for a more beautiful world.

HONOR HIS MEMORY!
JEWISH CULTURAL CENTER OF MEXICO

---

[2] Yiddish spelling: Yankev Eybrams = Y. Eybrams = J. Abrams.

JOSEPH SPIVAK

The Life's Journey of Jacob Abrams

Jacob Abrams came to America in 1908. He was then twenty-two years old and had been brought over by his sister, Manye. When their mother had died sometime around 1891, Yankele[3] was not yet five years old. From then on, during the course of more than seventeen years, he suffered hunger and want. The only bit of joy in his life was his sister Manye, who was devoted to him like a mother. In 1906, Manye came to America. She quickly began working and saved a cent here and there until she succeeded in bringing Yankele to her. At the same time, Manye herself was not in the best of situations. Although she was always lively and cheerful, she had heart disease. The life with her stepmother—the shrew—in her father's house had eaten away at her heart.

Since my acquaintanceship with Jacob Abrams came through his sister, Manye, I will begin there.

How I Met the Abramovskis[4]

Although I come from the same city as did the Abramovskis—from Uman—I had never met them there and it was first here, in America, that I became acquainted with them.

In 1905, I lived through the pogrom[5] and also the revolutionary uprising in our city. Uman had many students and the revolutionary parties there were extremely active. At the time of the uprising the city theater was open day and night; revolutionary speeches were being given there the entire time. I was greatly inspired by this, although I hadn't joined any particular party. When I came to America in 1906, I organized the Uman Revolutionary Circle here with the goal of raising support for the revolutionary parties in Uman. Our circle was very popular among the young people from Uman and when Manye Abramovski came to America, she soon joined the circle.

---

3   Yiddish: diminutive for Yankev (Jacob).
4   In Russia, the Abrams' family name was Abramovski; his sister Manye kept this last name in America.
5   There were two pogroms in Uman in 1905: one was 6 August that is described in this text, and the other was 3 November, with four Jews killed and fifty wounded.

Manye had an intelligent face with large, sad eyes. Her personality evoked respect from every person. Everybody was in love with her.

Our circle later decided to join with the Workman's Circle.[6] As all members were required to be examined by a doctor, Manye, because of her heart condition, couldn't become a member of the Workman's Circle. However, she remained a local member in our organization.

I was the branch health officer. My assignment was to visit members during times of sickness and do whatever was possible to help them. One day, the branch doctor let me know that Manye Abramovski had suffered a heart attack. I lived in New York (Manhattan) and Manye—in Brownsville (Brooklyn). Nonetheless, I quickly left to see how Manye was doing. Manye lived alone in a room. No one knew that she was ill and none of her friends had visited her. I was the first person to come see her.

Manye had always had a spotless appearance but now, after several days of being sick, her face had become pale and her dark eyes—softer. When I entered her room, it seemed to me that a goddess lay there in bed, the glory of God reflected in her face. From then on, I never left her sickbed. My interest in her became more than just as a friend. I watched over her until she got better and was out of bed.

I became strongly attached to her and later, she to me, and soon after that, Manye consented to be my wife.

Until that time, I didn't know Jacob, Manye's brother, very well. Only after Manye became my wife did I become closely acquainted with Jacob. I also met Manye's uncle and aunt (Esther Kretshmer), who had brought the Abramovskis to America. Esther Kretshmer had always been a bright light in Yankele's life. Back in Uman, when Jacob would get tired of sleeping on the floor at his stepmother's house—or just in the street— or when he could no longer endure the hunger he suffered, he would go to Aunt Esther. He couldn't get much to eat there because she was very poor; however, he always got a piece of bread with onion and for him, this was enough. Of a much greater value to him than food was, naturally, the motherly affection and closeness that Esther showed him—something that he never found at his father's house.

---

6   Yiddish: Der Arbeter Ring, an American Jewish nonprofit organization first formed in 1900 by Yiddish-speaking Jewish immigrants from Eastern Europe.

Here in America, Esther Kretshmer also played an important role in Jacob's life. When he came to America, he stayed at her house. Esther was very poor. Her husband, a teacher back home, fancied himself an aristocrat. He tried unsuccessfully to make a living at various things and his occupation was now washing out old, used medicine bottles and selling them to druggists. This brought in very little money and the aunt had to help out with the earnings. They lived in three rooms on Cherry Street on the East Side in an old, dilapidated house. There the Kretshmers lived with their four children, and Yankele also lived there with them when he came to America.

Mary Damski and Jack Abrams

If Jacob had difficulties then in finding a way to make a living, he had no problem at all finding opportunities to express his young revolutionary spirit. Wherever there was a strike or a workers' assembly, Yankele was there. Wherever there was a radical lesson, Yankele joined in the discussion and there gave his viewpoint. There was no lack of strikes or assemblies during 1910, when the needle-trades workers went through their historical revolutionary period. Yankele was everywhere. Here he gave lectures at gatherings of striking workers, there he stood in the picket line, and he soon became very popular with the striking workers. In one of these picket lines he also met Mary Damski, who later became his faithful life companion.

Mary Damski came to America in 1909 and soon started working at the Tuttleman Brothers factory, where blouses were made. In 1910 when a large strike broke out in the needle trades, one in which eighty thousand workers took part, Mary was also one of the strikers. On the picket lines as well as at the meetings, she met a young man who made a strong impression on her. Later she again met this young man at a meeting at the Cooper Union where Leon Deutsch, the secretary of the International Ladies Garment Workers Union,[7] gave a speech. Mary and Jacob became close friends and subsequently they would often go together to assemblies where Emma Goldman and other anarchists were speaking.

After the strike, Mary Damski lost her job with the Tuttlemans and began working at the Triangle Company. During the great fire in which over

---

7   The International Ladies' Garment Workers' Union (ILGWU).

a hundred girls perished in the Triangle Fire,[8] Mary was one of those rescued. When Jack (Jacob Abrams) was told of it, he quickly went to her and found her in hysterics after the tragedy. He calmed her and at that time they decided to become man and wife.

Jacob Abrams had had very little joy in his life, but on the first of May 1911, he walked into the room that he and Mary had rented for their shared home. This was the happiest moment of his life. His sister Manye and I had decorated the room with flowers and when he came in that evening, he became so exuberant that he began dancing with joy. It seems to me that back then, there was no happier couple on earth than Jack and Mary. Mary gave herself over to Abrams with her entire soul. It is hard to imagine that a woman could adore a man and be as devoted as Mary was to Jacob Abrams.

They both worked and earned enough for their daily needs. After work they would both go to meetings, assemblies and lessons. Mary was active in the needle trades union and Jack had then become active in the bookbinders union, with which he was associated for a long time. He also took part in different anarchist groups. Abrams found sympathy everywhere and with everyone, and became very popular among his friends. Jacob Abrams was of a restless and sincere revolutionary nature, and he did not let an opportunity pass by to help out in movements of a revolutionary character.

When America Enters the World War

When America entered the First World War and enacted the general conscription law, all the radical socialists as well as anarchists raised a protest against the law. Among the anarchists who fought against the law were Emma Goldman and Alexander Berkman, the heads of the movement. The *Mother Earth*,[9] the monthly journal put out by Emma Goldman, came out that month with a black front cover as a sign of mourning for American freedom. On the Jewish East Side, a group was organized against the war, the Anti-Conscription League, and opened offices on 173 East Broadway.

---

8   The Triangle Shirtwaist Factory fire in 1911: one of the deadliest in US history, it took the lives of 146 garment workers, the majority of them young, recently-arrived Jewish and Italian immigrant women.

9   *Mother Earth*: anarchist journal self-described as "A Monthly Magazine Devoted to Social Science and Literature," edited by Emma Goldman.

There enrolled all those who were principled against the war. The director of the group was A. Zogenstein; I was the secretary. The movement was very popular. Day and night, lines of young people lay siege to the office and signed up as members. Jacob Abrams was very active in the anti-war movement; he became Emma Goldman's right hand. He was the chairman at all her gatherings and one of the speakers. At one of the assemblies that the League had arranged at the large *Forward*[10] hall a large crowd was in attendance, with hundreds more outside who couldn't get in the full hall. Jacob Abrams was also one of the speakers that evening. When the meeting had already been going on for about an hour, policemen entered the hall under the leadership of Marshal McCarthy and halted the gathering. The police selected all the young people between the ages of eighteen and thirty-five—three hundred people in total—and detained them; the remainder left the hall. When those gathered in the street found out about this, it became a huge commotion. Several thousand people then gathered in the street and also in the park surrounding the *Forward* building. Meanwhile, we, Abrams and I, began vigorously protesting to the police for detaining citizens without a warrant. This prevailed; the police only took the addresses of those detained and let everyone go. When Abrams and I went out into the street, the thousand-strong crowd met us with thunderous applause.

Feverish activity was going on during that time in the radical circles, and Jacob Abrams stood in the very center of this activity.

U.S. vs. Jack Abrams

When the revolution in Russia overthrew the Tsarist government and the Bolsheviks withdrew from the war and concluded a separate peace with Germany, fourteen governments sent soldiers to the Russian border. Among the fourteen was also the United States government. This created a storm of protest among the radical elements in North America. Russia was the great hope of the entire revolutionary and radical world. As Emma Goldman expressed when she was being expelled from the country: "We go now to the east, where the sun rises." In those days, this is how all freedom-loving people felt about revolutionary Russia.

---

10   Yiddish *Forverts*: American newspaper first published in New York City as a Yiddish-language paper.

Abrams and his small group of young men and women didn't let the opportunity pass by and began distributing leaflets in which they attacked the actions of the government. However, printing shops refused to print such material because it was illegal. Abrams and his group then organized their own underground printing shop and they inundated New York with anti-government leaflets. Everyone had the impression that this was a large group with much potential, since they could distribute such a large amount of literature. The people from Abrams' group would go up on the rooftops of high buildings and from there toss down the forbidden literature. From this a rumor spread that the group even had its own aircraft. The police were desperate, because their best detectives couldn't find out anything. In the group was a new recruit, Hyman Rosansky, who was inexperienced in doing illegal work and the police caught him distributing the leaflets. In the police precinct, he was beaten mercilessly. He couldn't hold out and gave up the entire group. Everyone was arrested. Later some of them were released, but Jack Abrams, Hyman Lachowsky, Sam Lipman, Jacob Schwartz[11] and Molly Steimer remained locked up in jail. The arrestees were beaten cruelly and one of them, Jacob Schwartz, who had a bad heart, died from the blows even before he was taken before the court. The four remaining arrestees and also Rosanky were tried. The trial, which was entitled *The Trial of the United States vs. Jack Abrams*, was one of the most sensational court trials in the history of the United States. The courthouse was packed with spectators and the newspapers gave out all the details of the trial. The attacks by the accused against the government for sending troops against revolutionary Russia made a huge impression.

The sentence passed by the court was: for the three accused men—Abrams, Lipman and Lachowsky—twenty years; and for Molly Steimer, fifteen years imprisonment. Nonetheless, regardless of the harsh prison sentences, the convicted prisoners had accomplished what they had set out to do. The propaganda that had been spread across the country during the trial forced the government to withdraw the American soldiers from the Russian border. Jack's arrest and sentencing was a horrific blow for Mary. Her close friends feared that she wouldn't be able to get through it. However, she

---

11   Translator's note: Spivak refers to Jacob Schwartz by the Yiddish men's name "Yurke" (Yurke Schwartz).

stayed courageous and continued the work of her beloved Jackie. She also helped organize the defense committee for the liberation of Abrams and his friends. The same defense committee later conducted propaganda to reduce the sentence. After the group had served two years in prison, the government agreed to release them on the condition that they leave for Russia and should they ever want to return to America, they would have to serve out the remaining eighteen years of their sentence.

The fourth of December 1921, Jacob Abrams, Hyman Lachowsky, Sam Lipman and Molly Steimer arrived in Russia. Abrams soon became involved in anarchist work. He was employed there at a bookbindery. Subsequently he was made a manager of a large laundry—a job he had learned in the American prison. When I met with Abrams in Mexico in 1946, he described to me in detail the misery inflicted on him by the Bolsheviks. The laundry of which he was manager was rife with theft and fraud, and when he complained about this to a high official, he was punished for it.

While he was in Russia, one day Abrams had received a guest. His father had found out that his Yankele was a big shot in Moscow and came to see him. Abrams, although he bore a grudge against his father, received him amiably.

After Abrams and Mary had been in Russia five years, they succeeded in extricating themselves, leaving Russia at the end of 1926. They spent over a year in Germany and France until they managed to receive a visa for Mexico. In 1927, they arrived in Mexico.

Abrams' sister, Manye, had undergone some difficult times. Her heart became worse every day. Above all, the arrest and sentencing of her brother had a detrimental effect on her state of health. During the time that Abrams was in prison, she had to go to California: the doctors said that the air there would be better for her heart. Meanwhile, being so far away, she didn't have the chance to see her brother before he was deported to Russia. When we found out that Abrams and Mary intended to leave Russia, Manye was full of hope that she would now have a chance to see them. We began making plans and saving money to meet them in Mexico. Yet Manye's dream was not to come true: her ailing heart couldn't hold out for such a long time and in 1925, she died. In her last letter, written the day before she died, more than anything else she lamented the fact that she would not be able to see Jack and Mary.

Abrams in Mexico

In Mexico, a new epoch began in Abram's life. There was no anarchist movement there, at least none of any significance. The language was foreign to him and he felt distressed. He must have activity, and thus he was drawn to the Jewish cultural movement. He began working with groups that were close to his own ideology and also, little by little, started to approach groups of other people: Mexican and Spanish.

For thirty years, Abrams was active in the anti-fascist movement. This gave him the opportunity to display his organizational abilities and indeed, before long he became the president of the International Anti-Fascist Organization. The main task of the organization was to support refugees from fascist countries who wanted to come to Mexico.

Abrams was a contributor to several Yiddish newspapers and journals; for several years he was also the editor and publisher of a Yiddish newspaper in Mexico. There, with his active participation, the newspaper *The Time* was founded and he was also one of the first founders of the newspaper *The Voice*,[12] where for many years he was one of the main contributors. He published articles on political and cultural topics, and also a series of interesting portraits of revolutionary fighters. He was one of the spokesmen for the Mexican Jewish community, one of the directors of the Jewish Cultural Center and appeared on stage to give presentations and lessons on different subjects.

Abrams' Fatal Illness

In 1924, Abrams had a cracked skull in an automobile crash. From then on, the Abramses began to go downhill. In 1945, he started having problems with his throat. At first it was not taken seriously, but his throat issues worsened from day to day; it got harder for him to eat and speak. He was treated with radiation and had two operations, but nothing helped. The doctor who treated him said that at the Philadelphia Temple University Hospital could be found the only doctor who could help him.

Through much toil by prominent personalities in Mexico and America, the American government gave Abrams permission to go to the hospital, with one condition: that he be guarded by a marshal night and day for

---

12   Yiddish: *"Di Stime,"* Mexican-Yiddish newspaper.

the entire time that he was in American territory. He was admitted to the hospital in June 1952.

From right to left: Jacob and Mary Abrams; Joseph and Manye Spivak (Abrams' brother-in-law and sister) in their youth in New York

After spending a bit of time under the care of the specialist at Temple University Hospital, things seemed to be improved and he went back to Mexico. Yet later, the disease became worse and he was forced to go back to Philadelphia. In April 1953, Abrams returned to the hospital for the second time. This time he was there almost two months. He himself felt better, but his friends saw that the end was coming.

The first of June 1953, Abrams came back to Mexico. Many friends met him at the airport. Abrams was in a good mood, although the tragedy was immense. A man, who for his entire life had lived to debate and to talk, must now carry pen and paper so that he could write down everything that he wanted to say, because he had lost his voice after the operation at the hospital.

Several days later his situation became worse and Wednesday, 10 June 1953, at five-thirty in the afternoon, Jacob Abrams died at the age of sixty-seven. The tragedy of his death was greatest for his most devoted friend and wife, Mary. For her, Jackie had become her god, her entire life; what was there left to live for, when he was no more? For the last two critical years, she had been at his side day and night, never taking her eyes off him for a minute, and now—no more Yankele!

This is the way the curtain descended on a man who had lost his mother at four years old; was later kicked out of his father's house and left in the street; who had wandered from city to city, from country to country, never ceasing to strive for greater freedom and a better life for the human race.

M. RUBINSTEIN

J. Abrams and His Role in Jewish Mexico

"Abrams"—everyone knew him this way. Simply, Abrams.

His forename was known only by close friends, but all of Mexico knew Abrams.

He came here with the first great tide of immigration from Europe; the first time in the final months of 1925.

Abrams and his inseparable lifelong friend, Mary then lived in Berlin, where they had come after the disappointment with the Russian revolution. They wanted to return to the United States but because of his political crimes (see about this in other works of this same book), Abrams was not permitted to enter. Abrams went back to Germany and lived there two more years.

In 1927, he came to Mexico for the second time and settled here for good.

The Jewish community was still small then, numbering several hundred families, but these were the years when (owing to the difficulties with visas in North America) a large number of Jewish immigrants came to Mexico from Eastern Europe.

It was a hard life for the first immigrants during those early years; they consisted of mostly young people—people who were torn from the old country, who longed for it and brought from there the warmth and style of familiar life. They were inspired by ideals and with longing, and in the new world still felt inept and alien, barely managing to communicate in the new language and not yet knowing whether or how they would be able to get settled in Mexico. They had to withstand bouts of solitude and loneliness, but based on the example of the first immigrants who had worked their way up to a better life, hope was nourished for a better future.

In the calm and solitude of the newly sprouted Jewish community, people clung to each other and gathered together in the evenings at the couple of clubs that were already there (On Tacuba and Palma, on Bolivar and Cinco de Mayo) and dreamed dreams ...

Abrams showing up in the Jewish Mexico of that time was an event. A man had come with public zeal, with a political past behind him, with exuberant energy—and an orator as well!

His attire had already drawn everyone's attention.

Abrams the anarchist and revolutionary spirit did not keep to any kind of convention; in his style of dress he also looked different. He wore a short jacket, big wide shoes, a dark hat and no cravat, only a black bow …

His step was quick and he was perpetually in motion; a restlessness propelled him and he entered Jewish Mexico with this restlessness from the first day on. He quickly found friends in the radical group already existing here and overnight became its promoter and one of its leaders. Through this group and his own momentum, he also began to have influence within other circles (in "Young Men"—later the Cultural Center[13]). It was soon discovered that Abrams is an orator, a mass educator, a man who knows how to win over a crowd—and he becomes the first speaker at gatherings, gives presentations, and is the first to take the floor at meetings.

Abrams immediately makes friends in the new Jewish community and is on familiar terms with everybody. His first place of employment in the new country is unexpectedly in a photography establishment. His actual occupation is bookbinding or printing, but who can make use of such an occupation in Mexico? Everyone had become first peddlers and then traders and manufacturers. Abrams, however, had already been through a lifetime of experiences; in Moscow he directed the Kropotkin printing shop (in the honeymoon years after the revolution, when the anarchist and other revolutionary movements were not yet severely persecuted by the communist regime). He organized the automatic laundry in Russia; in Germany he was involved in similar enterprises. Photography was a beloved field of his and from being an amateur, he becomes a photographer (to this day Abrams' photograph "Rodin" still exists).

However, it was the printing shop that was in Abrams' blood. He was a specialist in printed material and loved to see how the books and journals would look under his experienced, professional eye. He very quickly becomes the proprietor of a printing shop in Mexico, and he created each enterprise with a partner. Abrams had a penchant for collaboration, because the business side of a venture was foreign to him. He both knew how and loved to

---

13   Likely refers to the Young Men's Hebrew Association in Mexico City, founded in 1917 and probably located in the Tacuba Street building. It later became the Jewish Cultural Center in Mexico. Now part of the historical center of Mexico City, Tacuba 15 was an important Jewish community, social and education center for nearly twenty years.

organize and establish new departments, install machines, build workrooms, re-organize, modify and modernize, and he donated much activity to this passion. It went from a small printing shop to a big one and later, an even bigger one; so they printed books and newspapers, and here Abrams also found a place to satisfy his personal goals through the printed word. If he himself didn't write stylish Yiddish, it didn't matter—his colleagues stylized his passionate writing for him; Abrams was passionate, effervescent and tempestuous as much in his speech as in his writing.

Abrams did not consider his business dealings as a goal in itself. They were a way to make a living—business was already good, and all his thoughts and free time he gave to the communal activities.

Not having been previously acquainted with Jewish community life (as can be seen from the works of his friend and brother-in-law Spivak and of Molly Steimer), he first became associated with it here in Mexico. Abrams was one of those people who had a lot of faith in himself—he "knew everything." He gave lectures on political topics or spoke even about "free love" or sexual issues. The young immigrant audience drank up the spoken word and there had only numbered a few who could give it to them. In those days (at the beginning of the thirties) Abrams filled halls with listeners, and we still remember that at the end of 1935 when Abrams had come back from a trip to Europe, the halls of 15 Tacuba were so packed for his lecture on his trip that it seemed the entire town had come to listen to him.

Abrams was one of those community activists who did it all: if someone needed to put on a play, he was the stage manager and an extra; with the youth, he would lead conversations in a secluded shop somewhere on Friday nights about social science and give lessons on political economy. Here in Jewish Mexico, it was the community activists of the younger generation who were his audience and adherents.

Generally, in the first ten years of his public activity, Abrams had a great number of admirers and with the organizations in which he was active, he always enjoyed a great deal of sympathy for his devotion to community matters and the unselfishness with which he attended to them. From the very beginning, he created a name for himself as a truth-and-justice-seeker, and people would turn to him whenever a wrong had been done to someone.

One of the characteristic occurrences was when a Jewish cemetery didn't want to bury a child from a poor family who had nothing with which to pay the burial fees. Abrams raised a ruckus and waged a "struggle" against the "backwards clericalism" of the "tax collectors," and he won the battle ... this was the first reaction against the old-fashioned manner of the Burial Society[14] and the public sided with Abrams, of course.

Immediately after his arrival in Mexico, Abrams, with his revolutionary fervor had already brought about a ... boycott against "Young Men." It was during the trial in the United States against Sacco and Vanzetti, in which the death sentence was passed.[15] People wanted to hold a protest meeting at "Young Men" with Abrams as the speaker but the management didn't want to allow it at their site. It became a quarrel and Abrams was forbidden to enter the locale. The radical group declared a boycott and it became very exciting in the city. The public at that time was after all, young and hotheaded; they fought and finally after a long struggle, gained the right for everyone to have access the club.

A separate chapter is Abrams' work in the area of the struggle against Nazism, from Mexico and outside of it, which was in fact the first anti-defamation work in Mexico.

Immediately after Hitler came to power in Germany in 1933, when fascist propaganda was carried across the world, Abrams established an anti-fascist committee, that through agitation led a boycott on merchandise from Nazi Germany and it also directed a large anti-Nazi education effort. Several times the committee published a large journal under the name of *In the Struggle* (edited by Salomon Kahan[16]); Mexican and Spanish activists from socialist camps were drawn to the activity and funds were gathered to support the anti-Nazi struggle in Europe. Abrams carried out this multi-faceted activity and his work in the matter became known on the general street. In 1935 Abrams received an anonymous letter, probably from reactionary circles, saying that "they would get even with him." It became a little too hot around the anti-fascist committee, and friends and comrades advised Abrams to take a trip to Europe until the red-hot atmosphere cooled down. At the end of the

---

14   Hebrew: Khevre Kedishe, traditional Jewish burial society that arranged funerals in accordance with Jewish law and custom.
15   Nicola Sacco and Bartolomeo Vanzetti: Italian-born U.S. anarchists convicted of murdering a guard and paymaster during a 1920 armed robbery of the Slater and Morrill Shoe Company.
16   Kahan, Salomon: Yiddish essayist and musicologist.

summer of 1935, Abrams and Mary left on a visit to Europe. They were in Lithuania and Poland, traveled incognito through Germany and stopped in Paris, France. In December of the same year, Abrams comes back to Mexico and throws himself with all his energy into the communal activity.

In the beginning of 1936, Abrams' fiftieth birthday was celebrated and the holiday was transformed into a demonstration of admiration for the esteemed community activist by all radical circles and the entire Jewish community. Abrams was then at the zenith of his public career and he was full of plans for further activity.

In Spain, the Spanish civil war broke out and Abrams placed himself at the head of an action to help the Republicans against the Franco fascists. At that time appeared the communal newspaper *The Time* that was established at Abrams' house and per his initiative, functioned as an organ of the radical and intellectual Jewish Mexico. Through this newspaper, edited by Moyshe Rubinstein, Abrams conducted persuasive activity, writing about different topics; in the Jewish quarters there was a struggle against malevolent actions and immoralists, as was already done earlier in the journal *Mexican Jewish Life* (also co-founded by Abrams), and in general a reasoned persuasion was being carried out, against the growing fascism, for freedom and for democracy and against the threatening peril of war.

In 1938, when multitudes of Spanish Republicans began coming here as political refugees, Abrams became head of an International Committee in which Jews, Mexicans, Spaniards and Americans collaborated to support those anti-fascist immigrants who were being persecuted by party dictators. At that time, a substantial number of Jewish immigrants also arrived and a committee was formed to receive them at the Trades room (from which later developed the central committee). When a group of immigrants would arrive, among them those fleeing Nazism, a reception was prepared for them and they were served ... rolls and tea. Abrams protested against such a wretched philanthropic treatment and demanded a better attitude towards them. In a certain measure, it was thanks to this that the reception and the initial help for immigrants became placed on a better community foundation.

Thus was Abrams active as much in the Jewish public life as in the general political activity. At the end of 1937 Trotsky comes to Mexico and Abrams sees him as the greatest of political immigrants. They are introduced here and become friends. Although he was not in agreement with Trotsky's ultra-revolutionary stances towards international politics and universal issues, he helps Trotsky with his life in exile. Abrams was of long acquaintance with the famous Mexican painter Diego Rivera, who as a supporter of Trotsky, succeeded in obtaining the right of exile in Mexico for Lenin's friend. One day Trotsky, who lived off the royalties from his books and weekly articles for the *New York Times*, sent for Abrams to come to his secured apartment in Coyoacán and confided to him that he was without means to live and in need of a loan. Trotsky was expecting to eventually receive money from the publishers in Europe and America who had published his works, and Abrams produced a substantial sum for the "world revolutionist," guaranteeing that Trotsky would, with gratitude, repay it very quickly. And so it was. Trotsky kept up the friendship with Abrams until the last day of his life, and during their get-togethers in Coyoacán they had many spicy conversations. From those times we have learned a series of interesting facts about Trotsky's life in Mexico, but this was not the place to tell them. Yet there was one detail that was connected with Abrams, and a moment can be taken here to look at it.

In the autobiographical records, the reader will encounter the distant relationship Abrams had with his father since leaving Russia for America. From Mexico, Abrams almost never corresponded with his father. The old Abramovski lived his last years in Kiev and he was already a very old man when Abrams, at the end of 1938, received a letter from him in Russian with a very characteristic content. The old father writes him that he was already a very old man and he has for him, his son, one sole request: since he has heard that the counter-revolutionary Lev Davidovitsh Trotsky was in Mexico, if he wants to make his father proud and allow him to die in peace, he asks that he "eliminate" Trotsky.

Abrams showed the letter to Trotsky and "Leybele" laughed loudly at the idea that now the "epigones" have reached the point, he said, that it was right to exploit an old man for a great political state murder. This was at the time of the second Purge in Soviet Russia when Pyatokov[17] and the other communist leaders had been condemned and Trotsky had long been on Stalin's "list." Once while in our presence Abrams reminded Trotsky of this, but Trotsky took it lightly, too lightly. What happened in the end is well known.

---

17   Georgy (Yury) Leonidovich Pyatakov: Bolshevik revolutionary leader during the Russian Revolution, and member of Trotsky's faction, the Left Opposition.

* * *

Abrams earned good money for the printed Yiddish word in Mexico. In his printing shop, he showed more interest in printing a Yiddish journal or newspaper that in the actual printing business. In the beginning of 1939, he, together with me and his partner Mr. S. Mindel, cofounded *The Voice*. For a number of years, he published weekly articles in the journal covering political subjects and reactions to current matters in society. A favorite topic of his was bashing Stalinist politics, particularly during the time of the Stalin-Hitler treaty; he also wrote very often against Nazism and Hitlerism. During that time he provided the newspaper with cartoons of a political nature and during the Second World War, published many encouraging articles about the inevitable end and defeat of Nazism and the fascist Axis.

When the first news reports about the Nazi slaughter of Jews in Poland and Europe arrived, Abrams was shocked. He was the commissar of the first campaign committee to rescue Polish Jews, and it didn't bother him—the true free-thinker and anti-cleric— to work together with elements of the Orthodox Jewish camps, because help and rescue for those suffering was to him, more important than anything else.

Over the course of the war, Abrams was literally feverish over the climatic events: he would lie in his bed until late at night glued to the radio, and at daybreak would go down to grab the first morning papers to get the news from the war fronts.

On the street, in cafes, in the neighborhood and at all people's gatherings, Abrams was always the center of political conversations. He even led discussions over the telephone, debated and explained, and hundreds of friends listened respectfully to his words.

Abrams was so intent on finally being able to see the downfall of Hitlerism that in every piece of news and improbable indication, he saw a sign of the "beginning of the end." One day, during the second year of the war, we were out with a group of friends for a Sunday stroll, along with Abrams and Mary. We were walking along Alameda in the large municipal gardens. Across from us on Hidalgo Street, large placards from some sort of company had been put up with huge letters saying "Hitler has been killed!"

Abrams was the first to dash across the street to read the text of the poster, and we were right behind him. He was so surprised that he didn't read the smaller print and began dancing with joy in the middle of the street, hugging each of us with the greatest of joy. It turned out that this was a day in the month of December that in Mexico is called the "Día de Los Inocentes" (similar to April Fool's Day on April 1), when one could trick another in good fun. The poster with its headline was a joke and drew the public's attention.

Abrams' disappointment was unmatched, but we consoled ourselves that soon the tasteless joke would become a reality—and several years later we, along with Abrams, lived to see this. Unfortunately, all of us lost loved ones among the six million Jewish victims of the blood-soaked Nazism.

In the middle of the war years, Abrams discovered that among the Germans interned in La Perota, Mexico, were a number of anti-fascist Germans. As the chairman of the International Committee against fascism, Abrams intervened with the authorities, received the help of the STM,[18] and went himself to La Perota and obtained the liberation of the German anti-fascists. Later, several of them returned to Germany and as anti-Nazis, occupied high positions both in West and East Germany. Among the group of anti-Nazis were both socialists and communists, but in order to free innocent Nazi victims, Abrams saw no difference between them.

Abrams was held in high esteem among the circles of Spanish Republican refugees. He worked with members of the ideologically anarchist group CNT[19] and also with the socialist groups helping to create material support and jobs for the refugees. This was just as he had done with the socialist circles by taking part in aid work for the labor committee and the aid groups for refugees associated with the *Free Voice of Labor* in New York.[20]

Abrams also helped to bring several friends and comrades to Mexico from the inferno in Europe, and many would turn to him for help and support while getting settled in the new land. For each person he found time and an encouraging word, and helped with advice and action when and where he was able.

In his social work Abrams was not picky, because he naively believed that since his intentions were good, he should do everything he possibly could.

---

18 Translator's note: reference unknown.
19 *Confederación Nacional del Trabajo* (National Confederation of Labor): a Spanish confederation of anarcho-syndicalist labor unions.
20 Yiddish: *Freyer Arbeter Shtime*, the longest-running Yiddish language anarchist periodical.

Consequently, it was natural that he would often be misunderstood and criticized even in his own milieu. Abrams was a person who let himself be easily influenced; he believed people but did not always meet with sincerity. Because of this he made mistakes, but he would be forgiven because people knew that he truly believed in what he did. He often unloaded his former revolutionary fire on local social quarrels, and sometimes it seemed to be an exaggeration, so to speak. So, for example, it happened with his speaking out for the rights of the individual when a campaign one time publicly released the names of those who refused to contribute. Abrams considered this as an assault on the rights of the individual and he fought with word and print against every sort of imposing upon others actions that were not in accordance with their way of thinking. For him the issue was not a question of defending the incorrect actions of an individual; rather, he did not want the community to be tempted into actions that could call into question the freedom of society.

People had differing opinions regarding the actual matter; they split hairs over whether or not drastic steps could be taken against Jews who didn't honor their communal duties. Yet they knew that in this instance Abrams took his position very seriously, because the "struggle for personal liberty" was an inborn character trait of his since the times of his anarchist activity, one for which he had paid with years in prison (see pieces on this in this book).

It was natural that J. Abrams, with his extensive activity, should have made mistakes. He was mortal like everyone else and had his virtues and defects. Abrams himself would not have wanted people to say that he didn't have any human weaknesses, or to label him as a saint. We had occasion to meet and work together with him on a daily basis for many years, even though the last time before his death we were not on good terms, so to speak. Yet always with us, as it was with almost all acquaintances, friends and comrades of Abrams, there was and remained a veneration for him, because for the most part Abrams approached social issues with seriousness and devotion—and everyone appreciated this quality in him.

* * *

Abrams didn't have within him any type of narrow nationalism: his upbringing and his entire life had kept him far from this. By nature he was an internationalist—and simultaneously a person with a warm Jewish heart—a humanist and sympathizer with all human suffering. During the years of the struggle in the Land of Israel against the English colonial authorities, he became well acquainted with the literature about the HeChalutz movement,[21] which greatly appealed to his trade unionist position and his socialist dream of communal life. He talked with admiration of the kibbutzim in Israel and even wrote about them. As a former anarchist, he had no kind of "state interest," of course.

Abrams had read much political literature and possessed a rich library, formerly with English and Spanish texts and later also Yiddish. He was familiar with all mankind's problems, and his holiday was—the holiday of the working class, the first of May. He never failed to write a holiday article about the Chicago Martyrs[22] and at the same time expressed his conviction in a world of social justice and fairness that must come.

*   *   *

Abrams was a unique figure. Here he was not in a familiar place and against his will, didn't occupy himself with what he really cared about. He sought to derive meaning from the communal cultural atmosphere that he had helped create, and found within it interest in life.

During the last years of his life, Abrams was especially active in the management of the Jewish Cultural Center; one always met him and Mary here, and it was here that he organized cultural ventures, gave lectures (although now for a smaller audience than before), brought films to show and helped to publish several books and the yearly journals. His departure was a great loss to the Cultural Center and the institution will remember him well in its history.

Abrams, the truly dynamic community activist and official, found himself during the last two years of his life in a state of chronic illness that devoured him. He, the orator and rational persuader, the constant conversationalist—contracted a disease of the throat and was not allowed to speak! How bitter the irony of fate can be!

---

21 Hebrew: *the pioneer*, an international association of Jewish youth whose aim was to train its members to settle in the historical Land of Israel.

22 The Chicago Haymarket massacre in 1886 is generally considered as the inspiration for May Day.

* * *

Abrams played a peculiar role in the Jewish community of Mexico. He was one of the pioneers of the community and builders of its culture, and he was one of those who left a clear stamp on its environment.

Abrams personified a special type of community activist, that of an old-time revolutionary and one who breaks down barriers, an eternal fighter against injustice, a persistent demander of fairness, an awakener to the struggle for a more beautiful world and a better society—a person who lived among the world's problems and in a natural way identified with the wronged and the oppressed.

Justice was what drove him, and stubbornly naïve, J. Abrams brought this drive to expression in his public activity. Even when he made a mistake, he was sincere in his conviction. The anarchism from his youth was also an essential expression of internal striving for a better human society. Through word and writing, he yearned for distant heights and sought, not always finding them, ears and minds for the thought of liberal socialism and a world of justice.

J. Abrams was a universalist. He showed up at the end of the twenties to a Jewish Mexico, unsettled after the storm of the First World War. He was one of the first whom the Russian revolution had disappointed and whom an agitated Europe had expelled. He came here to a Jewish environment and in fact found himself. His universal way of thinking did not become weaker and his belief remained rock-hard. Rather, he began transplanting his ideas in the new Jewish surroundings, conforming himself even partially to the new environment, and he also became a Jewish community activist—because without public activity, J. Abrams couldn't breathe.

For over a quarter of a century, J. Abrams lived, strove and fought ideationally in Jewish Mexico. Here he acquired countless friends—and regrettably, was pitilessly befallen by the adversities of life in what was for him an alien public atmosphere, especially in his later years.

When after much physical suffering he closed his eyes for eternity, on the sickbed in the hospital where his faithful lifelong friend Mary never left his side[23]—a chapter of Jewish life concluded in Mexico. Taken was one of those who had helped to shape this very life, and who wanted to see a life full of culture, one that was ethical and elevated. It is a loss that Abrams went away, that he disappeared from among the living—but he will be long, long remembered.

All honor his illustrious memory!

---

23 Translator's note: according to most accounts, Abrams died at home shortly after he left the hospital.

The Last Words of J. Abrams

Before his death, J. Abrams was bedridden for many months. During the course of his difficult and painful illness, Abrams, the man of the fiery word, lost his ability to speak. Yet he yearned to express himself and many times quietly whispered to his faithful life companion, Mary, encouraged and comforted her, and in a deeply human way expressed his appreciation for her truly motherly treatment of him. On the last night before he was to leave the hospital, Abrams gathered enough strength to write down the following, pouring out his heart to his Mary:

"Philadelphia, Monday June 1, 1953.

Today was the last night of one hundred and eighty-two long nights in Temple Hospital. It's very hard to sleep—not because I'm in pain, but because of waiting for the morning, when I will leave the hospital and you, Merele,[24] will be liberated from your torments. It's true that I was the sick one, but you were the one that endured so much hardship and did everything for me, with so much love and devotion that more than once I asked myself: Why do you do all this? What have I done to deserve it? Perhaps the luxurious life that you lead because of me? Had it had been a rich life, you would not have been able to be so devoted: then you would have found nurses for the patient and you yourself would go off to enjoy the luxury, perhaps inquiring by telephone: how does he feel, that guy that because of him, I enjoy a sumptuous lifestyle …

Yes, dear Merele, in our poverty and moral lifestyle we lived a rich life, and when such a difficult moment arrived, like a mother you watched over my sickbed and with a sweet tear of hope brought forth better times and longer days. Who can understand this? It is not simply to be understood, but to be felt! My dear Merele, you have shown so much love and wholeheartedness that you don't yourself know how rich you are. I have to admit that during the long years that we've been together, I also didn't know it.

More than once, in my physical anguish, I've put the question to myself: Is it worth it? Yet when I see how you arrive so very early, oftentimes with your eyes swollen from crying the night long, without having taken a bite to eat because you weren't hungry and had forgotten to eat, only seeking what

---

24   Yiddish: diminutive of Mary

you could do to make things easier for me—I would say to myself: Yes, it's worth the trouble, I must live!

Then I bit my lips and swore—I will not abandon you! We will keep on living, and go on to live the course of our lives.

Now I will write about this feeling: you released a tear, and with it made the roots of my life sprout again, and I received a new life. We will continue living and our garden will again be full of flowers.

In regard to our friends and comrades and especially Eyde,[25] I have so much to say about them, but I will do it at the right time and in the right place … meanwhile I embrace them all and I don't tell them my thanks, because in my heart I've built a palace of love and seated all of them there. When I have the chance to talk with them—seating them on the flower-covered beds in the love-palace of my heart—I will tell all of them everything that I feel towards them, if it can be expressed in words.

Where can I find the words, dear Merele, to be able to express my inner admiration for your soulful faithfulness, for the richness of your soul, and for the deeply heartfelt love that you have demonstrated for me. I feel this with pride, no matter how hard my situation may be.

May we have the opportunity to continue this chapter. Meanwhile, may it be the last time that I lie in the hospital …

Your Jack"

---

25 Translator's note: presumably a woman's name, possibly Ida.

The Funeral of Jacob Abrams

On the morning of Thursday, 11 June 1953, the body of the deceased Jacob Abrams was brought to the hall of the Jewish Cultural Center, where he had been particularly active as of late. For the entire time, members of the board and friends stood an honor guard around his casket, which was draped in black and covered with red bows. At one o'clock, the funeral service was carried out by more than a hundred people who had come to pay their last respects to the dead. Appearing on stage with touching words and eulogies to J. Abrams were P. Lisker and H. Krishtal in the name of the Cultural Center and of the Society for Culture and Aid.

From there, the funeral moved to the Nidchei Yisrael[26] field, where a large crowd of friends and acquaintances were gathered. Appearing here with short speeches of mourning were: R. Vaysfeld, Augustin Zukhi, N. Aks, Julian Gorkin and Dr. Y. N. Shteynberg. The speakers talked of what a great loss it was that one had gone away who strove his entire life for a better world and a happier humanity, fighting for these both courageously and proudly. Also emphasized was Abrams' aid work for the victims of fascism and other political immigrants, many of whom will mourn for Abrams as if he were their own close friend and companion.

The funeral was conducted—at the request of his wife and the close friends of the deceased—without ritual, in the same free spirit that he had lived. The directors of the Nidchei Yisrael community demonstrated fitting tolerance in this instance and with this made it possible to guard the honor of the dead. The funeral participants left in deep mourning, taking with them in their memories Abrams' good deeds, with which he was immortalized in his surroundings.

THE TOMBSTONE PLACED AT JACOB ABRAMS' GRAVE

Over a hundred people—members of the Mexican Jewish Cultural Center, of the Bundist organization in Mexico, of the Society for Culture and Aid, writers, representatives of the Jewish press, as well as personal friends of J. Abrams, gathered together on Sunday, 13 June 1954, at the Jewish cemetery

---

26 Hebrew: literally, "dispersed of Israel," likely the name of the congregation that managed the cemetery.

to unveil the tombstone at J. Abrams' grave. The mourning ceremony was organized by the Jewish Cultural Center of Mexico on the first anniversary of his death.

The tombstone was erected by the widow of the deceased, Mary Abrams, and by several personal friends of the deceased; it was a simple, yet impressive monument bearing the inscription: "J. Abrams, who fought passionately for freedom, justice and tolerance."

The grave was covered with red flowers.

Dr. A. King, chairman of the Jewish Cultural Center, opened the mourning ceremony with a moving introductory speech. Further speakers were: Pesach Lisker in the name of the Jewish Cultural Center; F. Zukhi, famous liberal-socialist writer and personal friend of J. Abrams; and Y. Krishtal, in the name of the Bundist organization in Mexico, the Society for Culture and Aid, and of the journal *Forward*. With impressive words, they described J. Abrams' personality, his tireless and unflinching struggle for the ideals of liberty and socialism, and his service to the Mexican community. Dr. A. King concluded the mourning ceremony.

MARY ABRAMS

An Interesting Episode During Jack's First Years in Mexico

In 1927, Jack organized a protest meeting against the sentencing of Sacco and Vanzetti. Jack stood on the platform in the anarchist club on Palma; there were several hundred people in attendance. Jack was the sole speaker and the hall thundered with applause. At the end of the meeting when the audience had begun to exit the hall, detectives came to Jack and arrested him (along with the poet Glantz[27]).

The detectives were very courteous and allowed me to go with Jack. After a short interrogation, one of the detectives came to me—it was already three o'clock in the morning—and asked if I would like to bring something from the house for Jack—a blanket and pillow—and he went home with me to bring the items.

The poet Glantz was at that time the chairman of the evening; he was released a day later and Jack remained incarcerated. He was threatened with being expelled to Russia again.

A couple of days later, Jack was brought to the district attorney. When interrogating Jack, he asked him who were Sacco and Vanzetti. The government knew who Jack was and also that America had deported him; the district attorney's question was no more than some sort of way to find out more about Jack himself. Yet when Jack began describing the great martyrs, there were tears in the eyes of the district attorney. The prosecutor was a highly intelligent person. When Jack finished talking, the attorney told him that the communists had denounced him to the authorities.

A few days later, Jack was set free. Then the communists once again denounced him, saying that he was directing fierce propaganda for anarchism to the Mexican army. Jack was again arrested and questioned. This time, on his side Jack demanded that the communists who had denounced him be summoned to the hearing in his presence.

Several of the communists were brought in. They said that they didn't know anything about it, and that they didn't even know Jack. The denunciations,

---

27 Jacobo Glantz: Yiddish Mexican poet.

they explained, must have been made by someone on his own. So Jack was once again released.

THE FIRST OF MAY WITHOUT JACK

Today, the first of May, is forty-three years that Jack and I have shared our lives together. Therefore, for us, the first of May had a double significance.

Mary and J. Abrams

I certainly never thought that this May first, I would be decorating Jack's grave instead of his room—as always, with red roses.

This May first, I no longer heard Jakele's[28] murmured "Merele."

Today, Jake will no longer stand on the platform at the Cultural Center, ready to speak about the first of May. Today, his dynamic voice no longer carries across the hall.

Jakele no longer feels his physical and moralistic suffering; he feels it no more—not the suffering of the world, and also not the beauty of it. He no longer feels the caresses of the springtime breezes, the singing of the birds, not the whisper of the waves on the water that he had loved so much.

Now it's all finished. He is finished with the stormy conflicts of society, he's done with the day-to-day struggles of life; Jake has been released. On his current path, he is no longer escorted by the "protectors of justice"; America is now safe from peril.

My wish was always that I should go, and Jake should stay behind. My whole life has been wrapped up in him and even now, I am wrapped up in him. The longing is unbearable. No matter how strongly I hold on, I am still collapsing. I'm losing the ground on which I've been walking my entire life.

I still can't believe that everything is finished; that everything is over, to me it seems like an evil witch's prank. That Jake should no longer be able to speak a word—this is impossible!

How terrible it is that I was not with him during the last minutes of his life! How should I exist without Jakele?

Unless—to fuse myself with the memory of his personality, with the memory of the great love that I always had for him, and with the memory of the love that so many friends and comrades had for him—

This is the only thing that is left for me in life.

(Mexico, May 1954)

---

28   Yiddish diminutive of "Jake" – another one of Abrams' nicknames.

JOSEPH PAUL

Jacob Abrams in Temple University Hospital

On 18 October, 1952, I received a letter from the Poet Isaac Berliner,[29] in which he introduced Abrams to me and asked me to use all means possible to obtain an entry visa for Abrams to the States, because no one could cure him in Mexico and the best place for him therefore, could only be the Temple University Hospital where he, Isaac Berliner, had received an operation. I had not yet finished reading over Berliner's letter when Dr. Wolf Neiman[30] telephoned me and said that he must see me on a very important matter: he had also received a letter from Berliner about Abrams.

Dr. Neiman came at noon and from him, I learned about Abrams—who he was and why he was not allowed to enter the States. I needed to get a visa for Abrams just at the time when Senator McCarthy was rising to prominence.

That same day, that is, the 18th of October, I saw Dr. Jackson, one of the greatest cancer specialists at Temple Hospital. I went to him because I wanted to avoid the politicians; I left them as a last resort. However, it turned out that Dr. Jackson knew Abrams, who had already been under his observation once at an earlier time. On 21 October, I already had a copy of the letter that Dr. Jackson had sent to the American legation in Mexico. In the letter, Dr. Jackson reminded them that Jacob Abrams had already been under his care once and requested that the legation give Abrams a visa. And since Jackson knew "the deal" with Abrams, he added that certainly "we will cooperate in every instance—per the instructions that you give," etc. This meant that Abrams would be in the hospital under Jackson's supervision.

Several days later, I waited at the airport for Abrams, his wife and the escort, who was charged with paying careful attention that Abrams didn't, God forbid, call for a revolution ... I visited Abrams every day in the hospital, where I also became acquainted with his devoted friends from New York and

---

29   Isaac (Yitskhak) Berliner: Yiddish poet and writer, born in Poland, he immigrated to Mexico and was one of the early pioneers of the Ashkenazi cultural life.

30   Translator's note: the actual spelling of the names of Dr. Neiman and the other physicians are unknown.

Philadelphia. Dr. Neiman was also there every day. In addition, Abrams was visited by the eminent physicians Jonas and Vaises, my good friends. From them and from Dr. Norris, Dr. Jackson's assistant, I was always kept informed of the status of Abrams' health.

When I met Abrams, his voice had already been eaten away by the cancer. He tried to make sounds, but they were unintelligible and I thought: how tragic must this man feel who has been robbed of the voice with which he has inspired thousands of people in lectures and meetings. When with his friends (I also considered myself one of these), he had to communicate with them through notes—in Yiddish, English or Russian.

So passed the days and weeks. Often it seemed that he was getting better, and he could already even say entire words. Of course, it was hard for him to control the airflow, and he pronounced every syllable separately. Mary noted that the "lessons" were very hard for him, and she often requested that it would better that he write notes and wait until the wounds healed.

Mary never left Abrams the entire time he was in the hospital. She would come very early to the hospital and leave very late at night—only when the nurse would come in and tell her that it was time to leave the patient's room. When Mary would go down to the street to grab something, she would only take a few minutes. When Abrams took a nap, she sat in the chair and silently cried. She also cried at night, especially late in the evening when she had to leave her dear friend. Yet as soon as Abrams opened his eyes, she quickly wiped away her tears so that he wouldn't notice them. Nonetheless, he did indeed notice that she had been crying. He gave her a penetrating glance, and suddenly her eyes lit up with joy. So went the days and weeks.

Abrams, however, suffered not only from the terrifying angel of death—cancer—but also from the fact that Washington required Dr. Jackson to renew Abrams' visa every fourteen days. Washington could not find its way to allowing the visa to be extended until Abrams was discharged from the hospital. This irked Abrams terribly. He wrote to me in a note: "What do they think in Washington? They tremble, that I'll escape? I assure you, that as soon as I'm able to leave the hospital, I will return to Mexico, where people nowadays live a lot freer than in the States."

Yes, he left the hospital and returned to Mexico, and with so much joy! But the happiness didn't last long and he closed his eyes for eternity.

Abrams is no longer among the living. Yet he will live on in this book, dear friends of the Jewish Cultural Center, that you are publishing. So to this monument to Abrams, I send you this small contribution.

J. Paul, J. Abrams and Mary Abrams in Philadelphia

MOLLIE STEIMER
To Twenty Years in Prison

WITH JACK ABRAMS—TO PRISON AND DEPORTATION

I met Jack Abrams for the first time on a Saturday evening in January, 1917, when I participated in the New York anarchist group "Freedom."[31] Right away I noticed that two persons were in fact leading the group: Bunin (Jesus) and Jack Abrams. Of the two, Jack was the energetic one and the one with more will to take action. Indeed, he soon won my sympathy: this was that sort of sympathy that a young girl willingly gives to the one who, in her eyes, is the embodiment of the ideal that he preaches, and for which he fights. Thus it happened that Mary, Jack and I soon became good friends and good comrades. We all became active and everything, it seemed, was going smoothly when suddenly—I can't now recall the reason why—a conflict erupted among the members and the group Frayhayt ceased to exist.

Yet the times were very serious—war was raging in the world. We privately reorganized, this time without Bunin. Belonging to the new group were—if my memory doesn't lead me astray—Jacob Schwartz, Rosa Bernstein, Bernard Sirnakur, Jack Abrams, Mary Abrams, me, and several others whose names I don't now want to say.

We would put out fliers from time to time, and also published a Yiddish newspaper called *The Storm*.[32] The tendency of the newspaper was a general anarchist one without specific "-isms," and back then we all sincerely believed that the social revolution was nigh.

Events were happening then very quickly. America entered the war against Germany, and in Russia the revolution broke out. We were seized with enormous enthusiasm. Then discussions began between us on whether or not we should unite with the allies and proceed with the war against German militarism. In an article for our newspaper, Bernard Sirnakur defended the position of Kropotkin and the famous Sixteen[33] that the war must continue, but after long debates we rejected the article and our paper continued to proclaim

---

31 Yiddish: Frayhayt.
32 Yiddish: *Der Shturem*.
33 The *Manifesto of the Sixteen*, a 1916 document written by well-known anarchists Peter Kropotkin and Jean Grave advocating an Allied victory over Germany during WWI.

to the world that the war must be stopped. Soon, however, we were no longer allowed to lead our agitation openly and freely: the Espionage Act[34] was put into force and that sort of criticizing the government became forbidden. The printing shops refused to print our propaganda leaflets and we were forced to cross over to an illegal existence.

We first installed a small printing press in the room of a friend of ours, but this didn't work because the noise of the machine was drawing the attention of the neighbors. We then decided to open our own small printing shop where Jack Schwartz and Lachowsky[35] would take on small orders for private print-work and in the meantime, we would be able to print our things unhindered. Near to the printing shop that we set up in Harlem, we rented an apartment with several rooms. Residing there were Schwartz and Florence[36] in one room, Jack and Mary in a second and I was in the third. In this way we strove to reduce our expenditures on food and rent, so that we could be in a position to cover the expenses of the printing shop.

At that time—July 1918—it became known that President Wilson had ordered ten thousand American soldiers to be sent to Vladivostok to take part in the military intervention against revolutionary Russia, which at that time had all our sympathies on its side. We immediately called a meeting of our group and decided to publish an appeal to protest against the intervention. Samuel Lipman was also at the meeting, although he considered himself a Marxist socialist. We in turn, were thrilled to have him with us because we knew him to be a true friend, and we entrusted him and Schwartz with putting together the proclamation. Schwartz wrote the Yiddish text and Lipman, the English. The written texts were first discussed at a group meeting and then they were printed. All in all, we were ten people in the group and several of us took on the task of distributing the leaflets in a determined district. In several days, the leaflets were spread across the entire city of New York, Philadelphia and other places. In the worker districts, we scattered the leaflets so densely that the newspapers wrote afterwards that our organization used an airplane to distribute them. Innumerable detectives were sent out to spy on us, but without success.

---

34   The 1917 Espionage Act.
35   Hyman Lachowsky
36   Schwartz's wife, Florence.

Yet here is how we were undone: one day Lachowsky brought Rosansky with him to help us distribute the leaflets. Lachowsky knew and trusted Rosansky. We relied on Lachowsky completely and gave Rosansky a package of leaflets. The next morning Rosansky was caught with the leaflets and was beaten by the police; he couldn't hold out and gave all of us up to the police. He simply told the police that on that same day, late in the afternoon, he was to meet up with us at the corner of Madison Avenue and 104th Street.

At seven o'clock at night on August 23, 1918, I had returned from work and arrived at the arranged corner. There Rosansky was waiting; I greeted him, happy with our great success (the press had already reprinted our exhortation and in the streets, people had begun talking about the intervention). Lipman soon arrived and right after him, Lachowsky. Suddenly we found ourselves surrounded by policemen who took us to their headquarters. At the same time, another group of police broke into our shared apartment and there found Jack, Schwartz, Mary and Rosa Bernstein. After a thorough house search the police wanted to arrest everyone, but after Jack explained to them that Mary, his wife, was sick and knew nothing about his political activities, and that Rosa was a nurse who came to look after Mary—both women were released at the house and the rest were taken to the central police precinct.

We were already there when they were brought in. Then, we sat there for hour after hour. The men were questioned and at the same time beaten; I heard the shouts and groans that came from the different rooms, and saw the detectives who were going in and out of the rooms—with their sleeves rolled up, cursing and berating. When I was taken for questioning after midnight, as I was passing by the room where our group was being held I saw Schwartz and Lachowsky badly beaten. Schwartz was keeping his mouth covered with a handkerchief that was soaked with blood. As is known, six weeks later he was dead. Different inspectors questioned me for several hours. They wanted to extract the location of the printing shop and when they saw that they would learn nothing from me, they took all of us to the Tombs prison,[37] where people were kept until trial.

The court proceedings stretched out over two weeks, and during the entire time we ourselves were not judged; rather the discussion centered around

---

37   "The Tombs," colloquial name for the Manhattan Detention Complex, a municipal jail in Manhattan, NY.

the question of whether or not the government of the United States had the right to intervene in Russia's internal affairs. The weekly magazine *The Nation* put very unpleasant questions to the government. The intervention in Russia was halted. Our objective was achieved, and whatever was done to us no longer made a big difference. We received the sentences of twenty years imprisonment for Abrams, Lachowsky and Lipman, and fifteen years for me with calmness.

They let each of us out on ten thousand dollars bail and an appeal was filed with the Supreme Court. During the months that we were out on bail, Jack continued his activity in the bookbinder's union. He would also give talks to the defense committee.

In October 1919, I was separately sentenced to six months in the workhouse on Blackwell's Island,[38] where for the entire time I was kept shut off from the world, without letters or visits; even my mother was not allowed to visit me. One day in January 1920, someone smuggled a note into my cell informing me that Abrams, Lipman and Lachowsky had been caught attempting to flee to Mexico. That same day a newspaper clipping was tossed in my cell reporting that our sentences had been upheld by the Supreme Court and that my three codefendants had already been sent to the prison in Atlanta, Georgia.[39]

When my six months in the workhouse were up, I was brought to New York, held there for two days, and then on May 1, 1920, transferred to the federal penitentiary in Jefferson, Missouri, where I was to serve out my fifteen years. What more was done in the defense committee as well as with the amnesty committee, and how the plan to exchange us for Russian war prisoners came about—I don't know. I had separated from the committee on the question of serving a petition and I was not kept informed on all matters. I was only told that the deal with the Soviet government exchanging us for Russian war prisoners would take place. On November 23, 1921, the government deported all of us from the United States and we were sent back to Russia.

(Berlin, March 1930)

---

38   Now known as Roosevelt Island.
39   United States Federal Penitentiary, Atlanta, Georgia.

J. Abrams in the American prison after the trial

Courageous and Brave[40]

In August 1918, the New York anarchist group Frayhayt, of which Jack Abrams was the beloved leader, published an appeal against the military intervention taking place in Russia at that time by the United States and its allies. At that moment, the sympathies and the enthusiasm for the great revolution were still very strong among the different groups of the labor movement in the United States, England and other countries. Despite the fact that the world knew that the Bolsheviks had driven off the constitutional assembly and violently seized the country's governing power for themselves, the military intervention of the allied countries against the young Soviet government provoked irritation and fury among a large section of the workers in England and America. People then still identified the Bolshevik government with the revolution. An echo of this mood was also the decision of the small New York anarchist group to protest openly against the intervention.

This appeal was published in Yiddish and in English, and they typeset and printed approximately ten thousand copies in their own small printing shop that was located in the basement at 1582 Madison Avenue in Manhattan.

The Appeals

The English version of the appeal bore the title "The Hypocrisy of the United States and Her Allies," and the important sections read as follows:[41]

> "Our" President Wilson has hypnotized the American people so strongly with his magnificent phraseology that they don't see his hypocrisy ... the President was afraid to announce to the American people about the intervention in Russia ... He used splendid phrases with regard to Russia and silently and cowardly sent troops to suppress the Russian revolution. Can you now see how German militarism has joined with allied capitalism in order to strangle the Russian revolution?

---

40 Translator's note: it is unclear who the author of this section is; presumably it was the publishers of this book.
41 Translator's note: the actual document varies slightly in wording.

This is nothing new. The tyrants of the world fight among themselves until they catch sight of the common enemy—the enlightenment of the worker class; as soon as they find a common enemy, they unite to smash him.

In 1815, the monarchical nations united under the name of the "Holy Alliance" in order to suppress the French revolution. Now militarism unites with capitalism—although not openly—with the goal of crushing the Russian revolution.

What do YOU have to say about this? Will you allow the Russian revolution to be repressed? You, yes, we mean you, people of America!

The Russian revolution calls on the workers of the world to help. Wake up, wake up, you—workers of the world!

The appeal was signed "Revolutionaries" and in the postscript was added: "We hate and despise German militarism more than the hypocritical tyrants and more than 'the coward in the White House,' and it is therefore an absurdity to say that we are pro-Germanic."

The appeal in Yiddish was entitled "Workers Awaken!" and was directed principally towards the Russian immigrants in America; it was also much more fiery and provocative than the English version, and supplied the legal basis for the sworn jury to bring back the unanimous verdict: guilty!

We bring the important excerpts from the leaflets, which we are translating back into Yiddish from the English translation found in the official transcripts of the court proceedings. Unfortunately, we don't have the Yiddish original with us now.

It first says in the leaflet that the beginning of Russia's emancipation was halted by "His Majesty, Mr. Wilson, and the rest of his friends—dogs of all colors." America and her allies want to march into Russia on the pretext of helping the Czechoslovakians, but the Russian immigrants will not be deceived this time, because they understand the true intention of the measure. The leaflet then clarifies to the "Workers, Russian immigrants" that the money they lend the government will be used to make bullets, "not only against the Germans, but also against the labor councils in Russia." The workers in the ammunition plants must know that they "produce bullets, bayonets and cannons to murder not only the Germans, but also their dearest and best who are fighting in Russia for freedom." Lastly, there comes a direct call to the workers to answer the barbarous rebellion with a general strike.

"... For three hundred years, the Romanov dynasty taught us how to fight; all rulers, from the smallest to the mightiest, should remember that the hand of the revolution will not tremble in the fight."

The leaflet is signed: "Di Buntarn" (in English, "The Rebels").

The actual history of the writing, discussing, printing and disseminating of the leaflets, as well as about the entire anti-intervention activity of Jacob Abrams and his group has already been reconstructed by Mollie Steimer in another place in this book. Moreover, Mollie Steimer stood in the center of the entire undertaking and also subsequently played an important role in court. In addition, her narrative about the arrest of the five and about their conduct at the interrogation and in court is of great significance to the description of the entire affair today, thirty-eight years after the event. Thus, the task left to us here is merely to try to reconstruct anew at least a part of the general picture that was then being created during the proceedings of the sensational trial. We do it on the basis of the books: 1.) *Sentenced to Twenty Years in Prison*, published in New York in 1919 by the Aid and Defense Committee for the Political Prisoners,[42] and 2.) A book of minutes from the court proceedings in the "District Court of the United States," division of the Southern District of New York,[43] October session of 1918: the title of the record books is *United States versus Jack Abrams, et al.*

The Arrest

Mollie Steimer tells here in her description how the main leaders of the group Frayhayt were, thanks to Hyman Rosansky, undone when distributing the leaflets; how they were all subsequently arrested, brought in for questioning at the central police precinct, and from there transferred to the Tombs prison. We will here add several details to Mollie's description.

The shared apartment that Mollie Steimer tells of was located on 5 East 104th Street. On August 23, 1918, at seven o'clock at night, as a group of detectives surrounded Mollie Steimer, Hyman Lachowsky, Samuel Lipman

---

42 *Sentenced to Twenty Years in Prison* by the Political Prisoners Defense and Relief Committee, New York City 1919

43 United States District Court, Southern District of New York

and Hyman Rosansky on the corner of 5th Avenue and 104th Street, another group of detectives followed Jack Abrams and Jacob Schwartz from the printing shop to their apartment and accompanied them inside. During the house search, bundles of the leaflets were found there. When arresting Abrams and Schwartz, three others were also detained—Boris, Aurin[44] and Prober[45]—who during the house search had come unexpectedly to see Abrams; the first two were questioned and released and the third, Prober, was arraigned together with the rest but was also quickly released. In this way there remained only five who were accused, but about this—a little later.

All those arrested were brought in two parties down to the police precinct on 240 Center Street, downtown New York, late in the evening. Rosansky had been first brought there the same day, 23 August, at two-thirty in the afternoon, when he had been caught with the leaflets. He had only been released later to go the place where he was to meet Mollie Steimer and the others, so that the others could be arrested as well. The interrogation went on for an entire night in Room 214, and the beatings occurred in other adjacent rooms. They beat Aurin, Lachowsky, Lipman and Rosansky (the last, apparently, during the day, surprisingly), but it was the fate of Schwartz to bear the worst of it, who in a letter dated September 18, 1918, sent from the Tombs prison, later described in exhaustive detail the tortures that he endured during the interrogation. Later, while Schwartz was sitting in prison, he became sick and was transported to Bellevue Hospital where he died on the night of 14 October—the eve of the opening of their court proceedings. Afterwards, an unfinished farewell note was found in his prison cell, written in Yiddish with the following words: "Farewell, friends. When you appear in court, I will no longer be with you. Fight without fear, fight courageously. I regret that I must leave you, but such is life. After your long martyrdom ..." The note shows that Schwartz anticipated his approaching death, and his friends asserted that the police brutality was the main cause of his untimely demise. Schwartz's letter and farewell note, as with his death in general, were at that time utilized extensively by the defense committee at a public, twelve hundred-strong mass meeting (October 25, 1918), at which spoke

---

44 Translator's note: *Sentenced to Twenty Years* notes three prisoners detained as shown here; other documents show Boris Aurin as one person, not two.

45 Gabriel Prober.

the attorney for the defendants, Harry Weinberger,[46] and the pro-Bolshevik writer well-known during that time, John Reed.[47]

The Trial

The trial at the Southern District Court was set for the tenth of October, but the actual court proceedings began on October 15, 1918. Only four of the accused were actually tried: Jacob Abrams, Samuel Lipman, Hyman Lachowsky and Mollie Steimer. As far as Hyman Rosansky was concerned, although he was sentenced to three years imprisonment, he is not considered as one of those being tried because in the course of the proceedings, the court utilized him completely as a witness against the four. It was apparent that the accused, as well as the jury, considered Abrams to be the initiator and leader of the entire venture, and this was also expressed in the court proceedings. Abrams' examination stretched out over two long court sessions. The plaintiffs for the government did everything they could to get the accused to agree to the charge's assertion that he, Abrams, and his group consciously called for people to disobey the government and sabotage its war efforts, and that this was called an act of state treason and a crime per the new Espionage law. Against this the accused, Abrams, with the help of his defense attorney, Harry Weinberger, tried to demonstrate that although he did indeed organize the printing and distribution of the leaflets, he had committed no crime against the law with it; on the contrary, the crime committed was wholly that of the President, who had begun the intervention on his own responsibility without the consent of Congress. Moreover, the defense attorney, per the express desire of all four accused, did everything possible to convert the court dealings into a propaganda arena against the allied military intervention in Russia. With his leading questions, Weinberger prompted the accused to give long, detailed statements about the economic and political system in Russia before and after the revolution, about the general debate between socialism and capitalism in the world as a whole, and about the driving forces of the war.

---

46   Harry Weinberger: a New York City lawyer and staunch believer in civil liberties, he acted as defense attorney in many civil liberties cases, including Emma Goldman and Alexander Berkman.

47   John Reed: American journalist, poet, and socialist activist.

It was Jacob Abrams, regardless of his language barrier and the frequent traps that were laid for him during cross-examination on the side of his accusers, who managed to keep the attention of the jury and audience riveted to his long political speeches and arguments. Towards the end, he even earned a word of praise on the part of Judge Clayton for his intelligence.

Mollie Steimer also kept the courtroom in suspense with her intricate explanations about the nature of anarchism, about workers and capitalism in our society, about love and marriage, and on other similar topics. She was also listened to respectfully. All four of the accused stayed proud and courageous during the entire length of the court proceedings. When the jury pronounced a verdict of "guilty," Jacob Abrams said:

"If it is really a crime to intercede for the people that you love; if it is a crime to believe in ideals, if it is a crime to stick up for one's one country—

Then I am proud to be a criminal."

Samuel Lipman, among others, said:

"The trial will go down in history not as a case of the government of the United Sates against five Jews, but rather as a case of capitalism against the working class ... the more lovers of freedom that you lock up in prison, all the sooner will be the end of poverty, misery, hunger, despotism and tyranny."

Mollie Steimer and Hyman Lachowsky spoke in the same spirit. After this came the sentencing: Abrams, Lipman and Lachowsky were each sentenced to twenty years imprisonment in the state of Maryland[48] and a fine of one thousand dollars; Mollie Steimer was sentenced to fifteen years in the Missouri Prison for Women and a fine of five hundred dollars; Hyman Rosansky was sentenced to three years imprisonment and a one thousand dollar fine—this was on October 25, 1918.

* * *

As Mollie Steimer tells, after the sentencing they were released on ten thousand dollars bail each until it was decided if their filed appeal would be ruled on by the Supreme Court. At the end of 1919, the verdict was upheld by the Supreme Court and the three convicted men were incarcerated in the prison in Atlanta, Georgia; and she, Mollie—in the Women's Prison in

---

48 The location was later changed by Judge John Knox to the Atlanta, Georgia federal penitentiary.

Jefferson, Missouri. What took place in the lives of the convicted during their time in prison over the course of almost two years—until November 23, 1921, when they were all exchanged for Russian prisoners of war and expelled from America—unfortunately, none of them has ever described. However, from the moment of their deportation and what followed next, that is, the journey to the "land of their dream," the hard life there, the great disappointment of the previous illusions and the flight from there back to the west—all this is colorfully and vividly depicted by Jacob Abrams in his description "Deep Conviction and Bitter Disappointment," that is reproduced here in this book.[49]

---

49 Translator's note: See section *Five Years in Soviet Russia (Deep Conviction and Bitter Disappointment)*

Abrams and his friend Schwartz, who died in prison

J. Abrams

The Person, Friend, and Fighter

ISAAC BERLINER

J. Abrams A"H [50]

J. Abrams is no longer among the living.

It is hard to believe that this man with so much dynamic energy would suddenly forsake life and fall into eternal sleep.

It is hard to believe, because —

Jacob Abrams definitely had no wish to embark upon a deep sleep. He loved life. His eye was always vigilant and he would notice—according to his point of view—the crooked and the straight of human conduct. His social sense was refined, and he was always ready to react to events in Jewish and general life.

Always militant and straightforward in his fight for a better world, J. Abrams possessed the strength to create around him adherents and disciples who looked up to him, listened to his words and followed his ideas.

He Walked Straight

An anti-fascist and in general an anti-dictatorship position—on this basis, J. Abrams constructed his community work in Jewish Mexico.

Abrams was not just a preeminent community activist in Jewish Mexico. He also surrounded himself with revolutionaries from different nations, and together they dreamed of a future liberated world.

It was to this anti-fascist building that Abrams, through his words, contributed his bricks. Yet all the bricks were of the same sort, because Abrams never changed his ideas, and would not allow his view of the world to be diminished by even one iota.

In general, Abrams was a real human being.

He did not deviate even a hair from his straight and narrow path.

He hated to move in zigzags. He walked ahead with certainty. And it was with just this certainty that he waited, with his anarchist-socialist aspiring, for the liberty and freedom of the human race on our bloodstained earth.

---

50   Hebrew: Olevasholem, "May he rest in peace."

Over a Quarter Century of Community Work in Mexico

I don't now want to seek the synthesis of Abrams, the human being and the Jew. Abrams was very far from Jewish tradition and national Jewishness.

His motto—an equal world for everyone—did not allow him to single himself out from the ordinary world. Therefore, the Jewishness inside him didn't smolder separately; rather, it became an integral part of the human race.

The narrow circle of adherents that had formed around him also did not relinquish this line.

For over a quarter century, Abrams did activist work in our Jewish community.

He was one of the leading personalities who carried out their activities with dignity and sincerity.

His authoritative word had a direct impact on the socialist part of our Jewish community.

One Cannot Go Against Fate

A few years back, he suddenly became sick with a malevolent illness inside his throat.

His companions and friends from here, as well as from abroad, did much to try to save him.

The best doctors from Mexico and the States brought to bear modern medicine and surgical remedies.

Abrams was—in the last, most difficult months—surrounded by love and kindness from his wife Mary and his friends.

The final six months he lay in a Philadelphia hospital under the care of expert doctors, and he received the best treatment. His wife, Mary, hovered near him day and night. A local resident there—the community activist and extraordinary friend of humanity, Joe Paul, a man with a great soul—helped much in Abrams' coming to the United States from South America, as Abrams was not allowed to enter due to past revolutionary sins ... the good Jew and human being, Joe (Joseph) Paul, also encircled the patient with brotherly kindness to ease Abrams' suffering. Also, Dr. Wolf Neiman—a

former resident of Mexico and old friend of Abrams who now lived in Philadelphia—never missed a day in coming to the hospital to see Abrams.
But —
One cannot go against fate.
Abrams is no longer of this world.

Abrams' Last Days in Mexico

During his last days, I saw J. Abrams in a Mexican hospital.
He lay there and suffered. He was in a great deal of pain.
Yet he could not cry out in pain, nor even groan ...
He had already lost his speech —
He was mute —
At the Philadelphia hospital, they'd had to remove the vocal chords[51] from his throat ...
They'd cut out his voice ...
Here is an irony of fate: the elocutionist has become mute ... (this reminds me of H. Leivik's drama, "The Poet Became Blind"[52] ...) Yes, a speaker without a voice is like a fiddler or a painter without hands ...
And —
It is also soothing for one suffering, if he can at least give a sigh ...
Abrams could not even complain about the terrible pain tormenting him.
Like a stoic he lay on his hospital bed, and his terrifying pain was almost visible from his still sparkling eyes . . . .
Yes —
J. Abrams became permanently mute. He has left this world. Yet with his word and his deeds, he contributed a considerable share to the construction of the Jewish cultural-social life in Mexico.
All honor his memory!

---

51   Translator's note: It is not clear from the Yiddish text exactly what type of surgery was done to his throat, only that the operation resulted in him being unable to speak.
52   Yiddish: "Der *poet* vert *blind*" by H. Leivick (pen name of Yiddish writer Leivick Halpern).

SALOMON KAHAN

1. His Faith Was Mankind

My friend, my brother,
Weary, suffering brother,
Whoever you are, may your courage not fail;
Believe— there will come a time,
When Baal lies crushed,
And human love rises anew
To rule the world.
                    Nadson[53]

There are people here who are deeply religious, although they themselves don't know it. To these who are of a religious nature—belongs Jack Abrams.

He was a believer, and the object of his belief was *mankind*. Along with Leonhard Frank,[54] he too was convinced that "man is good," and that only the injustices of the existing social order had transformed the world into a kingdom of wickedness.

So deeply rooted was his faith in mankind and in humanity's potential to yearn after all that is good, beautiful and uplifting, that he lived out all the years of his socially-conscious life with rock-solid certainty in the possibility of realizing the pinnacle of utopian socialism, which is anarchism as a social philosophy.

The deceased's anarchism developed in his consciousness as a worldview not so much as a result of *theoretical* study, as from his intrinsic belief in the goodness of humankind and in its ability to live in voluntary cooperation, without the lash of organized government's whip. With perfect faith, he believed that the state—even when it was a socialist state—was an unpardonable pressure against the free personality, and that this was against superior ethics and was an offense to humankind.

This deep belief in mankind and —although it is still far away—the

---

53 Semyon Nadson: a poet during the Russian Empire (most likely the Yiddish was a translation from Russian).

54 Leonhard Frank: a German expressionist writer and pacifist who wrote a series of anti-war short-stories entitled *Man is Good*.

certain triumph of anarchy in the highest philosophical sense of the word, was the most important driving force in the deceased's community activity.

There was nothing in the world that could uproot his anarchism; he had returned from Soviet Russia deeply disillusioned, but his disappointment in the Soviet reality did not diminish by one hair his belief that the redemption of mankind would still come. Yet the methods had to be, he remained convinced, completely different.

One of the most beautiful chapters in the history of the Jewish community activity here are the years of—per his initiative, it was established and in fact, administered by him—the anti-fascism committee. His enthusiasm and energy inspired all co-participants to the highest level and ensured that the committee activity would result in cultural elevation, as demonstrated in a series of public enterprises that are recalled yet today, almost twenty years later, as a watershed moment in the history of Jewish spiritual life here in this country.

How deeply he experienced Spain's tragedy! With so much zeal, he threw himself into aid work for the victims of Franco's fascist attack against the Spanish Republic and his victory over it! When the history of this chapter is written, the activity of the deceased as the chairman of the Mexican division of the International Aid Organization will be properly esteemed, and his spirited figure will then be lit up from the great splendor of his nobleness and true, unpublicized love of humanity.

Jack Abrams did not belong to those who proclaimed themselves passionately in love with abstract "humanity"; for him first of all existed the *concrete* fellow man around him who was suffering. It was to *him* that Abrams strove to be a comfort, him that Abrams wanted to encourage, and in him to awaken new hope.

He would not allow the prosaic reality to repress him spiritually; he would resist the grayness of day-to-day life with the celebration of future visions. Anarcho-syndicalism was the banner that he hung out over the construction of his attitude towards the world, and to human society.

And he never lowered this banner until his last breath of air.

(*The Voice*, Mexico, 17 June 1953)

SALOMON KAHAN

2. J. Abrams—The Oppositionist

Jacob Abrams was the great *adversary*.
His oppositional stance came from two different sources:
    A. From his romantic-anarchist world view in general, which was in its entire essence anti-centralist, and did not fit well into a social dynamic in which the tendency towards more and more obvious forms of centralization was its strongest driving force.
    B. From his constitutionally democratic being that organically could not tolerate any high-handedness, insolence or mailed-fist politics—in one word, everything that violated in whatever form the liberty of the individual personality and trampled on the will of the majority of a collective.

It is with *this* aspect of the public activist personality of the deceased that the *positive*—which stood behind Abrams' adversarial nature— must be especially emphasized, because a great many of the things he fought for are also just as important today, and therefore as timely as when Abrams took up their causes.

He first of all interceded incessantly for *freedom of thought* in the local Jewish street. On innumerable occasions, he expressed—in his own way naturally, and in a specific form—the great truth that lay in the classic warning phrase by the French thinker Voltaire:

"I may not be in agreement with any of the thoughts that you assert; however, if necessary I will defend with my entire life your right to freely express them."

The right to one's own opinion, the freedom to express it without being persecuted for it—such elementary things these are! And yet! How many times did we have the occasion to hear Abrams protesting with justification against the violation of those basic principles without which there can be no talk of democracy in social communal life, and without which the social fabric becomes converted into a caricature and a bitter farce.

It was Jacob Abrams who, with all his might, fought against the first attempts that were made years ago to bring brutality regarding other ways of thinking into our local life in the form of exclusion, boycotting, and eventually, excommunication.

Abrams had warned already years ago that with such behaviors, people would sooner or later place our Jewish community face-to-face with the peril of totalitarianism, and with the danger of it being such a type of situation that the high-handedness described in Mendele's "The Tax"[55] would pale by comparison.

For that reason, any time he had the chance to speak he emphasized the life necessity of *tolerance* to one's ideational opponent, as long as that person didn't want to abuse this characteristic trait of democracy in order to destroy it.

Consequently, Abrams also always pointed out the thought that no one—and truly no one—was permitted to think that he, and only he, had the monopoly on truth, and that only *his* lenses were the best possible ones through which to view the world and the problems that life brings with it.

If there was ever anyone in our local Jewish street who could not organically tolerate dogmatism and was always prepared to *analyze*, it was Jacob Abrams. He had, better than anyone in our local Jewish community, grasped the dangers that a dogmatic stance brings to the development of community life.

And was there one among us who was a greater opponent of fanaticism? One of the favorite weapons of the fanatic is: "Shut your mouth!" The fanatic doesn't seek voluntary, thoughtful agreement from the opposing side: the fanatic wants him *silenced*, he is aggressive; his weapon is not logic but "Accept my opinion," and woe to him who wants to think freely and analyze. Abrams was the antithesis of this kind of thing.

Jacob Abrams was the anti-fascist "par excellence" and the embodiment of anti-totalitarianism. He would suffer greatly every time that he would come across facts and phenomena in our Jewish life here that contained kernels of fascist tactics or disguised totalitarianism. With all the force of his powerful spirited personality, he would unmask them and fight against them.

This indefatigable fighter against dogmatism, fanaticism and every form of totalitarianism—and for democracy and tolerance in our community life; we will never forget him.

(*The Voice*, Mexico, 12 June 1954)

---

55   A reference to the story by famous Yiddish writer Mendele Moykher-Sforim, "Di takse" ("The Tax").

AUGUSTIN ZUKHI

J. Abrams—The Idealist

On June 11th, at the Jewish cemetery in Mexico City, several hundred people gathered together around the casket of Jacob Abrams. Those present consisted of members of the Jewish community and socialist and anarchist groups, who came to pay their last respects to the deceased. In accordance with Abrams' tendencies, life and work, the burial was carried out without religious rituals.

Jacob Abrams was of that generation that at the end of the last century and beginning of the current, had inscribed upon his banner the ideal of a socialist revolution. In 1908, the young Abrams came from Tsarist Russia to the free America. A book publisher by profession, he quickly became one of the liveliest militants in his union in New York. As a fervent anti-militarist and sympathizer with the ideas of Emma Goldman and Alexander Berkman, during the war years he declared himself against the war and against America interfering in the Russian revolution. For this position and for his revolutionary activity, in 1918 he was arrested. After spending almost three years in prison, in 1921 he was deported from the United States to revolutionary Russia. It is only in this last year that Abrams received permission to return to the United States.

After the end of the First World War, Russia was the mecca of the Promised Land where the socialist ideals should have been brought about. In a short time, Abrams was the leader of the anarcho-syndicalist printing shop Golos Truda in Moscow. Yet the dictatorship of the Bolshevik party that began to oppress everyone more and more quickly destroyed the illusions of all honest anarchist socialists. Under the iron boots of the Soviet Communist Party that smashed all liberties, there was no possibility of activity for people of Abrams' cut. As Alexander Schapiro[56] and other anarchist social revolutionaries and social democrats had already done, in 1926 Abrams was compelled to leave the fatherland of the revolution. The first stop for the new socialist and anarchist immigrants from the east was Germany. However, the Weimar Republic that the Nazis continued to undermine was not a hospitable terrain for the Russian social revolutionaries. Moreover, Abrams could not stay in Germany. He and

---

56 Alexander M. Schapiro: Russian Jewish anarcho-syndicalist militant.

his life-friend Mary chose, and then found their home in Mexico.

Yet in their new home, Abrams still couldn't be satisfied with a peaceful, bourgeois existence. His lively public spirit sought new activity for itself that would be suitable for a different circumstance. When the Nazi race persecutions started, Abrams began working tirelessly for those fleeing and placed himself in charge of an aid action in Mexico. On his initiative, collections were arranged which brought in considerable sums to support the refugees from Germany. Abrams often put the community requirements before his personal interests, which he thought were more important than his private matters.

At the outbreak of the Second World War, Mexico was one of the reception countries for political refugees. Together with tens of thousands of Spanish Republicans of every hue, a large number of victims of persecution came into the country from other nations. When a division of the International Rescue and Relief Committee was founded in Mexico, Abrams was chosen as its chairman. For Abrams, no type of national or ideological discrimination existed. He helped all refugees who were in need of aid.

Abrams remained an idealist until a ripe old age. He never renounced his humanistic ideals. His guiding star was his faith in liberty and human dignity. He never turned away from this star, following it all his life.

(*Free Voice of Labor*,[57] Mexico, 7 July 1953)

---

57 Yiddish: *Freie Arbeiter Stimme*.

M. RUBINSTEIN

A Human Being

He was an immigrant since childhood, leaving his father's house while still a young boy, and had already done much grueling labor during the years when the nouveau riche were springing up in America like mushrooms after a rain. His ardor brought him to the lines of those discontented with the world and its order, and there he forged his spirit—from then onwards utilizing that energy of his very youngest years.

With conviction, he did everything possible for a new world and a new people; for his anti-war agitation an American court took away his freedom—four years later he is traded to his homeland, Russia, where the revolution still cooked with an honest fire and where men of such fiery natures were still needed.

Nevertheless, he came to Mexico, through Berlin and Havana where he tried to find shelter for his temperament and work, until he arrived here; close to the land where he had committed the "great crimes"; he settled here actually as a joke, and he has stayed here ever since.

He hasn't yet made any money, and won't make any. He has no wealth and won't have any. He didn't work his way up to having a house, because he doesn't need more than a corner, and only a hard bed to lay down his bones.

He knows everyone in the city, and even more know him. Everyone has heard him and each one knows that he is a one-of-a-kind person. He is not a believer, rather—an atheist, and is more observant than the most pious among the pious.

Everyone believes him and everyone trusts him. He doesn't own his own thousands, and people entrust him to regulate matters worth tens of thousands. Friends mistrust each other—they rest assured that he will reconcile them; people feel uncertain—they listen to what he says and look for clarification from him on complicated questions.

If he speaks, people listen to him with bated breath. If someone maligns him, that person is flaunting a testimonial to his own madness because Abrams' conscience is spotless, as he never does a deliberate act detrimental to another. Like everyone, he has human weaknesses: Surprisingly, he himself is not inflexible and allows himself to be influenced; he believes everyone, and can be persuaded to various good things, even if they are against his own way of thinking. Yet somehow he has one thing that is entrenched in him like steel —and this is a sound and deeply humane morality!

He doesn't talk about morality, doesn't preach morality, but *behaves* like a moralist.

He is very restless, a bit of an odd eccentric. He is always creating something, building, doing, organizing. He has almost nothing for his efforts—he needs nothing; enough that he has a living, a bite to eat and a place to lay his head. He helps—he slips in when anonymous support is needed so people won't know where it came from. People often exploit his naiveté and do things to him that are detrimental; for good—he receives bad. He doesn't think long about the injustice done; a short while later he is again doing this person a favor and doesn't mention that something happened.

The city considers him a courageous person, although almost everyone does the opposite of him. They say that he is an extraordinary person, and that not everyone can be extraordinary. He is respected and esteemed. They look for an opportunity to have a few words with him, they want to be among his acquaintances; they meet him with respect and take their leave of him with esteem—and they admire his cheerfulness, his youthful appearance that doesn't match his years, his exuberant energy that is so out of step with his age—his optimism, his faith in goodness and justice, his contempt for bad deeds as much for Jews as for the political movements.

There are those who consider him an oddball, who see such types as abnormalities, especially in today's world of deception and hypocrisy. There are such who quietly accompany him with derision because they begrudge a person obtaining such a halo, and they are instinctively jealous of him. Yet they are few—their scorn will not be a big hit with the public, because people can quickly tell that this is spoken out of envy or hatred.

He is already, as was said, in his later years and has nothing. He is provided with nothing and doesn't want to be provided for. He lives only by physical labor and is envious of no one. Wealth is a waste to him; property—despised; the thread of personal happiness—also interrupted, and yet he is happy.

Without houses, without reserves, without bank accounts, without operating with large sums and tossing around banknotes; in one word—without earthly fortune.

Yet he has possessions that can't be bought with any amount of money: a good, spotless name that is worth more than great factories and buildings —a possession that was created by King Solomon with the profound incantation of "A good name is better than precious ointment."[58]

And where? In a country where men forget their own names, where they don't remember the Fathers[59] and transgress their rites, where men make money, where men don't rest, do no good deeds, where men think neither about God nor people. And who? Not a religious person, not a fanatic; a free spirit and a quiet man—small of body, large of spirit, good-hearted and literally without a drop of bitterness. And when he does something that deviates from pure good? It is when people in whom he trusts lead him to it.

Is he some sort strange saint? No, he is not some sort of oddity—but a decent human being, such of which there are few today.

(From the book *Topics of Mexico*, 1941)

---

58   Ecclesiastes 7:1.
59   Possible reference to *Pirkei Avos*, "Ethics of Our Fathers" or to the Patriarchs of Judaism: Abraham, Isaac and Jacob.

J. PAT[60]
Friend Abrams

"The entire life is a story that someone dreams"—said the Yiddish writer Dovid Ignatov. Each person is himself a story. Today I want to tell you a story about a person who not long ago left this world. This is friend Abrams of Mexico.

The name is well known by a significant number of labor activists, trade unionists, socialists and anarchists in America. He lived for many years in New York. Afterwards, he had to live in Mexico and indeed, now he has died there. He was one of my good, good friends.

In my life, I've traveled all over the world. I was in many countries and met people, many people, numbering up to the thousands. Yet when I close my eyes and want to see in my imagination those people that remain in my memory and my heart, those Jewish homes that are dear to my soul, the number is much smaller. To *this* small number belong Abrams, his wife and his home.

Who was Abrams? Born in a small town in Russia, in Uman in 1886, meaning that at his death he was sixty-seven years old. He looked much younger: his face—a very interesting one. His black hair was disheveled and curly. His eyes—large and deep. His expression was always a smile. He was a thoughtful, intelligent, Jewish working person, of a fighting nature—a rarity.

Beginning in his youth, still in the old country, Abrams was active in the revolutionary movement. He had to leave Russia, fleeing the police and prisons and came to America in 1908, arriving in New York. He was in the printing trades. He did his job but as always, he was occupied with the labor movement. At that time, he was well known in the American Jewish labor scene. A fiery speaker, a logical mind, a man with a quick wit, pure, honest, loyal, a good friend ... what more can one ask of a person?

He had transgressed during the time of the First World War. He was against war, against bloodshed. He agitated on the corners of New York against war. The American court then sentenced him to twenty years. He fled the prisons of Russia and ended up in a prison in free America. Why? He

---

60   Jacob Pat: Yiddish author, one of the founders of the World Congress of Jewish Culture.

had never stolen anything, never robbed anyone, never killed anyone, and not done anything bad. He only spoke out against the war. War—he argued— was an imperialistic, capitalistic thing. No matter who is victorious, which side is the loser, everything will be bad for the working class. We know this classic anti-war speech from that very distant time.

At that time, there was no Bolshevism in Russia. There was only revolution—Kerensky[61] revolution, peasants' revolution, socialist upheaval. It drew friend Abrams back to the old country, back to Uman, back to Minsk, back to Petersburg and Moscow. Instead of serving twenty years in prison, the American government allowed him to be deported to Russia that was then, according to Abrams' belief, a country becoming new, free and just. He was released from prison and deported to Russia with the injunction: he could not enter America again.

Abrams went off to Russia. However, it was inevitable that Abrams would be very quickly sobered up from his illusions. After a short time in Russia, he witnessed and acknowledged the brutality of the communist revolution. It was the time when the sailors led the rebellion against Lenin and Leninism in Kronstadt. He ran to Odessa, where people had also risen up against the dictatorship and violence. The "revolutionary Russia" became worse for Abrams than the twenty years of prison in America. It was time to leave.

And he ran, friend Abrams and his wife Mary, from Russia. Where to? America was closed. In Europe, he had nothing to do. He wandered through the European cities and in 1927, settled in Mexico. Mexico needed him. There he became a central figure. He was the founder of a Yiddish weekly periodical and the builder of Jewish community life. Fascism came to Europe, the Spanish civil war came, and Abrams was in charge of the anti-fascist committee in Mexico.

I saw him for the first time and we became friends in the year 1937, when I was in Mexico on assignment from the Yiddish schools in Poland. He became then one of my nearest and most intimate friends. He threw himself into the campaign for the Yiddish schools. We spent long hours, days and nights together. It was a pleasure to sit with Abrams, to chat with him about world matters, about freedom and slavery, about socialism and

---

61 Alexander Kerensky: Russian lawyer and politician who served in the Russian Provisional Government.

anarchism, about democracy and dictatorship. Yes, Abrams became in those days in particular a courageous fighter against communism in Mexico. The Jewish community there was in a certain measure infected with communism. The communists were seen and heard at every assembly, at every get-together.

Abrams was a brilliant speaker, an energetic chairman; unflinching and uncompromising, he led the struggle. I remember the assemblies we had with him in Mexico. Friends and foes, admirers and opponents, socialists and communists—it reverberated and raged in the hall. Abrams spoke. He was a hero of the revolutionary rebellion, he was a hero of the Odessa port; and on the New York streets he courageously struggled for his anti-war beliefs. He was certainly valiant on the daises of Mexico, fighting for freedom.

There comes to mind an extraordinary meeting I had with him. This was at the table of Lev Trotsky in Mexico. Abrams was well acquainted with Trotsky and a familiar visitor at his house. When I was in Mexico, I was interested in meeting with Trotsky and having a chat with him about world issues. It was very complicated to get into Trotsky's house; guards watched over him. Trotsky knew well that Stalin was lying in wait for him, so he had to be careful.

These were three or four remarkable hours at Trotsky's table. "Doesn't he seem to you," Abrams said to me, "like a Vilna expert on rabbinical law, a Vilna rabbi, or a Vilna rabbinical judge who rules on religious questions with an acuity, brilliance and severity?" Trotsky spoke coarse words—such as are spoken among soldiers in the barracks—about his former comrades: about Stalin and Molotov, Zinoviev and Kamenev. His tongue was like a razor. His coarse words were blended with much acuteness in brilliantly structured Russian sentences.

So Abrams, sitting at the table with him, said: "Comrade Trotsky, I'm only fifty-percent in agreement with you. I agree with what you say about your former comrades when you condemn them. However, here's where we part ways. I don't agree that if you were in Stalin's place, you would be better. Dictatorship has its own logic; perhaps you would be even worse."

To say such words to Trotsky, the keen polemicist with complete faith in his own truth, who sat at the table with a revolver by his right hand—not everyone could do this. Abrams could, and he continued to be good friends with Trotsky.

Mexico eventually became a place for Jewish cultural work, and Abrams was in charge of it. Abrams was active in each important aid campaign. From time to time—rarely as of late—I would receive a note from him; a brotherly greeting. A couple of months ago, he came to New York to save his health, to save his life in a New York[62] hospital. It was not so easy to enter into America—he had, after all, sinned during the time of the First World War and was sentenced to twenty years in prison. However, a serious illness—he was permitted to enter the country.

The New York hospital didn't help him and sent him back to Mexico. Now he is dead. One of the most interesting, important and colorful figures is gone. The Jewish labor movement has lost one of its most loyal sons.

(*Forward*, Mexico, 15 July 1953)

---

62   Translator's note: as told in other accounts, Abrams was at Temple University Hospital in Philadelphia, PA.

JULIAN GORKIN[63]
The Perfect Human Being

When I think about the truly good human beings that I have met in my life, one of the first figures that springs to mind is—the persona of Jack Abrams.

There are people here who are naturally good, just as one's skin is white or black. Abrams was by nature good from the inside out; he was consciously good from an intellectual and idealistic standpoint. He was truly a model of human kindness. I believe that nowadays, this is the best thing that can be said about a person.

Abrams was the first friend with my same ideology that I met when I arrived in Mexico in May, 1940. At our first meeting, I already felt that a friendship would grow between us that would last a lifetime. He was one of the first people to help me when the Moscow Kremlin brought a lawsuit against me in Spain, my own country—a lawsuit that almost cost me my life. When I thanked him, he just gave me a brotherly smile. I remember also that with his natural sincerity, he offered me a desk to help furnish my modest refugee's home.

Another time, I had problems with my landlord. As soon as Abrams found out about it—I don't know from whom—he was off to see him and paid him all the money that I owed. My opponents kept on spreading rumors that during the civil war I had smuggled millions out of Spain—Abrams, in a quiet but effective way was fair to me with his action. When several years later I was in a position to pay back the debt, he immediately handed the money over to the International Committee to Aid the Victims of Fascism.

Such satisfaction he would feel when he could help a friend! No one who turned to him went away empty-handed. I don't believe that there was a single day in his life in which he would not have done something in the area of human aid and solidarity. To give, to help—this was Abrams' luxury, his spiritual wealth, his "weakness." Is it then possible that such a person would not die poor? However, he was not one of those who believed in a reward after death. His kindness, which was not tied to any notion of future compensation, was therefore of the idealistic and elevated type.

---

63   Julián Gómez García-Ribera: better known as Julián Gorkin, an author and Spanish revolutionary socialist.

How often we would both painfully comment on the lack of human solidarity so characteristic of our current era. There were, however, times when humanity had mobilized itself: for the benefit of Dreyfus,[64] Ferrer,[65] and Sacco and Vanzetti. Yet when the Nazis carried out the horrible slaughter of over six million Jews, there was no one who would arouse and mobilize the conscience of the human race. And what about the world's silence towards the Soviet concentration camps? It was not enough for the totalitarian governments to continue destroying human lives and annihilating cultural treasures; they destroyed something that was even dearer: the human conscience and moral awareness.

In that time of crisis of human values, the existence of Jack Abrams was truly a wonder. His life, from his earliest years up until his death, was a continuous act of solidarity—in the best sense of the word—with his fellow man: each righteous struggle found a standard-bearer in him; each friendly hand that reached out to him would find a warm heart and brotherly assistance.

In Mexico, I had the occasion to work together with Abrams on the International Committee to Aid the Victims of Fascism. This committee consisted of activists from a variety of political tendencies, and people from different nations were active in it. We unanimously elected Abrams as chairman. Could there really be anyone else suited for this important and difficult office, when there was Abrams? No one merited it more than he did, and neither did anyone else possess his moral authority. He, in a fuller measure than any other committee member, personified the idea and consciousness of universal brotherhood and solidarity. In this lucky little corner of the "right of asylum"—which Mexico symbolized in the tragic years of the Second World War—our committee accomplished much, especially for the benefit of refugees from Spain who were old and sick. Many of them who still live today have Abrams to thank for it. He was the one who on his daily visits, would instill in them fresh courage and bring them new hope. He would dedicate much of his time to them, and also his best efforts. It was a kind of fatherly relationship that he had with them, and from the deepest resources of his heart there flowed to them unending kindness. The question of the nationality of the person asking for help never came up for him. Himself a

---

64 Presumably referring to the treason conviction of French artillery officer Alfred Dreyfus.
65 Presumably the trial and execution of Spanish anarchist Francisco Ferrer Guardia.

Jew, his heart bled due to the abyss of suffering of his people. Yet not for one minute did he limit his sorrow only to the Jewish tragedy, because Abrams belonged to all those "degraded and repressed," and his noble spirit embraced the whole world that was awaiting its redemption. In my entire life, I never met such a universal person as was Abrams.

After thirty years of a militant life in many countries, I was a considerable skeptic towards these so-called great human beings, who were known as such thanks to their great knowledge or because of certain specific services and events of their lives that furnished them with glory. On the contrary, I bow to the truly great people, that is, to those for whom justice and fairness are the leitmotif of their lives and the driving force of their deeds.

In this sense, Jack Abrams was the embodiment of a life-concept, and his name itself symbolizes an idea and a banner that flutters in the hands of freedom fighters. His existence was a continuing confirmation of the idea that true valor consists in living—being true to oneself and to the end comprehending the sanctity of life and the never-diminishing importance of not profaning it.

As one of these heroes, Abrams will live in my memory.

(Paris, October 1953)
Translated from Spanish by Salomon Kahan

SH. TSFAS

One Who Storms, One Who Fights

Death, in and of itself, is cruel and horrible, but even more cruel and horrible was the death of our dear friend of many years, J. Abrams. He had been struggling against death for the last several years. I remember as if it were yesterday, when the first claw of mankind's greatest enemy—cancer—entangled itself in Abrams' throat. At that moment he was standing on a dais speaking. He became stuck and couldn't speak again.

This was the terrifying beginning.

After that had begun a bitter struggle, an intense combat between Abrams, the perpetual fighter, and pitiless illness and death. J. Abrams, entirely courageous by nature, energetic and militant, did not become overwhelmed; he fought with all his physical and spiritual strength. He still had hope up to the last weeks of his life, when he had already lost the most precious thing that God had gifted him with: his speech. He would learn how to talk with his stomach; there was such a school in the States, he sometimes explained to us. On the day before he died, when I, along with Mr. N. Aks was with him, he asked the nurse for a mirror. He wanted to see himself for the last time. Was he concerned about his external appearance? Indeed, perhaps both things together ...

Cruel death finally defeated the esthetically beautiful and the ethically pure J. Abrams.

*   *   *

He didn't die rich, yet together with his life-companion, Mary, he had a rich life—a life with substance, with struggle, with complete awareness of why he lived and why he fought. It was not the rich life that brings sweet warmth, physical contentment and material happiness. No, in that precise sense he had a bitter life, a life of travel, wandering and homelessness. Cast out of America for anti-war activity while the First World War was still going on; fleeing from Soviet Russia because of the dictatorship and terror there; and also even here, in Mexico, he didn't always find peace and contentment, especially during the last years of his life when everything went downhill. Despite this, he was a rich person: rich in substance, in spirit, in conviction.

Friend J. Abrams was an interesting and beautiful personality.

It was twenty-five years ago when I went for the first time to a meeting of socialists and radicals, and I saw for myself a good-looking man with a full shock of hair combed straight back and a large, wide cravat. He stood, spoke and raged. I don't accurately remember what Abrams was raging about, but this is how he remains in my memory: Abrams raging, Abrams protesting, Abrams fighting. He was born this way: one who storms, one who fights. He never could make peace with injustice. Whether he had to fight against a mighty government and therefore sit in prison for three and a half years; whether he had to fight against a power made of steel, blood and iron—against the Stalinist regime; whether it was a struggle against the united campaign when it seemed to him that someone was about to be wronged—everywhere and always, Abrams stood in the frontlines of the battle.

I would say that he was the Don Quixote here on our Jewish street in Mexico. He fought against windmills in the depressing real life, and he was defeated. Reality was too strong and too entrenched, and the spiritually-pure Don Quixote fell.

With Abrams has departed a piece of Jewish history, of a young Jewish community such as the one here in Mexico; not the history of the economically advancing Jew, but the history of the cultural Jew, the Jew that built cultural society, founded newspapers, published journals, did cultural enterprises; the history of the modern and secular Jewish person who believed and still believes in honest and pure community activity.

Who doesn't remember how Abrams literally reigned over the presentations, lectures, and literary and social trials.[66] Abrams was always the defender at these trials. Here he defends "Bontshe Shvayg"[67] and there he unexpectedly defends the doctor (in a famous story) who shoots his patient suffering from cancer, in order to learn the secret of this destructive disease—just as if Abrams had a dark premonition that it would be this illness that would defeat him.

Abrams saw the world as an internationalist; I am afraid to use the word

---

66   In Eastern Europe in the 1930's—and perhaps even earlier—it was fashionable among Yiddish-speaking Jews to conduct "literary trials." A large audience would gather and listen first to a "prosecutor" and then to a "defender" making the case against and then for the conduct of a character in a literary work.

67   Yiddish: "Bontshe the Silent," a short story by famous Yiddish writer I. L. Perets.

"cosmopolitan," because this became a term of abuse used by his greatest enemy, Stalinism. Nevertheless, he always lived and was productive among Jews and in Jewish life. Deep inside, in the honesty of his soul he was a Jew, a Jewish revolutionary, and he agonized for the Jewish calamities and suffering.

He himself was a person who studied. In the mature years of his life, he began to study Yiddish, especially how to write Yiddish.

I had the honor to be his Yiddish teacher. It did not take me much time, and little trouble. Within a couple of months, Abrams was writing articles in Yiddish.

The Jewish Mexico lost a capable and honest cultural human being. We, his close companions and friends, lost a loyal friend, a true socialist believer and revolutionary.

His memory will always be dear and beloved to us, and call forth respect.

(*Forward*, Mexico, 1 July 1953)

DR. YEHOSHUA USTRI-DIN

Like a Hero from a Romance Novel

J. Abrams was one of the central figures of the first generation of immigrants in Mexico. He was one of those who laid the cornerstones of the development of Mexican Jewry. When he departed from us after a difficult illness and much suffering, a part of the history of the Jewish community here becomes concluded. We are closing an initial chapter of our life.

Abrams was a personality. He left a specific impression on whoever got close to him. There was a sort of distinctiveness about him, I would say. He was a different sort of person, a more beautiful person; he was like a hero from a romance novel. Abrams carried on his shoulders that which no one else would allow himself to take on as he proceeds down the path of his life.

The impression that Abrams (may he rest in peace) left on his fellow conversationalists would become deeper and more impressive over time. The more one met with him, all the more one desired to meet and converse with him again.

Abrams was one of those who went out into the world with burning enthusiasm in his heart. I am certain that opponents of the social revolution, although they themselves stood very far from social-revolutionary ideas, when they met with Abrams must have had a feeling of respect for his deep faith in a better tomorrow for humanity,.

However, life did not make a present to Abrams of any valid social coins. The Russian revolution, of which he dreamt, for which he struggled—didn't become his revolution. The Zionist movement that by hard-fought struggle achieved the new process of redemption in the current bloody era was also not his movement. Nevertheless, Zionists and, for a very long time, socialist ideological opponents, had an attitude of respect towards Abrams' person.

Because: this is it—the deep substance of a superior human being and a true bearer of faith and justice and righteousness; no one bows to him and no one despises him.

I personally very much regretted that our paths became so divergent that we stopped speaking to each other. Nevertheless, for me Abrams remained one of the most beautiful figures that I have met in my life. You sometimes read in a book a portrayal of an extraordinary person with extraordinary accomplishments, original thinking and an original way of life, and you think to yourself, "Oh, nonsense—I know that such good fortune only happens in romances; in life it never happens that we would find such a person in our path."

Yet the hero of romances became flesh and blood for me, thanks to the encounter with Abrams—an encounter that lasted several wonderful years. I would often meet with him about printing matters and in this way spend long hours with him.

Immediately after the emergence of the State of Israel, Abrams said to me: "You've ruined my fate for me. Until now I was an original Jew from an original nation. There was no government, no army, no police and no government statutes. See what you've done to me: no more original Jew!"

There was so much personal belief in this irony that I thought for a moment: there is a bit of socialist truth in it. Today I would add to it and say: a bit of Abrams' anarchist truth.

He departed suddenly, although we all knew about his dire state of health. May these words be a contribution to the beautiful personality, to the beautiful human being and good Jew that Abrams (of blessed memory) was; a consolation for his devastated wife and for his friends, and for all those who had met Abrams during the walk of their lives.

Abrams deserves a memorial marker. His memory must become immortalized with us, as best we can do for the "eternity" of this dearly departed. The community learned from Abrams. The structure of the community received a great many bricks from Abrams. I am convinced that none of those whom Abrams fought and struggled against bore any enmity towards him. No, no one could become an enemy of Abrams. So therefore, the central committee, along with the Cultural Center, should develop a project to honor the memory of J. Abrams.

We didn't have many Abramses!

(*The Voice*, Mexico, 17 July 1953)

The Writings of Jacob Abrams
Autobiographical Fragments

CHAPTER 1
Without a Childhood

THE MOTHER DIES—A STEPMOTHER COMES

My childhood ended even before the first five years of my life were over. My mother died very young. To this day, I retain a habit impressed upon me by her death. Every night when I lay down to sleep, I roll over so I face the wall, in the same pose my mother took before she died. At that moment she called me to her, gave me a kiss, and then turned with her face to the wall and was gone. From that day on, I became an adult. All my happy childish years vanished and I knew no more of childhood.

When my mother died, we lived in the city of Odessa. My father remained with me and my sister, who was four years older than I was. For a time, she took over the role of mother for me.

My father's parents lived in the Ukrainian Jewish city of Uman, Kiev province. He liquidated his little bit of possessions which had never amounted to much, and we all moved to his parents in Uman.

In that time, my sister already understood all that had taken place. I still had no idea whatsoever about it. My mother died—for me it was that, "Mama isn't here, but she'll come back soon." Yet when a few months later my father moved us to a new house and presented us with a "new mother," I immediately burst into tears and shrieked, "I want my mama!"

My sister refused to call her "mother." No matter what they did to her—she stood her ground. They worked harder on me to break me down, and from time to time I would say "Mama"—mainly when I wanted something to eat.

As the majority of them are, my stepmother was also a very bad one, especially to us children. She was bitter that while still so young she had to become a mother to two children, and worse, with the title of "stepmother." Moreover, if there was somewhere a bitter stepmother, it fell to me to have that fate. For seven long years, from this woman along with my father's assistance, I suffered a taste of hell, if it is as men describe it. My sister was not treated this way. Her argument was that a girl should be protected, but a boy—"break his head!" This was an expression of her brother, who was considered to be a learned Jew. Seven long years, with never enough to eat and sleeping on a sack in the hallway between one room and another. When there was a hole to be filled, they would plug it up with "Yankele"[68]—that is, with me.

In seven years, my stepmother had produced five children: three girls and two boys. From the first child to the fifth, I was the nanny. Be it day or night, when something was needed for a child, it was my task to go get it. To run around in the street with other children—that was taken from me. Every step I took was done stealthily, accompanied by childish lies and my not following the rules my stepmother had set out for me. My father, whose business dealings were scattered across the entire expanse of Russia, was very rarely at home outside of the two, three, or four times a year when he would come home for a few weeks. Then my life became a complete misery: my father would beat me without mercy in order to placate his second wife.

My father dressed all his children as was fitting for a successful Jewish businessman. I was the only one to go about in tattered suits and worn-out boots, on the claim that I was a devil, not a child, and if my clothes were sewn of iron they still wouldn't last. Therefore I suffered greatly. In the neighborhood where I lived there were many well-to-do families, and all the children were beautifully dressed. I was always dressed like the children of our courtyard watchman. With each year, this bothered me more. I did everything possible to merit that somebody should pay attention to me, but from my parents I couldn't garner even a drop of sympathy.

However, I received much attention from the neighborhood children. The tribulations of my home, exposing me to hunger and cold, the constant blows—all this hardened me greatly. I feared nothing. I was the best ice skater, could ride a horse, was a good swimmer, and could stretch from one tree to another and shake down the fruit. I was not afraid of dogs. In one word, to these children I was a true hero.

But my bravery also caused me great problems. The children of the neighborhood, who loved to go around with me, would often fail to go to school and when they would fail, they would put the blame on me. The mother of such a child would typically go running to my stepmother in a great fuss: "Why can't you restrain this prodigy, the ringleader, this brat?" After such a ruckus from a mother, my sister would quickly run to me and let me know and I wouldn't go home that day.

---

68   Yiddish: diminutive of Yakob, the Russified Yiddish version of Jacob.

My place of refuge in such a case was my Aunt Esther. She was herself an extreme pauper, but she was a very good person and it was to her I would run for help. I could not stay with her for long though, because every piece of bread that she gave me she had to take from her own children, who themselves never had enough to eat. My uncle had gone off to England some time before. She was the sole breadwinner for her three small children and she eked out a living sewing skirts for people. Therefore, after such a stint of hiding, I would not go straight home. Earlier that day I would sneak into my own house when the stepmother wasn't home and make a "Witch's Sabbath"[69] in the kitchen. I would gather up the fish, and if it was Friday the fresh-baked challah, and carry them off to my aunt.

My aunt, a kind and intelligent woman, would always chastise me for doing such a bad thing. It always made me happy to hear her maternal reproach. It was very welcome to listen to her lecturing me that one is not permitted to be bad, and that it wasn't correct that I would do such wrong things. Finally, we would make a grand feast. My aunt would usually not take even a taste of that which I had brought, but we children would devour it with both cheeks full. In the years from when I was five until I was twelve, such episodes were repeated many times. Moreover, with every year, my life in my father's house became harder and harder.

When I turned ten years old, only then had my father realized that I should go to school. My stepmother did not want to consent to it—"Who will pay for his education?" Nonetheless, on this point my father set his foot down and sent me to the Russian city elementary school. This for me was a new hell: a lad of ten years old put with children no older than six or seven. But because I was placed with younger children and wanted to quickly escape to an older class, I studied with the same fervor with which I had led my street life. In my first year I worked hard enough to move to the third class. I earned top grades, but when at the end of the first semester of my third class year I brought home A's and B's, my stepmother exclaimed, "So already you have a new scholar, enough! Doesn't it say there, that he can read and write? So he must be sent out to be trained as a clerk." My father tried to resist her demands, but when the grand lady remained intractable,

---

69   Yiddish: shvarts shabes ("black Sabbath"), a Sabbath on which a calamity occurred either that day or during the preceding week.

it was no use. Sure enough, soon after Passover I was given for three years to a dry goods store of one Ephraim Yampolski, who had earned a name for producing good men.

A CLERK IN A DRY GOODS STORE

I was not yet twelve years old when I became an errand-boy in a dry goods store. Actually, I was not in the store; I was kept mainly in the house. Ephraim Yampolski was a rich Jew with a large household, a phaeton with horses, cattle—all things for which a boy could be useful.

For me, the work, together with the coachman, the foreman, and with the Jewish cook who worked there, opened up a new world. First of all, it was the pleasure of hitching up the horses, mixing the food for the cows, and spraying the garden with water; secondly—the food. There everyone lacked for nothing, above all, me. The cook, each time she gave me a plate of food, would heap curses on my stepmother. Neither did she spare a few of the same blessings for my father; while serving me a piece of meat she would say: "Eat! May they choke there, eat!" I had known how to eat from before, but being there I perfected it as an art, so much that after being there for a few months, I had almost doubled my size. Suddenly, I was renewed.

Nonetheless my sister, who was already a young lady, would cast a shadow on the pleasures that I had so recently received. In those days my sister had already joined the Socialist movement. She would always tell me, "Certainly today you're not hungry, they give you food, but you must do something with your life, so you don't remain a servant for an overfed rich man." I didn't understand her grievances and her discontent, but I sensed them. I loved my sister very much; she had always defended me with so much love, and I felt that she was right, that to groom the horses and mix buckets of food for the cows would lead me nowhere.

It was then that a calamity suddenly happened. The owner had sent me to buy chaff for the cattle. In those days, it cost twenty kopeks a sack. The owner didn't tell me how much to buy; he only instructed me that I must bargain and not pay more than twenty kopeks. At the first chaff wagon that I approached, the peasant asked the proper price. Yet since I had sometimes heard that if you buy more, the cost is cheaper, I quickly became a merchant and asked how much he would want if I bought the entire wagonload of sacks of chaff. The peasant agreed to lower the price several kopeks, and I told him to deliver the chaff. He asked me if I had sacks. I didn't know what to say on this, but given that I was certain I had absolutely made a good deal, I showed him a place where he could pour out all the chaff.

Finishing up the task and with that—my great accomplishment, I got into the wagon and led the peasant to the storehouse where he would be paid. I jumped down from the wagon a happy lad and breathlessly told the owner that I had paid less than twenty kopeks.

"That's all good," the owner said, "but why didn't the cook pay him?"

"Because she didn't have enough money; it comes to several rubles. I bought a lot! When you buy a lot, it's cheaper …"

What happened next, I don't know. I was standing outside of the storehouse with blood running from my nose, and I heard the peasant shouting that he must be paid.

So thus came to an end my first position as a clerk in Yampolski's dry goods store. From the welcome I received from my boss, it was clear that there would be no talk of my returning to work. For a long time I stood and cried, wiping the tears from my face and the blood from my nose.

It was still early. I couldn't go home tearstained and my entire face smeared with blood, and at home— they would immediately begin interrogating me and I would receive yet an added portion. Slowly, I walked away from the rows of dry goods stores and began heading downhill to the river. I went up on the bridge, bent over the railing, and again began crying. This was a grief that I couldn't hold back; I had never cried like that. When my father would beat me with a strap until I was bloody I would cry out, and soon afterwards would go out in the street and forget that I had a father and that he had beat me. But this time was different. Not even understanding how it all happened, I felt that I had lost everything all at once. I would again have to go to the stepmother to quiet my hunger and I would not even hear how curses were thrown at her, as Ephraim Yampolski's cook would do.

I went down to the river. At first I thought of bathing. I stood there, looked at the water, and the desire to bathe left me. I placed my foot on a stone the peasants used to wash their laundry, bent down and taking water in my hands, washed my face a bit and then set off towards home.

The cold, fresh water from the river had refreshed me and also changed my mood. With each minute I began going faster. When I came up to the main street, Khreshchatyk, I slowed down, looking around me to see if my father was about, as this was the place where he would often stand in a group with other idlers from the city.

Coming up to our house, I remained standing outside. I waited in case my sister came out. Although I knew that she would not leave the house before noon, nevertheless I stood there and waited for a miracle. I didn't wait long; I went and sat down in the park in the shade and quickly fell asleep. When I woke up, the sun was already overhead. From the sun I knew that it was late, that my father was already at home and taking his afternoon nap as was his custom. Now was the best time to go into the courtyard and summon my sister. But before I stepped over the doorstep of the courtyard, my sister came out and she stopped, petrified. Before I could utter a word, I started crying again.

MY SISTER MANYE

She asked me questions and I kept on crying. Through tears I told her what had happened to me that day. My sister was the only person from whom I never concealed anything, no matter how bitter the truth. She encircled me with both arms, pressed me to her heart, and began chastising me: why was I crying? "Shush, shame on you, you're already a big boy and moreover it is not at all your nature. Stop crying." However, the more she lectured, the more I sobbed. At last she said, "Come away from here. The stepmother will come out soon and she'll wake up our father; then we'll both have …"

The mention to me of our father and stepmother stopped my tears. We set off down a back lane, sat down and thought of how to erase my crime and my being struck by my boss. Eventually my sister said to me, "Listen, Yankele, I didn't want you to become a clerk; it was only that your father was ashamed to have you as a tradesman—so now let him be ashamed. I have a good acquaintance who works with Azrelyant at the bookbindery. I'll call on him and ask him to persuade his boss to let you learn how to do bookbinding."

Thus speaking, we went to Azrelyant. My sister went in and I remained standing outside. After a long wait, I was summoned into the bookbindery. The proprietor considered me just as if he might buy me. Afterwards, he said that I was still really a small boy, but I seemed to be a clever rascal and he believed that I could master the tasks. After confirming that I could read, he said that after Sabbath—that is, Sunday—six o'clock in the morning, I could come learn to be a bookbinder.

My sister was already quite an impressive person. She discussed something with her acquaintance about things that I didn't understand. Well, I did actually understand a little. I knew that my sister met with printers, with bookbinders and also with students, that she came home late, and that they were doing something dangerous. Exactly what is was that my sister was doing, I didn't know. I did know that everyone held her in very high regard, that she was not like other girls, and that she was both a very good person and a smart one. When my father would get angry with her, he would shout, "You don't like the emperor, right? You want to take his place; you've even torn up his picture, haven't you, of him standing with his entire family? Remember," he would threaten her; "someday you'll be rotting in prison!" Normally she wouldn't answer him. If she occasionally did answer him, she would tell him that he preferred a pogromist to a person who is not in love with his Malinovski (one of his Christian partners).

As we were going back home, she pointed out to me that no one need know that I no longer worked for Yampolski. In the case that they did find out, then we would figure out what to do. Sunday I would report for work and her acquaintance, Yode, would see to it that I learned the job. "But you need to be more serious," she pleaded with me. "Don't be such a show-off. Can't you see that you're on your own and that no one concerns themselves with you? I can't help you. If I could ever earn enough, I would take you out of that house."

This was the first time that my sister had entreated me to grow up, to stop being a trouble-maker and to quit fooling around. I could see that my sister wanted me to make something of myself. I saw too, that she also had no one and I needed instead to focus on being able to help her.

I LEARN TO BECOME A BOOKBINDER

I became a bookbinder. That is, I went to the workplace. The bookbindery was very large. There they did all the work for the seminary, the agronomy school and also for all the important people in the city who would send there to be bound publications such as *Memoirs*, *Russian Wealth*, and other books that had been brought into the city. I threw myself into the work with great zeal. Unfortunately, I had few opportunities to train. More often I was sent around with bundles than actually doing the job. The only times I would help out at the counter were the hours from six to about nine in the morning. It was the same in the evenings, from six until almost nine o'clock at night. Obviously, it was these hours during which I picked up a lot about the work, quickly learned how to sew books, detach the covers, etc.

Everything should have been fine. I was very fond of all the boys there and the workers, particularly my sister's associate, Yode. He would treat every boy like a grown-up worker, and if the boss would strike a boy, it would be the greatest of scandals. Yode would tell him that if he would not break the habit of slapping, he would not be a bookbinder for long. We, all of us boys, knew that the owner was afraid of Yode. Being that Yode was a close acquaintance of my sister, I felt that I too, was just a little bit important.

It just so happened one day that I was sent for a pail of water. I took the bucket and saw that in the bottom there was still a little water and at the same time, that two girls were passing nearby. I was seized by the urge to pour the bit of water on the girls. When I upended the bucket of water, the girls stopped and complained that someone there had poured water on them. Seeing me with the water, one of the girls said that I was the prankster who had done it. Yode came to me and asked if it were true. Just like with my sister, I couldn't lie to Yode. Yode then spoke with the girls, asking that they forgive me. However, it wasn't the girls who needed to be convinced of my innocence, but the owner. The girls had already left the bookbindery but he still refused to change his mind. "Get away from here! Get lost!" he kept on shouting. In the very moment that Yode was in the midst of reasoning with him, I picked up my cap and jacket and walked out of the bookbindery.

To tell the story to my sister Manye was very hard for me. Only a short time ago, she had reasoned with me that I needed to change, that I was already a big boy. Yet here I had committed such a piece of work, turning a bucket of water on two girls. I had also placed Yode in a situation where he must argue with the owner and moreover, I didn't wait until the end to see if I could have stayed working in the bookbindery after all.

No, I couldn't go home. Now I was entirely on my own. Neither my sister nor Yode, who had become my loyal defender—now they also would not forgive me. If I weren't hungry, I would go to the Sofiyivsky Park,[70] to the enormous park in which I knew every corner. There I would even be able to spend the night. I had a deep love for the Sofiyivsky garden. More than once

---

70   Now known as the Sofiyivka: the National Dendrological Park of Ukraine

I had passed the night there, mainly weekend nights, and on Sunday I would stay there as long as my belly could hold out.

THE EMPRESS' PARK IN UMAN

The park was called the Empress' Park.[71] It was not just a park but also a great cultivated wood, with wonderful tree-lined paths, paved roads, fountains, large and small brooks and a waterfall—one which God himself created. The entire orchard was immersed in flowers and a large part of it—in fruit. This fruit was not easy to acquire. It was under the supervision of eight hundred agronomic students and protected by many servants and a limitless number of menacing dogs.

The garden had always tempted me. In spite of the barriers that encircled it, I always managed to find a way to get in and pick the best apples, pears, sour cherries and all the other fruit. The hardest ones to fool were the dogs. I found a trick to deal with them: I never climbed over the fence. I would dig a hole in some corner under the fence, lay there, and click my tongue. I would call out to the dogs and oftentimes they would come, sometimes one, sometimes two. When they would see me lying there and clicking my tongue, they would start wagging their tails and sticking out their tongues like good brothers. I would start petting them, play with them, all the while lying stretched out on the grass. Thus playing with them for a while, I would make my way to the trees. More than once, when I would start to pick the fruit, a dog would betray me and begin growling, as if to say: "Everything yes, but no stealing." Yet when I had been accepted as a good brother, it was not hard to pass by them and fill my shirt with fruit.

The hardest thing that I had to manage with these canine friends was crawling out from the garden. They could not understand why I would be crawling out of a hole. It was something a dog does, not a person. Each time that I tried to crawl out, they would raise the alarm. Finally I figured out how to cheat my four-legged friends. I would begin playing with them by throwing them a big apple or some other piece of fruit, and when they would run after it to catch it, I would quickly exit my den.

My most pleasant times in the Empress' Park would be on Saturday afternoons. These were the times that no Jew was permitted to enter. On

---

71 Russian: "Tsarytsyn sad," another name for the Sofiyivsky Park.

Saturdays from noon until late in the evening, they played music there; also on Sundays. These two days Jews could only go on the front exterior paths and very few Jews actually went there during these days when they weren't allowed in. At the main entrance would stand a pair of policemen and also a student patrol. They would ask, "Jew?" and not allow them in.

For me it wouldn't be hard to go through this exam. First of all, I had many gentile friends that I could go in with, and secondly, I could just not tell them I was a Jew. But to deny I was a Jew, that I would by no means do, and therefore I didn't want to go in during their watch. I would go by myself and enter the garden right under the noses of the police. Sometimes I would walk away for several versts[72] and then cross over. Other times, when I was suitably dressed, while whistling and kicking up a row I would push my way through with the crowd. In such ways I went to the Empress' Park whenever I wanted, and indeed, when no Jews were permitted to enter. It would happen on more than one occasion that I would get my ear tweaked. This typically happened when I declined to stop when told and started to run instead. When I was caught with the help of some passer-by, I would receive the proper punishment.

To this garden, which I knew like my ten fingers, was the place I went to after abandoning the bookbindery. Yet this time I didn't go with the same happiness with which I always would approach it: whistling, skipping, overtaking everyone in the street, tearing twigs from the trees and whipping them through the air. No, this time I made my way to the garden dragging my feet. My heart wept. It didn't bother me that I wouldn't become a bookbinder or even that I was now on bad terms with Yode. What hurt me was the suffering of my sister. She had told me that it was already time that I became a responsible adult, that is—mature—and I had intercepted two girls and poured water on them. With that thought I arrived at the foremost avenue of the garden.

Going no further than the first bench, I sat down to rest. I could feel that soon I would break into tears. This was after all, my second traumatic experience in two months. This time I didn't cry aloud.

The first bench stood next to a well-trodden trail leading to the Dubinka[73]

---

72   Russian: obsolete Russian unit of length, equal to 1.07 km or 0.67 miles.
73   Russian: Dubnyk, one of several forest tracts located inside the park.

and the deep wood that lay around the Empress' Park. Peasant men and women were constantly passing by, often enough so that I was not alone. I sat on the bench until late. The sun was nearly set; I was afraid to venture deeper in the garden to find fruit. I was suddenly gripped by some sort of dread. It was the first time that I had been seized by terror. Still, it could have been due more to the remoteness and uncertainty than to fear. I remained seated in the same place. It was already nearly dark; the wide paths were slightly illuminated by the sunbeams that had pierced through the trees. With each minute it became darker and darker. The cool forest breeze penetrated deep into my bones. I began to feel a slight shiver running through my entire body. Moreover, not eating for the entire day was apparently intensifying the effect of the coming night.

I became despondent. I would already have gone home, but it was now too late to make the journey on a weeknight. On the weekends the long road that led to the town was lively, but during the entire workweek one would not see a living soul. All the courtyards were locked and the entire street would seem like a Jewish cemetery with lavish gravestones on both sides of the street. The street was a hard uphill climb, and I felt such a fatigue, as I hadn't eaten all day and from the chill air, feeling that I was done in and could go no further. I began weeping intensely, frightening myself by my sobs. I had never cried so noisily as this time. With my sleeve I wiped the tears that poured from my eyes, and started out along the path that led into the woods.

MYSTERIES OF THE DUBINKA

Alongside the woods spread a large green meadow with tall grass. Many days and nights this green meadow had been my resting place; it was known as the Dubinka. In summertime all the holidays were celebrated in this spot. Here it was mild, and even by night it was warm. The Dubinka had been cleared and was not filled with trees; the sun shone on it the entire day and soaked it with its rays, therefore it stayed warm even in the evenings. It was to the Dubinka I now headed, so that I might warm up and pass the night.

With the first few steps I took down the narrow path, I heard my name being called. "Where are you going?" someone called out from among the trees. The voice was familiar, but not one often heard. I stood still, looked around me, and a disquiet overtook me. The voice spoke again: "It's me, Poleski." And there, under a tree on a stone, I saw Poleski. He was a boy about four years older than me, a gymnazist[74] and the son of wealthy parents. There was now no father in this family, but the mother received enough money to raise her four children: two boys and two girls. The family lived in the same courtyard as we did, and my sister would visit them. My stepmother was not happy that my sister was on such friendly terms with them although my father, who thought of himself as a great aristocrat and spoke only Russian and Polish in the street—he was indeed happy, as for him it was an honor.

No one knew where Poleski was at present, the father of the four children, if he was dead or had something happened to him and he was exiled. What they did know was that he was a well-known lawyer in the city of Kiev, a wealthy man, who had met with some sort of misfortune and the family had moved to Uman; here the mother raised the four children. At home were still two girls and a boy. The oldest son was a student in Odessa at Khersonki University, however people said that he was no better than his father who perhaps was, of all places, in Siberia.

In general, the Poleski family was a mystery to the courtyard. Mrs. Poleski was not friends with the wives of the courtyard, and the children also kept their distance from the other children. The only one who found favor with this reserved family was my sister Manye. It had gone so far that she spent more time with the Poleskis than at home.

My stepmother would literally burst with resentment. "What do they see in Malke?"[75] she would exclaim. "Why do they relate so well to her? They speak to no one, everyone has to make do with a nod of the head, and with her they make a big fuss. They don't make a move without her ..." For me, my stepmother's rage was a total holiday. I didn't myself know why it was it had that effect on her, but when I wanted to see her get upset I would run in with the news that Manye had just then left with Madam Poleski. This news would be enough that if a child should be moving about near her hands, she would pull out a piece of flesh pinching them and to me she would shout that I should never again dare to sniff around Madam's door.

My father, as it happened, was instead impressed; he would boast of it and brag to people that his daughter was the real leader of the house of Poleski,

---

74 Yiddish: a student who attends a gymnasium (European secondary school up to the level of a junior college).
75 Hebrew: queen.

the greatest lawyer of Kiev. Although he would quietly say to my sister that one of these days she would suffer some disaster because of them—that she would meet the same end as the father and his son.

"Hear me out, Manye," he would say to her. "Do what you want, you're already a young lady and are very intelligent; you speak like an adult. I won't humiliate myself for you. I have indeed the police superintendent and even the chief of police in my pocket. They receive a living from me, not I from them. Nonetheless, for such things I won't go to them. You're laughing, then?" he would start shouting, while my sister would smile at him. "And you don't need my help either? Have you no fear? I've heard this before. But one fine day when they throw you in prison, you'll sing another tune." Such conversations usually ended when my stepmother would arrive and my sister would say, "Sha, that's enough, your wife is now here."

And now Madam Poleski's son was sitting opposite me on a rock under a tree, holding a twig in his hand. Not looking at me, he asked, "Where are you headed to?" I told him that I was going to the Dubinka. To his question of what would I do there, I answered him, "Nothing." Then I told him, "I feel cold, and as the grass is always warm there because it is heated by the sun, I'm going there to warm up."

"Why don't you go home?" he inquired.

"Because I can't," I answered.

"Something with the stepmother again?" The entire courtyard knew that we got along like cats in a sack.

"No, not this time." I briefly explained to him what had happened.

"So sit here near me, and in a bit we'll both go to the Dubinka, And later, we'll go home together and you'll sleep with us."

This became a little too close for comfort for me. I—with Poleski, with a gymnazist, sleep at his house? He of course, was a lot older than me; he was always so well-dressed, always so flamboyant … spend the night at his house? No, I thought. Yes, my sister was indeed a constant visitor there but she was a lot older than I was and completely different—she was nothing like me.

"No, Poleski," I said. "I'll go by myself to the Dubinka and later I'll take myself home."

Before he managed to answer me, someone came by, told him something, and then kept going. The manner in which the passer-by asked a question and how Poleski answered him, to me seemed strange and I began to be afraid.

"Sit here then, like I told you," I heard Poleski's voice. "Right now you can't go to the Dubinka by yourself. We'll go together."

It sounded like a command, and I remained sitting. Then he told me, "Here are five kopeks. There by the gate a peasant woman always stands with bagels. If she's still there, buy five bagels and we'll both eat."

Without replying even one word, I went to the gate. I knew the gate very well. People were always there, and at the gate was also a place to water the horses of the peasants going by and those of the proprietors. By the gate were indeed invariably women merchants standing until late at night, wanting to take in a few groshen. I was certain that I would find something—if not bagels, then something else for five kopeks.

I literally ran to the gate and was back in a few minutes with the bagels. The bagels were threaded onto a stick and thus I handed them to Poleski. He looked at me: "Why do you not eat a bagel?" I pulled off a bagel and began chewing, and despite how hungry I was, the piece of bagel choked me. "One bagel is enough for me," I said. "You take the rest."

"No," he spoke up, "I'll take one and you put the rest in your pocket." I said nothing more. Tears were beginning to choke me; I was not aware that I was chewing. Meanwhile, I continued to see how someone would show up, ask something, and leave once more. Every time that a person appeared, he would ask Poleski something, that one would say something to the first, and the questioner would leave again. My tears dried up by themselves and my throat became clearer, and I began swallowing one bagel after another.

The passers-by began to come more and more frequently; they were a diverse lot. Some were ordinary folk like the people I met in the street, also fruit sellers from the Sofiyivsky and certainly from the Empress' Park, but also gymnazistn.[76] My fear became suddenly transformed into curiosity and optimism. I wanted to learn what it was that the people asked and that Poleski answered. However, this was impossible. A person would ask some sort of question from the side of his mouth and Poleski would answer in a whisper with his face kept down, and the questioner would be off again.

It gradually became quite dark. It was no longer possible to see the faces of the persons arriving. I settled back and sat and waited for this to finish. I was no longer trying to figure out what was going on. The bagels had

---

76 Yiddish: plural of gymnazist.

quieted my hunger and I was warm once more. I had become indifferent to the whole story of the day's sorrows and no longer being alone, I felt somewhat more secure. I started to doze off, sitting on a hard stone near my unexpected defender.

Suddenly I was awakened from my dreams. I had heard the voice of my sister. To me she said nothing, asked nothing; instead she got all the details from Poleski. I didn't dare to say a word. I then saw that she was standing with Joseph the locksmith. I knew him very well. He would come to our courtyard and wait for her and my stepmother would say, "The black tomcat is waiting for you now, the tall one," and accompany this with a score of curses.

When they left in the same manner as the other questioners, I stood up and wanted to leave. "What are you going to do?" Poleski asked.

"I want to go home," I said.

"You'll go with me!" he answered and for the first time looked directly at me. We set off in the woods in the direction of Dubinka.

Soon someone asked, "Who is he?"

"Manye's brother," he replied.

I FELT THAT I WAS NOT ALONE

As we went deeper in the woods, it became even darker. At the Dubinka I could see, as if through a haze, that there were many people. They were sitting on the grass—some lay against a tree, some back-to-back, and some reclining, resting on their elbows. No one spoke; from time to time a murmur would be heard that blended in with the rustle of the leaves as they were moved by the light summer breeze.

I was seized by a scary happiness. For a moment I was reminded of my stepmother, of my precious father who broke my bones in order to satisfy his wife for whom my weeping was often the best gift, a pleasure that I would destroy when my father beat me. She would say, "Here is a budding murderer, he is beaten and yet remains silent. Who knows what will become of him?" ... Compared to that, all of this here seemed like a dream. So many people, at night in the woods. Different kinds of people: high school students, university students, workers. Joseph the locksmith stood in the middle of them and spoke to everyone. I understood his words but what he wanted, I didn't know. He mentioned that because of the first of May[77] there were now many people in prison, young people sitting under arrest, and still more would be sent away to Kiev, and more, and more. He didn't speak loudly, but with anger. He often screamed quietly, addressing everyone with a new argument, demanding that each should befriend each other. I was very pleased with all these things, though I didn't know why. For a moment I felt that Joseph too hated my father and stepmother and indeed, that was why she couldn't stand the sight of him and called him the "black tomcat." Some day when I was as big as he was and could scream as he did and had such large hands as his, I would show what I could do.

I suddenly felt that I was no longer afraid, not of my father nor my stepmother. If something happened to me, I would tell Poleski or even Joseph the locksmith and they would stick up for me. It couldn't be otherwise then, I thought, so that people who stick up for others, must also stick up for me? This idea made me so happy that I wanted to break out shouting, whistling, which by the way, I could do quite well. Were I not sitting near Poleski and were he not the entire time with his hand on my shoulder, I would certainly have carried this out.

From that night on, a change took place inside me. I felt that I was not alone. Now, all the people that I had seen that evening as shadows between the trees whom I wouldn't recognize in the street—now all these people no longer felt like strangers to me.

For many days, that evening kept coming back to me in my thoughts. Especially when going home, several times Poleski warned me that I must confide in no one where I was—not even in my sister. "Not even in my sister?" I said in surprise. "She herself was also there and she saw me!"

"It doesn't matter. Of such things you can speak to no one, not even the people who were there and who saw you."

"And if my sister asks me about it?"

"Pretend that you don't know."

To be frank, I didn't understand it but I did really enjoy the game. Actually, I wished that the boys whom I ran around with would ask me and I would tell them nothing. But how could it be arranged that I wouldn't tell them, yet nevertheless they should know? For this, of course, I could find no solution.

---

77   Possible reference to a large political demonstration of factory workers in Kharkiv, Ukraine on 1 May 1900 that resulted in many arrests.

WITH A TRAINED STOMACH

A few days after these events, I had not yet gone home. I was certain that if they even thought of me, there would be no talk of going to look for me. The only one who would miss me was my sister. However, as she had seen me with Poleski and since in general my not coming home was a normal thing, she would sooner or later meet me somewhere, as had happened more than once. I wanted her to find out from Yode that I no longer worked in the bookbindery, because then it would be easier to speak with her about it.

The several days that I wasn't at home I spent with my Uncle Fishl. He was a middle-aged man, a hard worker, a blacksmith. He earned very little and had a house full of children. He was by nature a kind person, and a very good one. It was said of him that one could even climb on his head while he was engrossed in his books. My father always laughed at him and called him, "My brother, the philosopher." When I would go to Uncle Fishl, I was always a welcome guest. The piece of bread that I consumed there was one that in truth someone else lacked, but they were never stingy with me. My aunt, a simple Jewish woman, would always weep and wipe her nose with her apron, saying, "Better to not have been born, than to be without a mother." After this speech she would always serve me the best portion, adding to it "And may she choke there!"—meaning my stepmother. Consequently, I would always eat there with a double appetite.

In the city of Uman, everyone strolled exclusively on Kreshchatik. This was a long street in the better part of the city known as the "new city." On both sides of the street stretched two rows of shops of the high-end sort. The larger section lay on one side of the street and on the other, where most people did their strolling, were two bakeries. One, an inexpensive one, was called *The Chignon*. There one could find bagels, a large four-cornered white bread for six kopeks (actually called a chignon) and a cheap pirozhki (a cake) that one could buy two for five kopeks. On the other end of the street, reaching up to the city theatre, was found a French bakery called the *Frantsuzskaya Bakery*. There one could get the best, but it was expensive. It was for officials, rich people, aristocrats, and even those who were destitute. Some customers truly were very poor, but they shopped in the French bakery.

There between the two bakeries lay Kreshchatik Street, along the entirety on which the entire stroll would take place. Even we boys, who were called the "bosiaklekh" (little tramps), would also run around on Kreshchatik giving a hard time to whomever we could.

Saturday night I went over to the street, but not in the manner that I always did. This time I stood by the window of the *Chignon* and tried to avoid my friends with whom I would always go roaming. This time I wanted to stay alone and meet my sister and—either I would tell her or she would again ask me about that which she already knew.

I stood by the window because the street was generally almost completely dark. By the light of the sole street lamp hanging in the middle of the street, it was hard to make anyone out. Really, all the light came from the two windows of the bakeries. I stood for a while in this manner, and eventually the baked goods began speaking to my stomach. But my stomach was already well-trained; it knew that it couldn't expect much of me. It became more and more difficult to stand there and smell the aroma from the pastries that the *Chignon* would prepare specially on Saturday night for those out strolling.

I didn't wait in vain. It was already a bit late when my sister arrived with Joseph the locksmith. I started towards them but they had already spotted me and right away came to me.

"I wanted to see you so I stood here," I answered her, all the while looking at Joseph.

"Perhaps tonight you'll come home?"

"What do you mean, 'perhaps'? Isn't father at home?"

"No, he's away."

"Do you think I should go home, then?"

"Yes, come home. I'll be there soon too. I must ask you something."

Saying these words, my sister looked at Joseph, and they both smiled. I had the feeling that not only she, but also he knew what she was going to ask me. Also that something from the story pleased them, about how I had lost my bosses.

From Kreshchatik to my father's house was only a few streets and I didn't walk there, but ran. I was afraid that my sister would get there before me. When I opened the gate, I met the peasant girl who worked for us. I found out from her that no one was at home and that the "Mamshekhe"—the stepmother, was at a neighbor's. Hearing of such luck, I ran into the house like one poisoned, quickly made an inspection of the kitchen, and stuffed into my pockets whatever I could. I didn't dare sit down to eat in the kitchen because if the stepmother came home, that would be the end of my feast. When I was loaded with enough provisions, the major portion of which was bread—enough for three boys like me— I went out through the gate and sat down on a bench that stood near the fence with my mood now completely turned around.

My sister arrived later. When she came, I was still sitting on the bench by the side of the gate. She asked me if I'd been in the house yet. I told her that I had already been inside and that the stepmother hadn't seen me. I had grabbed something to eat from the kitchen and eaten it up right there where I was.

"Listen, Jacob," my sister began telling me in an earnest tone, "I've already told you that you are a young man and that there is no place for you in the house. You must learn a trade so that in time, you can earn a living and have a place to eat and sleep. This father of yours doesn't concern himself with you or what will happen with you. And the stepmother, you know all too well ... you must become more mature and serious."

"Manye," I started to say to her, but she interrupted me.

"I know all that happened. I have no complaints against you." She then hugged me and began crying, "Hear me, Yankele, I don't care what people say about you. I know it's all stories. But I want you to stop living like a dog in the street. Look—do something ..." she left her sentence unfinished and then began again, "Father is coming home. So tomorrow we will do something. I've spoken with Zelik and Samuil. They will bring you in to Tseytlin in the printing shop. There you'll learn to be a printer and in the evenings you'll send out the *Uman Page*. For this they'll pay you six rubles a month and you'll no longer have to be hungry."

I EARN SIX RUBLES A MONTH

All that night I tossed and turned on my usual resting place of some rags by the door, and couldn't go sleep. The thought that I would earn six rubles a month, twenty kopeks a day, would not let me sleep. I barely lasted until morning so I could be taken to the printing shop. More than anything else, it was the printing shop itself, the "printing house," where I could have stood by the window for hours without end, watching how the machine would print and how the men would lay the paper inside it. This was a sight that kept me riveted to my spot. Now I myself would stand here by the machine and feed in the paper ...

I could hardly wait until the moment when my sister would bring me to

Tseytlin at the printing shop; finally she was ready to go. She looked at how I was dressed and tilted her head, as if to say "It could be better." Not a surprise! My black shirt was shiny with wear, my boots were worn, and the rest was equally wretched. These were the clothes that I wore both on holidays and during the week. Their true color had long since ceased to be detectible.

"Jacob," my sister said, "comb your hair a bit. You should know that the Mister Tseytlin likes people to be dressed correctly."

Once again I wet my hair and began combing it, but it couldn't be done: they simply could not be made to lie down. They all stayed standing on end like a "yozsh" (thorn). "Ready!" I told Manye and we left the house.

The printing shop was not far, and in a few minutes we were there. Zelik, the one who was to speak with the owner, Mr. Tseytlin, was waiting by the door. When we arrived, he told us that he had already spoken with him and that everything would be fine. We went into the office. The owner sat at a wide table with sheets of papers strewn across the entire table. Seeing my sister, he stood up and offered his hand to her. She pointed to a chair and asked if she might sit. Mr. Tseytlin was tall with broad shoulders, gray-headed, but with a thick head of hair that was completely disheveled. He wore heavy clothing and as I later found out, was near-sighted.

I felt pretty good, because of his hair that was so unruly. It no longer concerned me that I couldn't make my hair smooth as my sister had ordered me; neither could Mr. Tseytlin.

In my brief years during which I had already lived through so much, I had developed an audacity that feared neither someone bigger nor one stronger. When Mr. Tseytlin called my name I went straight up to him, reached out my hand and said loudly, "Zdravstvujtye!" (Hello). He shook my hand and with his other hand pinched my cheek. For long afterwards, I would feel the friendly pinch from Mr. Tseytlin.

He was a Lithuanian Jew and in the city was considered an expert in Russian, but with Jews he spoke only Yiddish. This was the first time that a stranger had spoken to me in Yiddish, and I answered his questions in Russian.

"Look," he said to me, "I love that people speak Yiddish. If you keep working for me for a while, you'll speak better Yiddish than you do right now."

In that moment it seemed to me that Mr. Tseytlin was of all things, my father. He spoke to me as if to an equal, gave me a pinch on the cheek, and even had an interest in the manner that I spoke.

"I have enough apprentices in the printing shop," Mr. Tseytlin declared, "for the most part boys from parents who don't need their income. They stand about and learn. But I need a boy who can be sent everywhere and also at night can glue the addresses on the newspapers."

My sister told him that she understood quite well all that was said, that I was definitely in need of work and would do everything, and that the six rubles for the evenings would really mean a lot for me. He stood up again, apparently to signal the end of the conversation, patted me on the head and spoke to Zelik, who had not moved during the conversation: "Take him in and tell him what he will be doing."

Neither my sister nor I had expected that I would be staying in the shop so soon. We had left the house without eating. My sister even wanted to say that we would come later, but I was so happy that I gave her a sign with my hand saying "No."

IN TSEYTLIN'S PRINTING SHOP

Tseytlin's printing shop was the largest in the city. Besides the daily newspaper, the *Uman Page*, also printed there were all the playbills from the theatre and circus, and the entire print-work for the neighborhood sugar mills. For the newspaper alone were employed many typesetters, compositors, printers and still other production help. In addition to the staff printer, there were also proofreaders from the newspaper and correspondents from several cities. Day and night, the print shop was as busy as a beehive. Tseytlin was not a printer himself; the printer was a relative of his. However, Mr. Tseytlin loved the hustle and bustle of the printing shop and the people who busied themselves about it. He was an affable man, a good man by nature, and everyone took advantage of him. He seemed more like a teacher or a doctor than an owner of the business, even less so of one where so many people came and went every day.

A new world opened up for me. No one criticized me. From time to time, I would be sent on an errand and then I would do as ordered. I had to wash the machines, blow out the boxes of fonts and at midnight when the newspaper was done printing, I would glue labels on them and then glue the addresses on the labels. At six o'clock in the morning, I would carry the newspapers in a droshky to the train, and a portion to the post office.

I stayed in the printing shop nearly day and night. During the day I was an apprentice; I was not paid for this. After ten to twelve hours of work, I could go home and come back at midnight to ship the newspaper. From eight o'clock at night until twelve I had free time; I could go home and rest. Yet my love for my home was so great that I preferred to climb on top of the table that I used to prepare the newspapers for shipping and go to sleep until I was awoken to pack the newspapers. Given that the paper would be late five times a week and instead of midnight would be ready at three in the morning, I actually got enough sleep. Moreover, I received so much love from the printing shop and from all the people who worked there that I never wanted to leave.

Above all, from the first day I no longer knew hunger. I was, after all, the one who everybody sent on their errands. When one of them had a sudden craving for something, he would send me to buy it. Usually when someone sent me, he would make me a partner to the deed. During the day, I principally lived off of the chief compositor. He was not from Uman; they had brought him down from Kiev; Abramov, it seems, is what they called him. He was the highest-paid compositor. He earned 50 rubles a month—such a sum in Uman was enough for a family of ten people. However, he was built such that he himself could eat for ten. He was immensely big and stout. He would constantly send me out to buy food and each time when I would bring him his beloved salami, pickles and black bread, cut it up and serve it to him on a paper, he would immediately allocate me a portion and say, "Kushay!" (Eat!). In time I got so accustomed to being a partner to his meals that I spared him having to say "Kushay"; I would give myself a portion and eat equally with him.

On the other hand there was one who because of him, I nearly lost my job. This was the night-correspondent, Bernshteyn. Now this Bernshteyn had the habit that when he finished with his work, he would come into the printing shop, push me off the table where I was sleeping and stretch himself out there. I would have to remain lying on the floor. I had protested several times and the night-compositor even berated him for it, but it didn't help. He came from a privileged family and he was a relative of the lawyer Vinitski who financed the newspaper. I suffered much because of his actions and gradually built up a lot of bitterness against him. I would be fast asleep after a day of running around, cleaning the machines, sweeping the printing shop and other such tasks, and he would suddenly show up, strike me with a blow to wake me up, and take my spot.

In the past, I had always had plenty of mischievous ideas and with their help had caused much misfortune, mainly to my stepmother. These days, since working at the Tseytlin printing shop, I no longer made use of them. I had worked hard to keep them in check. But the actions of the night-correspondent Bernshteyn had reawakened in me the desire to play a trick on him. I gathered up several dozen pins and pounded them into the middle of the table. I cut off their heads with pliers so that the pins were sharp on both ends. I lay down to sleep along the edge of the table. Like always, he repeated his coming in during the night and chasing me off the table. I didn't even have time to curl up on the floor when Bernshteyn let out such a wild shriek that the gentile who turned the great wheel of the machine stopped in shock and the machine stopped along with him.

Everybody came running and Bernshteyn cried that needles were inside him from his side and from all over. Geler, the Jewish proofreader from the newspaper and also a prankster, had no love for Bernshteyn. He went to him and frightened him even more by saying that one cannot play with such things, that if the needles began to travel through his body, it was all over for him. Bernshteyn ran out in a panic. In about an hour he came back much calmer. He had gone to a doctor, who had told him that he was only a little cut up. When he had left, I had begun removing all traces of the pins. The printer from the machine noticed this, and by the next day had told everyone that I had gotten even with Bernshteyn.

The entire printing shop laughed. Each one told me "Bravo!" though I had the feeling the matter would not conclude so smoothly for me. Sure enough: someone told Bernshteyn. Originally, he grabbed me and started beating me, but he wasn't successful—the others interceded for me. He demanded from Mr. Tseytlin that he expel me from the print shop. Tseytlin listened to my grievance and then lectured me strongly for doing such a thing. "You could really hurt someone!" he told me. "Now remember, don't you ever dare to do such a thing again." Then, as I heard from the older workers, he had scolded Bernshteyn and warned him to leave me alone and not come near my table, and that I was right, not him.

This was the first time in my life that someone had decided that I was the one who was right, and because of this my boss Tseytlin grew even greater in my eyes, as if he were a god. I became very attached to the print shop. The print shop had taken the place of my mother, Tseytlin had become my father, and as someone who loved them both, I protected each thing that belonged to the print shop.

Little by little, I learned the ways of working there. The night workers stopped watching me. After that, when they finished the newspaper they would often set up a composition, set it in the machine and print it out. Then they would divide up the bundles among them and carry them off. Although I was completely loyal to the print shop, I never told Mr. Tseytlin. Not because I didn't want to, but because I was afraid he would say that they were right, not I.

THE FIRST ILLEGAL LEAFLET

What I did want was to get ahold of a leaflet and see what they were printing, and what it was that people were carrying away in small packages. This turned out to be impossible, because as soon as they finished printing them they would tear everything down, even removing the traces from the machine cylinder and rummaging through every cranny to ensure that nothing, God forbid, remained. One time I dared to ask Samuil the bookbinder to give me a leaflet. He laid his hand on my shoulder and said that if Malinovski, the police superintendent, found it on me he would turn me into a pile of rubble.

Samuil then looked at me and smiled. "So, do you still want a leaflet?" he asked.

"Yes," I answered. "I'm not afraid of the police superintendent."

I had heard much about Police Superintendent Malinovski, although I had never heard why he was such a bad person. I couldn't possibly imagine that he was worse than the stepmother was. I'd also heard about him from my father. My father was on absolute good terms with him and they had done some business dealings. As Samuil had not scared me with Malinovski, I continued to ask him for a leaflet.

When I received the leaflet, it suddenly occurred to me that it would be good if my stepmother should read the leaflet. I was certain that when she read it, she would die of fright. Not so much because of what was written there, but because of what I would tell her: that the police superintendent would turn her into rubble. But how to get her to read it? I had promised that I would not show it to anyone and that after reading it, I would throw it away in the street so that some other person might read it. Nevertheless, I couldn't resist the pleasure of scaring my stepmother with it. As soon as I was through with work, I ran home.

When I came into the house, my father was seated writing and she was puttering around the house screaming at the children. My entrance went unnoticed. On the other hand, the children cheered up to see me. The small fry, who were in the middle of getting dressed, threw themselves at me. One had a shoe, one was half-naked, and everyone was asking me for something. The stepmother noticed the scene around me and out came her tongue: "Just look who is here. What a surprise. I don't know what got into him. Just see how happy they are with him, with such a sour apple. Off work so early? Couldn't you come a little later? Who needs you here at all? He still thinks that somebody misses him here."

My sister greatly resented the reception the stepmother gave me, and she intervened. It became a quarrel between the two of them. My father put away his writing and said to my sister that it was not her concern, and that she should give me a glass of tea and let me go back to where I came from. "I have enough problems in the house without him," he said.

Such scenes would always make me sad at heart and end with my crying and leaving the house. This time it didn't even begin to bother me. Rather, it only pleased me. I just wished that my sister had not mixed herself up in the middle of it. I took out the leaflet from my pocket and began reading. My father asked me what I had in my hand. Instead of answering, I put it back in my pocket.

"What is it?" my father repeated.

"Nothing," was the answer.

"You should tell me right now what you have there, or else I'll wring your neck!"

With these words, my stepmother appeared. "You should have wrung his neck a long time ago," she chimed in.

I now put away the leaflet again, positioning myself by the door so I could flee and said to my father, "You see this leaflet? When Police Superintendent Malinovski finds it here, he will put an end to your wife!" Proclaiming these words, I quickly left the house. When I was already by the gate, my father stood by the side of the door and threatened that he would yet settle the score with me. My sister had also left the house and was laughing heartily. It made her happy that I had finally openly defied my father's wife in front of him.

I never again went to my father's house. Not because I was afraid of him, but because I felt independent and no longer needed them. A few months later, I once met my father in the street. He stopped me, promised me golden fortunes, gave me some money to buy a new pair of boots, and said that I could never come home again. I responded with silence.

I AM BANISHED FROM THE PRINT SHOP WITHOUT KNOWING WHY

I would have worked in Tseytlin's print shop for years, and became a skilled printer. After all, this was the first place where I had made friends and comrades. Moysai Tseytlin was a brilliant man. Even when he would sometimes scold me, it became just a formality. Afterwards he would ask if I truly wanted to become a printer and would give me some extra kopeks that would be enough to eat on for a few days. Nonetheless, things soon unfolded very differently from how they started out.

During the several months that I worked at the printing shop, I became a good brother to everyone. They trusted me completely. They no longer hid from me the leaflets they would print at night. On the contrary, they had reached a point with me where during the night, I myself would be told to typeset a leaflet. Thus without know exactly what it was, I gradually became an accomplice in the underground printing activities.

Since Uman was the center that served many neighboring towns with illegal literature, it was decided to open an illegal printing shop just for that purpose. From all the printing shops in the city, people took fonts and other things needed for such an undertaking. From Tseytlin's printing shop, as it was the biggest, it was decided to remove the bostonke[78]—such a small printing press was just right for the objective.

The small printing press was taken out at night. Moysai Tseytlin, who supported the underground movement with all his being, was compelled to let the gendarmerie know about the late-night theft. At that time there was a decree in force from the authorities that if anything disappeared from a printing shop that could serve the underground movement, the printer must report it immediately. If he did not, he was in danger of not only being arrested, but of also losing his fortune. That Tseytlin must inform the gendarmerie about the stolen bostonke, everyone in the printing shop had agreed to this. Before he reported it, they decided to send me away from the workplace. Since I always worked at night, they were afraid that if I was at work when

---

78   Reference unknown; presumably a small Russian printing press.

the gendarmes came to investigate, I could be frightened into telling all. If I remained silent, they would take me to the police station and beat me; they would break my ribs, and I would have no one to take my part. Therefore—all had quietly agreed—I must be sent away before the gendarmes arrived.

Of course I knew nothing of this plan. Tseytlin called me in and began screaming at me, tore me to pieces for some minor detail and cursed at me in a way that I had never heard from him before. It was completely out of character for him. Finally he told me that my feet should never cross his door again. I was owed six rubles a month; he would give me ten, and out from there immediately!

For a long time I didn't know why Tseytlin had kicked me out of the shop. I went around in a fog. My sister, Zelik and Samuil consoled me with the thought that I would be found a job in another printing shop. They said that I already knew the work and shouldn't take it to heart. Yet I was not as upset that I could no longer work with Tseytlin in the printing shop, as that Tseytlin was angry with me. I truly loved and missed Moysai Tseytlin. I kept on arguing that someone had slandered me, the proof of this being that now when I stood by the printing shop and greeted him, he would not even look at me.

Meanwhile I remained in the street. The first few days I slept at my Uncle Fishl's. I also gave him the ten rubles and he would give me a few kopeks each day to get by on. For me it was immensely sad and terribly hard to be alone. I already missed my friends and comrades. During this time Samuil and some others from the printing shop were arrested. When I would ask Zelik when they would take me to another printing shop, his answer was, "Very soon."

One time Zelik told me that those arrested had been freed and that I would soon be sent to Torodosh's printing shop. Since in the meantime I had nowhere to live, they would take me to one such Polovina, an acquaintance who had a vacant room. No one lived in the room except from time to time when someone would come and stay there for a few days. Therefore, there was an empty bed available. I could move in there, but on one condition: I was not permitted to tell anyone where I lived, not even my sister.

During the time that I worked in Tseytlin's printing shop, I had seen so many incomprehensible things that I had learned not to ask any questions. No one ever told me a thing, but gradually I became aware of the situation. I perceived that all of these events occurring: that Tseytlin had expelled me, the arrest of the workers and later their release, the fact that I would be working again because they were free— all these things were somehow connected together, and that they were one and the same. In one year I matured ten; I gained courage and stopped crying when things got hard. On the contrary, during the difficult days I often became even more cheerful. I suddenly saw that I was not alone. What I wasn't able to see, I managed to hear. I now knew that family problems such as mine were found in every corner. I no longer felt isolated. All my new acquaintances, I felt, were my brothers and they had the same concern for me that my sister did.

CHAPTER 2
My First Contact With the Underground Movement

POLOVINA

Polovina, who I moved in with, was a young man of about twenty. He was one of the Jewish students that because of the educational quota[79] couldn't attend the university. He studied independently and was an external candidate; each year he went to take the exam. This was allowed, and the classes he finished were credited to him by the department with which he studied.

"Polovina" was his nickname. People had started to call him this since his "second half," his faithful friend and roommate had been arrested, and Polovina remained alone ("Polovina" in Russian meant "a half"). No one seemed to know what his real name was. Everyone loved him very much for his devotion to his friends and to that which he served. I understood this from the first day that I met Polovina; I sensed in him a loyal friend. From the first minute on, he knew all about me and took care that I should lack for nothing now that I was his tenant. Polovina did not live in the apartment himself. He would only come there from time to time. This would happen when someone came from out-of-town. Living there, I learned little by little that this was the "Yavotshne Lodging" or the "Reporting Place," as it was called then, for the entire Russian oyezd (district). When someone came to Uman, the first thing they had to do was come to the lodging and I was the one who would let Polovina know. Then the necessary contacts would be made.

The new arrivals, the majority of them from Kiev, would not stay long there unless someone was sent for a specific period of time to set up a certain job. As the time passed, I was given the opportunity to meet many people at the apartment, people with many different perspectives on life. Among them were workers, students, energetic people and resolute ones—all of them were such that being with them for a few days, I received so much love and all whom I would come in contact with took a strong interest in me. This could

---

79   The Jewish quota in Imperial Russia limited the number of Jewish students to no more than ten percent in those cities where Jews were allowed to live (i.e., the Pale of Settlement), five percent in other cities, and three percent in Moscow and St. Petersburg.

be due to the fact that I was still very young—not yet fourteen years old—and already engaged in such a task as facilitating introductions for the center.

FANYE THE BLACK

Among those who came was one who gave me my first instruction in socialism. This was a woman who everyone knew as Fanye the Black. She did indeed have a very dark complexion and aside from her dark skin, this woman was a man in every sense of the word: wide shoulders, large hands, a lion's head and she spoke with a deep voice. When she left with somebody, that person had to run after her; to keep up with her was impossible. She was a teacher by profession—not just for the movement, but a real schoolteacher. Fanye the Black was then twenty-some years old, but she looked much younger. Her assignment was to establish the underground press in an appropriate manner. Until she set up the necessary connections with people who needed to work there, she lived at the Yavotshne Lodging.

The first few days were very hard for me. It was not comfortable to be together with her. I would come in very early and go straight to sleep, or extremely late when she was already asleep. Fanye the Black, who was a girl with much experience, understood that I felt that as a man, it was not comfortable to sleep with a girl in the same room. She began utilizing the mornings before she would leave to strike up a conversation with me. Yet no matter how talkative I would usually be and how much I had liked to tell about the bitter experiences of my past—with her I was very skimpy with my words. Somehow I didn't want her to know about the entire path of my life, that it was built on extreme hunger and insults. If she knew everything about me, I thought, she would understand why I was at the lodging. She would know that hardship had brought me there, and this I didn't want. By now I no longer felt that I was at the lodging because I needed a place to sleep. Now I wouldn't have changed places for the finest of quarters, but she would not have believed me. Therefore, I avoided speaking with her and wanted to say as little as possible.

Yet all the things that I hadn't wanted to tell, Fanye already knew from other people. She only pretended not to know. Just from time to time, she would ask a question and I would sidestep giving her an answer. She would fall silent and ask no more. Then she'd smile and begin speaking of other things, things in which I was very interested.

As a teacher, she saw me as raw material with which she had become greatly inspired to develop. Bit by bit I began to understand what my role was and what I was to do there. In addition, I learned why people became involved and why they published the leaflets. I discovered what sort of thing Russia was and what Russia needed to become, and who was to blame for the fact that she wasn't as she should be. Fanye would often give me entire lessons in Russian history, along with explanations of how the lives of the ethnic minorities in Russia were and why Jews were persecuted. She taught me that any person who has a soul must do something against this, and that we were those persons. I slowly began to feel like I was one of these people who had a soul, and that rather than bad things being done only to me, Russia was bad everywhere. Thus, when things became better in Russia, it would likewise be good for people like us. Stepmothers and bad fathers—these were nothing. Fanye the Black would often say that all children would have good teachers and everything they require when life becomes good in Russia, and then what kind of influence would a bad father or stepmother play?

I believed her with all my heart. The way that she described to me how it would be when Russia became the way that the Socialists, or as she called them, the Social Democrats, wanted it to be, I was positive that this was truly how it would become. I became strongly attached to her. I no longer avoided her, rather I would wait hours for her to come and tell or teach me something. Often I would ask her about things that I didn't understand from the pamphlets that she would let me read. Fanye now took on the role of mother and teacher in my life and so she was called in our group: "Yankele's mother." I was very happy with this.

I became the main assistant in the work for which Fanye had come to Uman. We began setting up the underground printing shop on Bovolipke, the very street where the Gendarmerie Administration was located. There an apartment had been found and slowly all the tools were brought together in one spot from all the different corners. Fanye wanted to be on this street because she gave "urokn" (private lessons) to the children of the district chief of police who lived on that very street: in this way, she believed, no suspicion would be raised when she was often seen on the Bovolipke.

I also became the official typesetter for the printing shop and was also put in charge of the apartment. I was provided with food and in this way my problem was solved. I felt completely thrilled with my new position.

Fanye the Black was not happy about this. She felt that I was losing my independence too young. One time she told me: "Listen, Yankele, it is really good that you occupy yourself with the secret apartment and with the printing shop. Nonetheless, for you yourself, it is not an appropriate outlet. You would do better to work in a printing shop and become a printer. All of those things that you do in the secret printing shop, you must do in your own time." She spoke to me at length about the necessity of having one's own occupation and of being a complete person.

For the short time that I was with Fanye, she completely dominated me. Her words were holy to me. I sensed in her the friend or sister who wanted only good for me. She had only to command and I followed. Just then, in that same week, I went to go work in Torodosh's printing shop, which had been set up by my friends from Tseytlin's printing shop.

AT TORODOSH'S PRINTING SHOP

From the first day that I went to work there, I seriously understood for the first time the great value of my former boss, the printer Tseytlin, from whom every day I had received so much love. Now I actually had two bosses, because Torodosh had a partner, a certain Perlman. Torodosh was out and about in the street more than in the printing shop, so for that reason he was more well-known and the printing shop was under his name. The two men, Torodosh and Perlman, were considered the best-dressed people in the city. They dressed according to the latest fashion and it was said that they received shoes and suits from abroad.

Perlman was indeed very handsome. He was young, with two red cheeks like a girl's and the tips of his twisted mustache reached to his nostrils. He was the machinist in the printing shop and famous for being the most expert machinist in the city. Torodosh physically was an average man, but he was conspicuous because he shaved his mustache. In those days it was known that only actors went without mustaches: they couldn't have mustaches because they had to wear makeup. As he sported no mustache, Torodosh was called an actor. He was very happy with this title and actually had an acquaintanceship with the actors who would come on tour to the city. Hence, all the print work for the theater was done in the printing shop.

I began working for Torodosh for the same salary that I had earned with Tseytlin—six rubles a month, but now I only had to work during the day. If it sometimes happened that I had to work late on a theatre playbill, I would be paid several more kopeks. The playbills would print in two parts because there weren't sheets of paper available that were large enough. My job was to glue together the two halves of the playbill after they had printed so the theatre would receive the size needed. The Torodosh printing shop was a model of cleanliness. This cleanliness was accompanied by the discipline of the two partners: both were ample and expansive. The floor sparkled no less than the machines and the writing tables that stood in the office. The daily regimen was modeled after this same way of doing things. Should someone come in a few minutes late or speak a word during work hours, both owners would become enraged. They themselves led this way—they always came in at the exact same hour and spoke to no one at the printing shop unless it was about the work. Here was a printing shop that was the complete opposite of Tseytlin's shop: there complete anarchy ruled and everyone came and went as they pleased.

The first few weeks were not easy for me. I simply couldn't understand why no one was permitted to speak to each other or smoke a cigarette in the middle of the workday. Slowly, after I had been warned several times that I would be fired, I got into line. I began to feel like I had a say about things; that I could come and go like everyone else and work the same twelve hours with a two-hour break. I felt like I had equal status with everyone else. Moreover, I learned a great deal in this highly disciplined printing shop. I began to be a good loader for the printing press.

The playbills that I would glue every week, I would then have to take to the theatre myself. In the beginning I had no great desire to do it. I even tried protesting against it, but since to Torodosh my protests were a low priority, it fell to me to deliver them once or twice a week to the theatre. In such a way did the playbills bring me to the door of a type of lifestyle that for children of my age was very strange. When I brought the playbills, I could not only go into the theatre when I wanted, but also go up to the dressing rooms where the artists, circus clowns and acrobats would change. I had the opportunity to get to know all their intrigues, shameful romances and treacheries. There I also saw the disdain with which all actor-types looked upon the theatregoers.

THEATRE INTOXICATION

I became a regular resident in the theatre, so much that not only could I come in for free, but I could also bring someone else. I would walk around back and open the rear door installed there in case of fire, meet my friends there and let them into the theatre. The theatre began taking up all my free time. I would come back to the Yavotshne Lodging very late and often neglect to set the type for the leaflets that would be left for me. I would promise to do them and break my word. I became intoxicated with the environment, the commotion and the invectives of this hidden life. Bit by bit, I became the errand boy for the actors. No matter where they sent me, I ran there. I would walk through fire for them.

Rather than go to sleep at night, Fanye the Black would often wait up until I would come in from the theatre. Each time she would initiate a conversation about my losing my way among the actors. I would listen and be silent, sometimes even promise that I would not go there anymore. In the moment in which I made the promise, I sincerely believed that it was over. With this decision I would go to sleep: I'm never going back to the theatre. The next day at work, my mind would go back and forth the entire day on whether or not to go to the theatre. As I walked out the door of the printing shop, the decision was—no! Yet when I turned to go to the lodging, instead I would change direction and head to the theatre.

Fanye now tried a different tactic with me. She stopped speaking to me. Not just about how the theatre was ruining me, but altogether. I was very glad that she had stopped asking me about the theatre. However, that she wouldn't speak to me about any other thing grieved me. Now when she did say something, it seemed as if from a stranger and sounded like a sign that I actually no longer had business living at the lodging.

Meanwhile, at the end of summer the Russian troupe "Tarski and Dobmarova" arrived. I had already heard people speak of this great theatre artist who was heading toward Uman. As great as my desire was to win back Fanye's friendship, which was tied to my not going to the theatre, suddenly now I couldn't do it. To stop going to the theatre when such a great actor had come—I couldn't bring myself to let it go.

The Tarski troupe was truly something different from what I'd seen up until then. All the non-theatre people would come backstage. Each night came students and teachers, and the majority would spend time with the artist Karlamov and also with Patshina. Tarski, who was the theatrical director and owner of the troupe, distinguished himself by his beauty as much backstage as onstage. He was tall, with broad shoulders, a fair complexion and a mop of disheveled black hair. He also sported a small, thinly shaved mustache, an exception among actors. He had a voice that attracted everyone's ear, but he used a language that one would hear from a coachman on the street. He was not embarrassed to speak in such a way, even in the presence of ladies, but surprisingly, no one was insulted. To the contrary, the ladies and female students were his biggest followers. As Karlamov surrounded himself with the intelligentsia of the city, so did Tarski with the female elements.

After playing for a few weeks, it was announced that they would produce the piece *Revolutionary*. From that day on, the theatre became a beehive. It was not possible to go backstage. Everyone was talking in an uproar over the new play. The work *Revolutionary* portrayed a great revolutionary in some other country who had incited the people, was condemned to death, and was pardoned before he could be hanged. Beforehand there had been difficulties in obtaining the permit to stage the piece. Finally they received the permit, and playbills for the performance *Revolutionary* were hung over the four main streets.

In the midst of such commotion I also could be found, under everyone's feet. Even if no one had sown me there, there I did sprout. I listened to everything and learned everything. I would always look people in the eye; perhaps they would send me on an errand or ask that I bring them something. It was all good as long as I could feel that I also was part of the ensuing hubbub. I had a lot of audacity and would often call out a word that snapped people's attention away from their surroundings and forced them to pay attention to me. Karlamov, the star of the troupe, soon noticed me and would often send me on an errand and tweak my ear, and I literally glowed when he would want me to serve him. Then one time, such a story came to pass:

In the last scene of the piece *Revolutionary*, the revolutionary is pardoned as he stands on the scaffold about to be hanged. A small boy who is actually the son of the man to be hanged, runs in with a rolled-up paper and cries out, "You are free!" People began bringing boys for the "big part" that consisted of running up to the stage and shouting "You are free!" All the boys that assembled together in the theatre were in uniform: some from the Russian city elementary school, some from another school, young students from the gymnasium: all were well schooled. Notwithstanding, when they were supposed to run in and shout their lines, they would get frightened. One would run in and forget to cry out, another did shout his line but while standing in one place rather than saying the line while running as the script dictated.

I was always present during the scene and kept myself in Karlamov's view. I felt that I could do the scene well, but to tell him this—I didn't dare. First, because of the way I was dressed and second, perhaps they really did need a student to do such a thing?

One time at a try-out Karlamov suddenly asked me, "Could you do it?" Before the words were out of his mouth, I started running to the stage and cried out the few words. Everyone was in agreement about my candidacy. They had me repeat it a few times and it turned out that I was the one who could do a good job.

I now found myself in a new role: I was an artist. I felt like one, and also told everyone that I would be playing in *Revolutionary*. I promised many of my young friends that I would open the rear door of the balcony so they could come see me play the part.

Because of my new position, I had completely stopped going to the lodging. I was not only somewhat ashamed, but also afraid and for the several days before doing the show I went to sleep at my Uncle Fishl's. There I could tell all about the miracles of the theatre and didn't forget, of course, to tell about the role that I would play in *Revolutionary*. The role was always in my head, whether at home or at work. The few words "You are free!" never left me for a minute. My impatience grew with every hour. In the evenings when I needed to do the scene, I waited with quivering breath.

Two or three days before the opening performance was to take place, I had left work early that day and gone to my uncle's for supper. My uncle was not much of a rich man and with so many children, the suppers were made from whatever was available. That evening as I stepped across the threshold to my uncle's apartment, I found the entire household in a joyful mood. On a box in the corner stood the tin-plated samovar, boiling like it wanted to join the party. On the table was a large bowl with onions and herring—more onions than herring—doused in vinegar. Each one sat with a piece of bread in his hand and on top of the bread rested a piece of herring. They ate the onions and licked the herring.

The little children received me with much gaiety. They slid over on the long wooden bench to make room for me and I became a partner to the onions and a fellow licker to the herring. Onions with vinegar was a dish that always satisfied me. I lost count and was off at a gallop, just as if there was a prize offered for eating onions. My aunt continually diced up a new blue onion, wiping the tears from her eyes that the onions had provoked while at the same time thanking God that onions were not dear.

After I washed down the meal with a few glasses of hot tea, I was off to the theatre. Generally I was never late, but this time I was the first person to arrive. The guard had long considered me as one of his own although tonight that didn't even matter: he knew that I would be playing this evening in the rehearsal; I myself had told him so.

People gradually began coming in and it was getting hectic. Fearful that I would be forgotten, I planted myself right next to Karlamov's door and peered in the faces of all who passed by.

Soon Karlamov came. He went inside and summoned me. I hastily followed him in. He gave me a few coins and told me to buy cigarettes. When I gave him the cigarettes, he was laying stretched out on the narrow couch in his room. He sat up, called me over and began asking me about myself. I was silent for a few seconds; I didn't know what to say. "Speak, why are you quiet?" he said in surprise. I lifted my head and began talking to him. He immediately gave me a shove backwards and covered his nose with his hand. "You've gorged yourself on onions!" he shouted angrily. "Get out of here! Scram!"

Like one who'd been shot, I ran out into the street. I stood in front of the theatre entrance, tears choking me. I cried aloud, something I hadn't done for a long time. I wept not only because I'd been thrown out of the theatre—and perhaps I hadn't been banished, just simply scolded. I wept because I suddenly remembered that it was for the theatre that I had lost my best friend, Fanye the Black.

CHAPTER 3

Odessa

THE HEART WEPT AND THE FACE LAUGHED

Odessa was the city of which every youth from our neighborhood dreamt. Each one had something to tell about Odessa. For this it wasn't necessary that he actually had been in Odessa; it was enough that he had heard something about it from someone else. He could then let his fantasies run free and a wonderful story would come to him, exactly as if he had been there himself.

Each time that I would hear someone speaking of Odessa, I felt a kind of trembling. With me, Odessa was a distant relative. I had a history with the city. After all, aside from being born there, it was Odessa that at four years old I lost my mother. I scarcely remembered the city; nevertheless I felt and also said that Odessa was my city and I would someday go and live there.

I was very patriotic towards Odessa. In the case that someone said something bad about Odessa or asserted that she was not as beautiful as people claimed, I would literally defend her tooth and nail to prove that she was the most beautiful city in Russia. Exactly how I wanted to think of Russia and remember her—that is how Odessa appeared. Since I now felt a little more confident in myself, Odessa had become my dream and my thoughts were constantly occupied with how I would get to the City of Wonder.

Now the time had come. In any case, I had destroyed my ties with the people who had instilled in me feelings of courage and independence, and also self-esteem. Indeed, the pride that they had awakened in me would now not allow me to go to them and say something in my defense. I must go away—this I decided. But how to get there? A ticket from Uman to Odessa would cost four rubles and sixty kopeks. Such a sum, of course, I didn't have; practically speaking, I had nothing. There was only one person to whom I could turn—a person with whom I could always share things; who always understood me—that person was, naturally, my sister Manye. I decided to tell her everything that had happened with me in the theatre, and also about my decision to journey to Odessa.

When I arrived at my father's house, everyone was already asleep. As always, I slipped quietly into the foyer. I looked around for a place to lie down and quickly went to sleep. The first one to notice me was the stepmother;

her racket woke me up. "He's here again!" she shrieked. "The treasure has returned! He's already moved in, this prodigy of yours!" I was already used to her complaints and curses and it didn't bother me when I would receive such a welcome.

My sister came in the foyer and said not to answer the stepmother. She wanted to know why I had come again and what had happened to me. I couldn't answer her: the tears began choking me. The only thing I was able to express was that I was going to Odessa.

"To Odessa with what?"

"I don't know," I answered. "You have to help me. And if not, I'll go on foot or travel by wagon."

Meanwhile a shriek was heard from the other room. The stepmother was calling my sister. "Where have you disappeared to?" she exclaimed. "Were you rejoicing with the treasure? You'll see enough of him yet, such brilliance won't get lost. Come to the room, I need you!" Manye motioned with her hand that I shouldn't leave; she still wanted to talk to me. By this time, the little children had discovered that I was at home, and they completely forgot about the pinches that their "loving" mother would give them if they clung to me. They rushed into the foyer, delighted to see me. It was with great difficulty that I sent them off to go wash and eat so the stepmother wouldn't scream at them and perhaps even beat them too.

A few hours later when no one was in the house, my sister began questioning me, asking advice both from me and from herself on how to get me to Odessa. She didn't try to dissuade me; rather, she agreed with me and said that perhaps it really would be better and that in time she would also come to me in Odessa. But the question was still: how? She had only a ruble and twenty kopeks; she had no idea where to get more. She would not ask my father. "You already know your father," she said. "And you know that he always likes to be contrary."

I then told her, "Twenty-nine kopeks will be enough to get me to the first station at Khrystynivka, and from there I'll travel as so many do: 'under the bench.' I've heard about traveling under the bench many times and I've thought that I would also travel that way; I'm not afraid to do so." My sister embraced me and wept. She knew that I wasn't afraid of such things, but she was frightened and for this reason hugged me and cried. We agreed that everything possible gotten ready for me and tomorrow, Friday, I would leave;

no one would be allowed to know until I had written my sister from Odessa. She would bring what she had gotten together for me to the station; I would be waiting for her there.

Exactly at the hour we had decided, my sister arrived with a bundle in her hand. She was already a completely different person: she met me with a smile and then spoke to me with her usual laughter to give me courage. She repeated several times that she was certain I wouldn't get lost. "Here is the money and in the bundle are some underwear, a towel, a roll, and some pletslekh.[80] I took them from what the stepmother always bakes for herself and hides; it just so happened that today she left the cupboard open and I took for you what I could."

With wobbly legs I made a dash for the ticket office to buy a ticket, paying with the ruble. As a result my pocket was full of change and I didn't have enough room to put in the ticket. I was in a panic that I wouldn't know where it was, so as I was standing there speaking with my sister, I was constantly slipping my hand into my pocket to touch the small, green piece of cardboard.

"Piervi zvonok!"—first call, the old conductor called out, naming the station where the train was headed. We embraced quickly and our happiness disappeared again. We cried bitterly and could have stood there for a lifetime if the same voice hadn't called out again, "Vtoroye zvonok!"—that is, second call. We could wait no longer. We kissed each other and I climbed up onto the railroad car. I remained standing on the car platform. Manye wiped her eyes and gave me a sign to be careful and laughed: the heart wept, and the face laughed. We were so preoccupied with this that we didn't notice the third call until the shaking of the railroad cars and the reverberations of the iron plates between them woke us up and reminded us that the plan to go away was now a reality.

UNDER THE BENCH

For the forty minutes the train took to travel to Khrystynivka, I never went inside the railroad car. I remained standing on the platform, engrossed in my thoughts. The conductor woke me up from this reverie when he came for my ticket.

Of all the things people told about Odessa, the one thing I had heard

---

80   Yiddish: plural of *pletsl*, a flat cake or cracker.

many times was how one travels without a train ticket, that is, how you travel with a ticket for only part of the way or with absolutely no money at all: under the bench. I already knew that those who travel under the bench must make sure that the conductor doesn't notice them when they climb aboard, so he won't be later seeking a misplaced passenger. All these stories debated each other in my head the entire time I stood on the platform. As soon as the train arrived at Khrystynivka, I needed to find out which train went to Vapnyarka because at that station I would need to change trains for the one that went to Odessa. It didn't take long, as I heard the conductor pointing out the train that went to Vapnyarka. Before the conductor could turn around, I had already gotten up on the platform and was hidden by the two passengers who had asked him a question.

The railroad car was still half-empty. I stood in the middle, not knowing what to do. Of course I knew that I must lie underneath a bench. But how did one do this, without others noticing? I began walking back and forth looking down under the benches but not daring to kneel down in case someone saw me. I decided to crawl under one of the benches in the middle of the car. I started to sit down but then didn't dare. An old peasant for whom those traveling under the bench were indeed nothing strange, said to me, "Don't be afraid, crawl in quickly!" What more he said to me I never heard, because I had already slid in and lay far underneath the bench.

An eternity seemed to pass until the train began moving. I was tired and had gone almost the entire day without eating. The bread and pletslekh had completely slipped my mind due to the excitement of the trip, and lying there I was rocked into a deep sleep. How much I slept, I didn't know; only that I woke up. I heard the snoring of the peasant and the squeak of the door through which people came and went. I tried not to go back to sleep. I knew that the train to Vapnyarka arrived at dawn. I felt that I had slept a long time, and I was very hungry.

I began slowly moving in order to reach the pack where I had the cookies. Lying as I was on my shoulders, I began nibbling them. As I lay backwards, I couldn't eat the dry cookies for long; they stuck in my throat and I quickly became full. For me, the time until Vapnyarka dragged on without end. My impatience and not knowing where exactly I was, prolonged the wait even more. The bundles that lay between the benches were, on one hand a good thing for me as they blocked me from view, but on the other hand, they also blocked out all the light and I couldn't tell when the new day would begin. I strained my ears as a dog does when he hears a stranger approaching so I wouldn't miss hearing it when they called out, "Vapnyarka." I suddenly heard a voice; it was the old peasant, who apparently was also traveling to Vapnyarka. "Come out, crawl up!" he said. "Now you can travel sitting on the bench; he has already taken the tickets!"

I cautiously poked my head out and then slowly brought out my body. I sat down on the edge of the bench; the uncertainty would not let me sit comfortably. There were only a few minutes left before we arrived at the station and the conductor would no longer return to the railroad car.

Changing trains for the one going to Odessa went much more smoothly. When I arrived at the terminal in Vapnyarka, the train to Odessa was not there yet. Thus I was able to sneak into a railroad car with the first passengers and a few minutes later I already had my under-the-bench train compartment and placing my pack under my head, I lay down as fine as if I were an aristocrat. I pricked up my ears to listen to what was taking place in the car. I heard people quarreling among themselves, shouting that the bundles shouldn't be laid under people's heads, and I thought to myself that my situation was better than was theirs. Suddenly my bed became narrower as I felt someone patting about with their hand, as if they were looking for something. I tried to slide in even deeper and I felt the touch of the searcher's hand. My heart stopped still, but the hand was quickly withdrawn. Then I heard a whisper from somebody's lips: "Hush, don't be afraid!" I didn't move a muscle.

A few minutes later I heard someone crawling under the bench. That there were others like me, made things seem easier. It made me happier too; I just hoped that I wasn't caught. I couldn't see who my fellow travelers were. Just over me sat a woman whose skirt took up half the bench, which actually protected me. However, the hem of her skirt was so besmeared and infused with the smells of the marketplace and of fish that it made me nauseated.

At that time, the train ride from Vapnyarka to Odessa took from eleven to twelve hours. I had been very edgy until I arrived at Vapnyarka. There I had drank some tea and snacked on the cookies; on this trip I felt much calmer than I did under my first bench. I slept for nearly the entire journey to Odessa.

When I woke up, the woman with the fish smell was gone. Instead of her dress blocking the light, my eyes were now dazzled by the light and by a pair of boots that never rested for a minute. I could see as far back as the second bench where my traveling companion lay, his eyes open and looking at his own ceiling of the bench over his face. I became calmer. There was no need to rush. I would do what he did. When I saw that he was ready to come out, I would too. However, I soon had another misery that did not allow me to lay still. This was the several glasses of tea that I had drunk at the terminal in Vapnyarka. I felt like my belly had become a piece of glass, and I couldn't move. I was feeling that should I make one careless movement, I would explode. Somehow I held out until we arrived.

I WANDER AROUND THE STREETS AND BECOME A BOOKBINDER AGAIN
Exiting the railroad car was a scene of terrible congestion. Everyone wanted to be the first to leave. Although I was very agile and could probably climb over people's heads, this time I remained trapped among the crowd and was swept along with them. My physical condition was such that I was twisted this way and that. But after passing through the terminal, I recovered and went out into the street. It was a beautiful day. The sun was already high in the sky. Together with the wave of people, I approached a dirt road that led to the different streets. I stood there, not knowing which way to go. I even had an address for one Noske, a paper-gluer, and knew that he could be found at a tavern called the Tsar's Village on Bolshaya Arnautskaya Street, but whom should I ask how to get there? Everybody hurried about so, and never in my life had I seen so many people on one street.

    I stayed standing where I was. From the bundle that my sister had given me, I took out a pinch of roll and also ate some cherries that I had bought for a few kopeks at the terminal, the first fruits of summer! Still I had absolutely no idea where to turn. Since I'd eaten the roll, my pack was now smaller. I tucked it under my armpit and set off down the first street, of which the inscription read Rishelyevskaya.

    I walked very slowly and felt no joy that I was finally in the city of Odessa, of which so many young boys dreamt. Rather, I had some regret that I hadn't stayed in the city where everyone knew me and I knew everyone. Were it not linked with so much hardship, I would have ran straight back. My heart wept quietly, but with great effort I kept my eyes dry. I told myself that here I must stay. With every new business I saw, I stopped and looked inside, as if I was searching for something there.

I continued on this street until I came to a second street that intersected it, a street called Bolshaya Arnautskaya. At that moment, I felt that I would find a treasure. I reread the inscription a few dozen times. I had asked no one and nevertheless found it. The only thing I didn't know if you should go up the street or down in order to find the tavern called the Tsar's Village. I didn't dare ask anyone. I was overwhelmed by a sense of fear that I had never felt before. I stood there and looked around me on all sides. Across the street I spotted a large sign with the inscription "Bookbindery" and in smaller letters, the name of the proprietor—Kopelman. I slowly crossed the street. The door of the bookbindery was open. I drew near to it and stood on the doorstep. I watched the people working there and suddenly felt strangely jealous of them; I literally devoured their every movement with my eyes.

Exhausted from the journey and all the emotional upheaval, it seemed I couldn't stay on my feet any longer. I myself didn't know how it happened, but I descended to the doorstep and sat there. Perhaps I even dozed off. I soon looked around and saw a Jew standing near me. He asked why was I sitting there and was I waiting for someone. I didn't know how to answer him. Now he became a littler firmer. "Get away from here!" he said. "You'll get nothing here!" I stood up but didn't leave. He stood and waited, reminding me again that I must leave.

"Maybe you can give me something to do," I said. "I'm not from Odessa …" My plea and my silent tears could be seen swimming in my eyes.

The Jew turned and walked a few steps away from me but he soon came back and asked, more calmly, where had I come from. When he heard that I was from Uman, he said that there in Odessa were many Umaners and asked which of them did I know there.

"I don't know," I answered. "I just arrived today. The only person that I know is Noske the Long One."

The Jew stood there, looked at me, and let me speak. He no longer suspected that I wanted to steal something and he listened to my story. Soon he knew not only that I was from Uman, but that I had a stepmother and that I had traveled to Odessa under the bench. Just as earlier I had been afraid to ask anyone a question on the street, now my tongue was loosened and I talked without stopping.

"So then, good," he said, "come inside. I'll see what you can do." He led me to a young man of about twenty. "Siomke," he said to him, "here is a helper for you. He is not a local; he is from Uman. He says that he can work—no doubt he can do more than a dead man can. He does seem to me to be a rascal and is not shy. See if he can do something for you."

The young man named Siomke was his son. From the first minute that I was brought before him, I felt that he was one of those like Zelik and Samuil; indeed, the very same as those I had worked with in the underground print shop. I remained standing by his table but he didn't give me any orders. He only asked what I was called, what kind of work I had done, and had I eaten yet. When he was finished with all his questions, he told me that since today was Friday and his father was very religious, I wouldn't work that day; I would begin on Sunday. During the time that he had been questioning me, I had felt a strange sense of closeness with him.

"Good," I said, "but where will I sleep until Sunday?"

"What do you mean, with us, of course, here in the bookbindery. Another boy sleeps here and works with us for meals. You'll sleep with him."

Now this Siomke, the son of the owner, was the true expert in the bookbindery and everything was done according to his instructions. Sunday morning when everybody was gathered at work, he called over one of the older workers and showed me to him, telling him that he now had a boy that seemed to want to work, although he didn't know if I knew anything.

Everything that I owned, I had brought with me. Therefore I worried about being smeared with the glue they had given me to glue the paper to the covers of the books. After smearing glue on the paper for a long time, my fingers were also covered with glue, making it hard for me to hand the papers to the master. Completely forgetting that they were my only riches, I wiped my fingers on my shirt. I had worn this shirt for a very long time, so much that it was barely held together, and now my hasty wipe on the weak cloth pulled it and ripped the shirt right down the middle. I suddenly forgot what I was doing. With both hands I hid the torn shirt and became very upset. The strange people around me, the severing from everyone who, no matter what, had always helped me, and now I'd lost my last shirt—with all this together I broke down, and feeling sorry for myself, started to cry.

Siomke came to me and asked me why was I crying. I showed him the torn shirt. "Don't worry!" he comforted me. "You'll have another shirt." That very same evening he brought me a new dark-red shirt. He sat down next to me and began asking what I did in Uman and why I had left the city. His questioning was so brotherly that in a few words, I told him everything. I didn't fail to tell him all the work I did as a printer and even about the underground printing shop in the city. We sat and talked for a long time; I didn't skimp on my answers. To each of his questions I answered with the entire history of my young life. In the evening, Siomke took me into the city. He walked with me for a long time and promised that he would see to it that I was introduced to several printers so that I could work in a printing shop, and that with time I would have even more friends in Odessa than I had in Uman.

I worked for more than a month in the bookbindery. During that time I met with many young people and this brought me closer to the life for which I had so much longed. Among the new acquaintances there was one with whom I was very close called Sherpovotski. He had an important role in the Social-Democratic Mensheviks.[81] I was introduced to them and my life slowly became more joyful.

AGAIN A PRINTER AND A RETURN TO THE MOVEMENT

Sherpovotski was a printer. He worked in the biggest printing shop, for Levinson. As promised, he brought me to work there. My salary was set at twelve rubles a month. The twelve rubles set me completely on my feet and I was truly independent. This same Sherpovotski gave me a place to sleep and board for six rubles a month. With the rest of the money I had all the necessary things and in addition, more than I could spend.

My independence awakened a new courage in me and with it, bit by bit I began going to the illegal assemblies and becoming involved with them as I had done before. On Friday nights, Sherpovotski, who was older and an external candidate student, taught us about socialism and what it meant. He followed the type of socialism that you didn't live for yourself, but for others. He had two things in his life: to prepare himself for the new world, and to prepare each person that he met for the socialism which he was certain stood ready on the threshold to emerge.

---

81 Russian: a faction of the Russian socialist movement, after a dispute in 1904 within the Russian Social-Democratic Labor Party led to the party splitting into two factions: the Mensheviks and the Bolsheviks.

Yakob Sherpovotski had in addition to us, other youth that surrounded him. All those for whom he was their teacher, must renounce all other pleasures because according to his point of view, to not renounce these—that was a crime. He was a man of high morals, and these morals he also pulled out of us. Slowly I began looking at Yakob Sherpovotski as a holy man and his word became law for me. On his part, he had confidence in me and would take me everywhere that in his judgment, I could be useful.

Over the next few months, my life in Odessa took on new worth. I was not directly involved in the more dangerous part of the underground work as I had been in Uman, but I was entrusted with things that could result in years in prison if they fell into the wrong hands. I was responsible for distributing in a designated sector each new leaflet published. I also had to attend my youth group and give reports on the work that I did and inform them on what I had mastered for that time period—something not just I, but each youth was required to do.

THE MUTINY OF THE BATTLESHIP POTEMKIN[82]

In July 1904[83] a rebellion broke out on the battleship Potemkin. A sailor had protested to his commander, complaining that they had been given worm-infested food. The commander had slapped the sailor. A fight ensued and the sailor was killed, triggering the beginning of the rebellion. The sailors arrested the officers, and they became the masters of the ship. The city socialist parties immediately began thinking of ways to exploit these events for even bigger revolutionary deeds. Representatives of all the socialist parties sent their delegations to encourage the sailors. They assured the sailors that the city joined them in their struggle and that they were prepared to give the sailors everything they would need. Meanwhile, the city began making preparations for the funeral of the murdered sailor. The

---

82 The Russian battleship Potemkin, part of the Imperial Russian Navy's Black Sea Fleet, became famous when the crew rebelled against the officers in the summer of 1905. The ship made for the port of Odessa, where disturbances and strikes had already been going on. When the Potemkin arrived in Odessa, events quickly worsened, resulting in violent clashes between demonstrators and government troops, a fire on the railway overpass and a pogrom, all of which left the city port burning and nearly a thousand dead.

83 Historical accounts based on the Gregorian calendar give this date as June 14, 1905 with the Potemkin arriving at the Port of Odessa on the morning of the 15th.

police didn't know how to handle the situation, and the city was handed over to the authority of the local military power. Initially, the general of the Odessa military garrison wouldn't listen to the request that the sailor be buried with honor, but the sailors gave him several hours' time to think over and accept their demand. If not, they warned that they would attack Odessa. As a demonstration that they meant what they said, they shot a cannonball at the Sobor (Russian Orthodox cathedral). The garrison general, although he did have troops, couldn't face off against the ship Potemkin, which was one of the largest and most well-armed ships that patrolled the Japanese waters. The general lost his nerve and allowed the funeral preparations to move forward.

In one day's time, the entire city was wrapped in mourning banners. A black and white ribbon was hung on every streetlight and the lamps were lit. On the day of the funeral, no one went to work. Student committees from the Kherson University together with workers went from one business to the next and forced them to close. From the railway overpass[84] to the cemetery, the streets were flooded with soldiers and the remaining parts of the city were patrolled by troops. By each police officer stood soldiers with rifles. The city was divided between the military forces and the socialist movement, and the streets were packed with equal numbers of adherents. Both the troop officials and the members of the revolutionary committees went around with ribbons on their right hands and helped to keep order for the funeral.

In the middle of the day, the casket of the murdered sailor was brought down. Thousands of people spontaneously united and the front rows locked arms, each one armed and ready to take on a fight if it became necessary. Revolutionary songs were sung during the entire way to the cemetery. The procession moved very slowly and the heavy black casket, changing hands many times, was covered with a red flag and red flowers.

All those on the street stood with bared heads. The police were completely panicked, and the Odessa police chief abandoned everything to the

---

84   Translator's note: The author uses the word "barentin" (transliterated pronunciation). I have chosen to translate it as "railway overpass," linking it to the Barentin Viaduct in France, a well-known railway viaduct that Abrams, who later lived in France, likely knew about. Historical accounts of this day confirm that the Odessa port did have a very long (4 km.) wooden railway overpass and that it burned to the ground on that day.

military power. The military had issued advance instructions in the meantime, not daring to begin a civil war at a time when the country was already at war. In fact, on the day of the funeral the city was in the hands of the socialist movement. The air was full of gunpowder; everyone felt how serious things were. Yet no one became frightened. The confidence of those who took part in the funeral drove away the fear.

It was already past noon when they arrived at the cemetery. Excited to a feverish pitch, none of the marchers intended to stay outside the gate. Thousands and thousands occupied the entire field, with still many more that had to stay outside because there was no more room. The grave had already been dug and it was encircled by a barricade of revolutionary guards. In spite of the large crowds, it was so quiet that you could hear a fly buzzing overhead. Everything was done in order. One speaker after another—representatives from all the different schools of socialist ideologies—warned the Tsarist autocracy that the beginning of the end was not far off. When the casket was lowered into the grave, it was already dark. The front rows began singing the revolutionary funeral march. The entire crowd picked up the chant and you could distinctly hear the pillars of tsarism groaning.

Meanwhile, the police, plucking up their courage, encircled the field and waited outside for those who had spoken at the cemetery and called for revolution. The socialist crowd delayed longer in the cemetery, waiting until it was completely dark so at least the police wouldn't be able to seize the leaders. Yet no matter how much they took care so that the police would do as little damage as possible, the police were nevertheless successful in making a dangerous pogrom and entrapping in their paws all the speakers and organizers of the political demonstration.

THE POGROM

The mood of the funeral had also carried over to the second day; almost no one who had taken part in the funeral went to work. You felt that something was quietly going on. The Russian underground was not sleeping. Everything possible was done to exploit the heightened mood of the large crowds to propose resistance against the reactionaries; you felt as though Russia also was ready for a challenge. First thing in the morning, a rumor spread across the city that the Black Hundreds[85] were planning a pogrom and that a gang of thugs was assembling under the protection of the police at the railway overpass.

The Odessa railway overpass stretched for thousands of meters along the shore of the sea. Hundreds of thugs arrived on the shore and got ready to carry out the pogrom. What followed would have been done by the police, under the pretext that there must be order in the city. Nonetheless, the mood of the large demonstration had raised people's courage to the extent that no one thought of fleeing and finding a secure corner; rather, they surged to the port where the hooligans were gathered.

In the fighters' organizations that had been trained by the socialist revolutionaries, there were representatives from all the factions ready to take part in the iron ring that had been created around the entire dock. They waited for the thugs, in order to pull them into a fight before they could spread to the city and bring the pogrom to the population.

Suddenly people began shouting that the railway overpass was burning, and in that moment the overpass became engulfed in flames. The tongues of flame shot so high that it seemed as if the flames would fuse with the sun—a sun that threw burning sticks and made the fire stronger and mightier with every minute. The thugs at the port were now surrounded on one side by the sea and on the other side by the fire, which with every minute was harder to pass through. The whole thing was perfectly planned out. People had started the fire by igniting casks of oil, which were then poured into each corner where material lay that could be lit even with a match.

A stampede broke out among the thugs. They began running wildly, trying to find a way through the fire. Those who stood ready, waiting to meet the rioters, did everything possible to stop them. They met them—some with knives and some with a whip; revolvers were also used against them. The news that a deadly fight had broken out at the railway overpass spread over the city as quickly as the fire had spread across the overpass. Everyone started running to the scene of the fight; men came in the thousands to help, and to put an end to the band of thugs.

---

85   A collection of anti-revolutionary, anti-Semitic groups in Russia active during and after the 1905 Russian Revolution. They were made up of landowners, rich peasants, bureaucrats, merchants, and police officials, leading brutal raids (with the tacit approval of the regime) against various revolutionary groups and notoriously, deadly pogroms against the Jews.

The military detachments assigned to Odessa were not primarily Russians, but Kalmykians.[86] This was the policy of Tsarist Russia: they always manned the cities either with Cossacks or with foreign soldiers. They sent Russian soldiers to the Tatars and among Russians assigned Tatar soldiers. This made it easier to incite the soldiers against the population, and the soldiers would beat them cruelly whenever it was the command.

The garrison in Odessa also received a decree to beat anyone whom they might meet in the street. They were told to quickly clear the streets and then go to the railway overpass and finish things with the organized gangs that were there. Cossacks and dragoons began executing the command and for hours, one after another, the streets flowed with blood. Like wild animals, they rode on horseback cutting down right and left whoever crossed their path. The wild ride of the Cossacks created a panicked stampede in the city. The gates of the yards became jammed and scores of people were forced to remain on the street under the whistle of the Cossack and dragoon knouts.[87]

Despite this, the self-defense brigades remained completely calm. The panic had not driven them from the streets; rather, they all pushed closer to the railway overpass in order to choke off the attempted pogrom that had been organized by the mayor so that the blame for the unrest in the city could be thrown on the Jews.

We, the younger ones who were assigned the task of helping with the self-defense, did not let the horrible situation get to us. Devoid of any fear and with complete devotion, each one did whatever he could to resist the armed Cossacks. Our weapons were the bricks that lay in decoration around the trees. Young friends—we began tearing out the bricks as we shouted, "Long live the city burghers, for having prepared these for us!"

AT THE BARRICADE

The "exchange" was a gathering point. Every organization had an exchange. People would meet there, get all the news, and receive instructions on what they were to do. The Social-Democratic exchange was located on Bolshaya

---

86   Kalmykia is a Russian republic. It was renowned for its cavalries: irregular Russian Army units of horsemen from the Lower Volga steppes, who had helped drive Napoleon's armies from Russia.

87   Knout: a heavy whip designed specifically for flogging.

Arnautskaya Street and also on Uspenskaya. On the same end of the two streets was a dairy business that was known by the name Bundist[88] Dairy Bar.

I was a member of the Social-Democratic youth and came often to the exchange. I would come together with many other young people from the same group, so that we could hear things and also receive the proper instructions. On the day of the pogrom, we went to the exchange a few times but there was no one there that we knew. At night when the Cossacks became wild, a group of us young people found ourselves at the exchange. We ourselves didn't see how it came about, but the plaza suddenly became barricaded. Carriages that were traveling down Uspenskaya Street were stopped and overturned, then used to block the entire width of the street. Each person began carrying what he could. People courageously broke into several yards, bringing out from there whatever could be used to block the street.

We began carrying the bricks that would serve as our weapons. The people who had first began building the barricade also had firearms—that is, revolvers—but these later proved to be very few.

Night began to fall. Scores of people encircled the barricade. All were seized by the desire to fight. People wanted to take revenge on the Cossacks for the bloody slaughter they had carried out during the day. Suddenly, in the distance we heard the gallop of the Cossacks' horses and the wild cries of the Cossacks. Everybody at the barricade began singing *La Marseillaise*.[89] The chanting of *La Marseillaise* brought forth a steely courage. Before the Cossacks drew near, we children began throwing the bricks at them we had prepared at the barricade.

In the first moment, the Cossacks did nothing. They remained sitting on their horses, at a distance where the stones couldn't reach them. Then they fired in the air a few times. The shots in the air drove off many people from the barricade, but there remained a sufficient count to take on the fight, if we had the means to do so—the couple of fighters with their revolvers had no

---

88 Yiddish: BUND, abbreviation for Der Algemeyner Yidisher Arbeter Bund in Lite, Poyln, un Rusland (The General Union of Jewish Workers in Lithuania, Poland, and Russia): founded in Russian in 1897, the Bund served as an influential member of the social democratic movement in Russia until after the 1917 revolution. Various manifestations of the organization continued in existence until shortly after WWII, when the majority of its members were killed.

89 The French national anthem that served as a rallying cry against tyranny during the French Revolution.

real significance. Nonetheless, no one remaining chose to run away after those first shots; it had brought out the drive to avenge the bloody day. More shots in the air were heard, and soon afterwards the Cossacks on their horses came bearing down on the crowd behind the barricade. A few shots rang out from the barricade side and what happened after that, I don't remember. I only know that when I recovered consciousness, I found myself in the Bundist Dairy Bar. Blood was flowing from my left cheek and a few teeth on the same side had been shattered; I also had a head wound. Both these "gifts" were received from a Cossack knout.

As I later found out, my life was saved thanks to a Bundist girl. She had fired at the Cossack while at the same time with the help of someone else, dragged me into the Dairy Bar and given me my initial aid. Later, in the nighttime, she had brought me to a Jewish hospital that was on the corner of Gospitalnaya. Many wounded had been brought to the same hospital and not only were we saved there, but they also hid us; each of us was taken out just before the police could get their hands on us. For all of this I had the loyal friend of the Liberation movement to thank: Doctor Zilverberg. Because of all this unpleasantness he had faced many obstacles; this had not deterred him from risking his own security to defend those who were involved in a just fight.

MOYSEY TSEYTLIN

After recovering for a few weeks, I was almost returned to health and left the hospital. A few of my youth friends came to get me and took me home. This was now a new apartment, one of a certain printer Moysey Tseytlin, who also worked for Levinson in the printing shop.

My prestige was now greatly elevated. The attitude towards me no longer was one towards a person whom no one knew; rather, I had already gone through the first trial by fire and this spoke for itself.

The apartment where I now lived was located on Bezimiani Pereulok (a side-street). This was a Bialystoker Jewish house. The owner of the house was an older Jew. When he came to discuss the business matters, the Jew would say that if he were our age, he would have done the same. "Even now I would have gone with you," he would say. "But to do something when you have a wife and children, may they be healthy, now I must leave it to you." He was not very religious; perhaps in Bialystok he had been observant. Here in Odessa, however, where the greater part of the Jews were not too much in the habit of bothering the Master of the Universe and where God, in truth, enjoyed life, my landlord did as everyone else did and had deep regrets that he was not a little younger.

Moysey Tseytlin, with whom I now shared a room, adhered to the path of the Russian Social Democracy called Bolshevism. In those years, people from different doctrines were not personal enemies and Bolsheviks and Mensheviks lived as good friends. People would debate about the differences between the two doctrines of the Social-Democratic movement. Until my acquaintanceship with Moysey I had known nothing about these differentiations, and even after a long time I still couldn't analyze them. Moysey worked to convince me to join the youth organization to which he belonged. To me, the differences didn't seem to be very important. I was more interested in my friends whom I would encounter every day, meeting with them at the exchange, and going together with them to illegal assemblies.

I learned much from Moysey. I learned where the differences between the Bolsheviks and the Mensheviks stemmed from, who were their creators, and who were Plekhanov, Axelrod, and Lenin.[90] Moysey explained to me that the Bolsheviks were the representatives of the labor movement and that I was following the doctrine that presented itself as intelligentsia, for whom the worker question was of little importance. When I would come to my group, I was always full of Moysey's arguments. The leader of our group, Yore, was completely pleased with my questions and he would give me well-prepared responses.

*   *   *

[The continuity of Abrams' autobiographical fragments here becomes, regrettably, disrupted. The next fragments bring us in at a new location and a later time. —Editor]

---

90   Respectively, Georgi Plekhanov: Russian revolutionary and a Marxist theoretician and founder of the social-democratic movement in Russia; Pavel Axelrod (born Pinches Borutsch): Russian Menshevik who sided with the Menshevik faction against Vladimir Lenin's Bolsheviks: Vladimir Ilyich Ulyanov (alias Lenin): Russian communist revolutionary, politician, and political theorist who served as the head of government for both the Russian Soviet Federative Socialist Republic and the Soviet Union, he led the Bolshevik faction against the Mensheviks.

CHAPTER 4
Back in Uman

AT NINETEEN YEARS OLD, A YOUNG MAN WITH PARTY SENIORITY

Three years later, I returned to Uman. The three years had had an effect on the small city; the pogroms and the harsh reaction had left their mark. The Jewish-Russian intelligentsia first began to wake up after the disappointment of the Worker's Revolution of 1905.[91]

The Uman prison and the "Arrest House" (jailhouse) were overflowing. Of the leading powers, very few were not under arrest. The mood among those remaining free was such that they went around not knowing what to do with themselves. The only thing they kept up was sustaining their link with those imprisoned: sending them food and all other things allowed in prison.

Yet on the contrary, among those imprisoned their spirits were cheerful, with the exception of two: Gervits and Vinokur. They had each received sentences of twenty years forced labor, and kept writing letters saying that the whole struggle was useless. It was the writing of desperation. Finally, on the same day they both poisoned themselves, leaving behind a letter saying that they made the decision to do it because they had nothing more to live for.

At that time I was a young man of nineteen years with the seniority of a responsible activist in the underground movement. I came from Odessa with a party-card from the Social-Democratic party and with their complete confidence.

In Odessa, I felt different than I did in Uman. The Odessa intelligentsia was also living under the cloud of disappointment that then ruled over all of Russia, but there was of course a difference between the Workers' Center of Odessa and the smaller city of Uman, which had almost no workers. In Uman all the work lay in the hands of the intelligentsia, and the mood there was bitter.

In the part of the movement to which I belonged, first in line were the representatives of the printer workers. Their number was about sixty or seventy. Not many of them had been arrested. Also in this section were representatives of the workers from the sole foundry then located in Uman.

---

91   A wave of mass political and social unrest that spread throughout Russia in 1905, including worker strikes, peasant unrest, and military mutinies.

Not much work was done by our detachment because leaders were lacking who had eloquence and the sharp revolutionary pen. Therefore, we would often be sent over directives and written leaflets from the prison, which needed to be printed and distributed. As I had expertise working in an underground printing shop, I proposed that a printing shop be immediately assembled. For this I pledged myself to come up with a box of fonts from a printing shop, should it become necessary.

Our group then decided that the commission seeing to the printing would be composed of three comrades and that we three should create everything necessary for the undertaking. Also that only the three of us would know where the printing shop was, and that we ourselves would do all the work.

WE MAKE AN ILLEGAL PRINTING SHOP

The Torodosh printing shop was considered at that time to be the biggest in the city. The shop owned many text fonts because it used to publish a daily newspaper; now the fonts were no longer used. Furthermore, it was also very easy to get into this shop, as one of our trio, Ziloykh, worked there. The printing shop also had a second entrance where the door could be left open and the required fonts carried out.

The plan was formulated and a night was appointed to carry it out. Ziloykh indicated the four boxes that we needed and left the door open. In a few weeks' time, this bit of work was completed and we were now rich with three full boxes of fonts, printer's ink and all the little necessities that we required. In the locksmith's shop at the talmed toyre[92] they had made us the needed cylinder, and in a month's time we had made ready the printing shop.

As we were preparing to print the first leaflets, everything was calm. Torodosh had not caught on that he was the one burglarized—that it was from his shop that we had taken the fonts and other materials. The printer workers, who had noticed the theft, immediately understood that this was party work and the affair was kept quiet.

One morning, the city of Uman was inundated with leaflets—something that had not been seen for a long time. The gendarmes leadership aimed themselves directly at the printing shops to discover where the leaflets had been printed. They summoned the owners of all the printing shops and

---

92   Yiddish: Jewish primary schools for poor children funded by the community.

asked them if they recognized the font type of the proclamation. All of them answered as one, affirming that it was their font. Even those who didn't actually have that type of font, also said that it was theirs. To the second question from the gendarmes: "Who is missing fonts?" they all declared that they were not missing any.

If Torodosh, from whom the fonts were taken, would have found us out, he certainly would have informed on us immediately to the gendarmes. He hadn't known; he was certain that they weren't his fonts and he conducted himself just as did the other printers. However, when he came to the printing shop, he immediately began reviewing what he owned and then he discovered the disaster. Torodosh was a Jew with a very narrow perspective. His entire life was dedicated to becoming rich and living an easy life; anything else was craziness. He immediately stopped the work, called all the workers together and informed them that if the boxes were not returned in a few days, he would hand everyone over to the police.

Ziloykh, who had taken part in extracting the fonts, went up to Torodosh and with his index finger on his chest, assured him that if he wanted to be the owner of a printing shop, he had better not dare do so. Ziloykh then turned to the workers and said, "He means to trifle with us about this, saying he will partner with the gendarmes colonel; our answer is that we will abandon the work and he can amuse himself with it."

Comrades began putting on their jackets, preparing to walk off the job. The printing shop became a chaotic scene. Torodosh began pleading that they forget what he said. Rather, it was that he himself agreed with what was done, it was just that he was afraid. He ran from one man to another, assuring them that what he said was in anger because still, three boxes of fonts cost a lot of money. What if someone said something or someone recognized the fonts? The men shouted to each other and it became calm. All remained in their places and they reassured him that in the event that something did happen, they, the workers, would take care of it and nothing would happen to him.

The gendarmes administration did not rest. Every day they arrested another printer; they dug up the ground. The jailhouse was packed. The majority of the printing shops were scarcely working. The five or six owners of the printing shops ran to the colonel, pleading with him to free the workers or else they would be ruined.

A BRIEF ARREST AND A VISIT WITH MY FATHER

One evening I was standing near the Buns bakery and a policeman came up to me and told me that the regional police superintendent wanted me. With those words, he quite firmly took me by the hand and gave a whistle. Soon a second policeman showed up and they led me away to the station.

The police were located opposite the boulevard in a large court. The firemen were on one side and on the other was a cell where they kept the temporary detainees: a cell with small windows that looked out on the boulevard. This cell was large with nailed boards along the entire length and breadth of one wall—a bed for the prisoners. In a corner stood a large bucket for bodily needs, called a "slop bucket." The wooden floor was rotten and the suffocating filth gave witness to the fact that since the square had been built, the floor had never been washed. The walls, from one edge to the other, were inscribed and adorned with the red spots of crushed bedbugs.

When they brought me into the cell, the police superintendent was no longer at the precinct building and I would have to be his guest for the night without the knowledge of my boss.

The cell was crowded. The long plank bed was covered with thieves and drunks. The air was thick from the smoke of cheap tobacco rolled up in newspaper-paper for smoking.

I was accepted by all as a good guest. The men sat up to give me a reception. Each one had something to say on my account. Mainly what everyone wanted to know was, did I have any cigarettes. "He doesn't have any cigarettes? So go screw your mother! He calls himself a thief and he doesn't even have any cigarettes."

This kind of welcome was by now nothing new to me. I had already heard it in Odessa, Yelisavetgrad,[93] and Zhytomyr, and it didn't surprise me. I knew that you either had to stay silent or use the same kind of talk in return, even if someone hit you for it and you were forced to answer in same.

One of them, an older gentile who was, it seemed, not there for the first time and had also been in other prisons—he was a village elder, a representative of the prisoners to the authorities. He sat down, considered me, and with a paternal look turned to me: "What, a political prisoner?"

"Yes!"

---

93 Now named Kirovohrad.

"Well then, find yourself a corner and lie down; that will be good." With this the incident was ended. I still didn't sleep the entire night. Not because of the bare boards that I was laying on—these I was already accustomed to. What tormented my thoughts was that perhaps the printing shop had been discovered, and that soon they would bring in the other two.

I ran different pretexts through my head in case they asked me about the printing shop. I knew that if they had brought me in because of the printing shop it would not go so easy for me, and I had to anticipate all possibilities. Thus I spent the entire night putting questions to myself and then answering them.

Before the day broke, all were fast asleep. The air in the cell was unbearable from what was coming from the bucket that everyone had used during the night. Using all my strength, I hauled myself up to the window that was as wide as the entire wall. The windowpanes behind the bars had long since disappeared. I squeezed the bars with my hands and pressed my face between the iron bars. The cold morning breeze revived me.

Sitting thus in the window, I began again to repeat in my mind the answers to the questions I would put to myself. The brisk breeze began lulling me to sleep. I was doing battle with drowsiness so I wouldn't fall out of the window. To keep this from happening, I began softly whistling a tune. As it was still cold outside and the quietness had not yet been disturbed, several of those passing by raised their eyes to see who the early-morning songbird was whistling melodies.

The time passed and bit by bit, those sleeping began standing up and cursing me for sitting in the window and blocking the little bit of air and light. The cell became lively. Some of them banged on the door, wanting the slop bucket taken out. Others wanted hot water. Each one told what he had dreamt, accompanying every few words with an ugly curse word. The older prisoner took off his shirt and began looking for the creatures that had bitten him the most. Others, envious that he found so many, followed his example.

From the other side of the door a commotion sounded, with the clanging of keys accompanied by the comments about one's mother. The door opened and two policemen came in the cell. The two prisoners standing closest to the door were honored with the privilege of carrying out the slop bucket. Then they pointed out two other prisoners to go bring the hot water. A policeman stood by the hot water guarding the other two. During the few minutes of the procedure the door remained open; this, along with the men carrying out the slop bucket, changed the air a bit inside the cell. But the prisoners raised a fuss, wanting the door to be shut because it was cold.

The sun was already high overhead when I was summoned to the district police superintendent. Two policemen led me across the large courtyard. Entering the administrative office, I saw my father sitting by the superintendent's desk. Before the superintendent could say a word, my father fell on me with a speech certainly meant for him. My father was a good brother to the district police superintendent; he received three times as much from my father as from the post he occupied. For this reason, the first questions were put to me by my father and not the superintendent. When I told my father that I didn't know why I had been arrested, he began cursing me again and turning to the superintendent, assured him that he had me well in hand, and that the superintendent could rely on him.

The district police superintendent, Malinovski, a great bribe-taker, understood that he would receive something in his hand and he turned to me very politely and told me that I needed to appreciate that I had such a father, and furthermore, that I should have nothing more to do with the "seditionists" (the political leaders). I stood there silently thinking to myself of the joy in having such a father, and wished the superintendent such good fortune. The superintendent assured my father that it would better if the chief of the gendarmes knew nothing of my matter, or he would not be able to free me.

As we left the yard, I asked my father how he found out that I had been arrested. "You don't know then?" my father answered. "Jews notified me that my son was sitting in a window of the precinct and whistling." Then he let loose his tongue.

"Maybe you think that I came to take you out for your own sake? As far as I'm concerned, you can rot there. Only that it's beneath my dignity that I allow you to sit there and people talk in the city, saying that Isumer lets his son sit in jail. The big shot can't do anything for his own son. Listen to me, I'm giving you some advice: pack up your things and go back to where you came from. If they should bring you in again, I won't come and get you. I don't need this pig Malinovski taking bribes from me and doing me favors."

After receiving this notice, I assured my father that I had not asked him for any favors and that I hadn't sent for him. As far as it being beneath his dignity that I be arrested and that people would say that he, the bigshot, couldn't help his own son, he could be certain that there would yet come a day when I would be sent away and he would be able to do nothing, and that would have to be good enough for him.

My father became angry, spat, turned away from me and quickly walked away. I began going on my way.

י. אייבראַמס'עס פֿאָטער

Jacob Abrams' Father

Five Years in Soviet Russia

(Deep Conviction and Bitter Disappointment)

[Translator's Note: This section begins in 1921, after Abrams' trial, conviction, and time in a U.S. prison. Abrams, his wife and co-defendants have been deported to the Soviet Union.]

AT THE BORDER

The ship Esthonia arrived at the shores of Libau[94] on December 4, 1921.

Our small group of five, deported from the United States to Russia, had kept together in a corner of the ship, ready to set foot on solid ground after a very stormy journey. All the other passengers had left the ship long ago. The officials had announced to us that we would be allowed to disembark only when the Soviet consul would guarantee that we would be allowed to enter Soviet Russia.

Because of the tone in which this was explained to us, it was already useless to ask more questions. Meanwhile, we were forbidden to go up to the deck until our situation was in order.

The few hours that we sat and waited for the Soviet consul seemed like long, hard nights. There was no one to ask when he would come, because the guard that stood near us was under orders not to speak to us. Nevertheless, I tried talking to him but he gazed at me with a pair of pleading eyes, as if telling me, "Don't make any difficulties for me; I'm not allowed to say anything."

Finally the consul arrived. In a hushed and cautious tone, he explained to our group that the Soviet representatives sometimes have to endure terrible problems. Therefore we must be very careful not to blurt out anything about where we were going and as fast as we could get down there, we should take the train to Riga. He gave us five train tickets to Riga and a prepared recommendation letter to the Soviet ambassador in the capital of Latvia. He parted from us in a friendly manner and left the ship.

A few minutes later the Esthonia officials arrived, looked over our hand luggage and announced that the train to Riga would leave a few hours later and that in order to avoid problems, we should take the first train and forsake Libau.

We arrived at Riga at night. It was already dark. The terminal was weakly illuminated and there were few passengers present. An official appeared and very politely informed us that we must stay in the hotel, which he pointed out to us. Naturally we obeyed him and fifteen minutes later, we were already at the hotel. We didn't lie down to sleep, instead sitting around discussing our continued journey, as our end goal was drawing near. It was decided that I would take responsibility for seeing to everything for our further travel to cross the border.

---

94   Libau, Latvia.

We barely lived to see the rest of the day. The poorly heated hotel left all of us blue from the cold. We finished talking and went out on the street a short way to get warm. Our light American clothing was not suitable to protect us from the freezing cold in which Riga was enveloped. Half-frozen, we went into the first decent restaurant that our eyes fell on.

After draining a few glasses of tea, we were refreshed and warm. We became braver and sat for long time, and then went back to the hotel. The hours dragged for us until it was time to go to the Soviet legation. At ten o'clock, as the representative of the group, I went to find out about our further travel.

At the Soviet legation, I was received immediately. Avstrin, the envoy, took the letter from the Libau consul from my hand without reading it and declared that he knew everything—who we were, where we came from, and where we were going. He ordered me to come back that afternoon; then he would let us know how we would be traveling further. He also repeated the same warning as had the consul in Libau: "Be careful, don't blurt out anything, so no one will have any excuses to pick a fight with you."

In the afternoon, we all went together for the answer. The feeling that we weren't alone, that there was someone there to give a friendly piece of advice, made the burden lighter and provided encouragement. Moreover, the growing realization that in no more than a few days we would be in the land of our hopes, in the free Soviet Russia, created brighter spirits. Even the stinging cold was transformed for us into a spring breeze.

The Soviet representative informed me on the second visit that everything had been seen to, and that the direct train from Riga to Moscow left in three days. I quickly thanked him, left his office with a light step and in one breath told my friends who were waiting in the corridor about our good luck; that we would travel directly to Moscow on a Soviet train.

When we sat in the restaurant that afternoon, the food was somehow tastier than usual. We had good appetites and it seemed to me that in my entire life, I had never tasted such delicious food. We drew the attention of others in the restaurant with our appetites.

We were the last to leave the restaurant. The days were short and outside the feeble lights of the lanterns were already flickering. After a short walk, we bought some sweets for a night snack and went to the hotel. In the large room that we all shared, we sat down around the table and plans flew on how to avoid delays caused by overzealous people.

Suddenly—a loud knock on the door. The same official from the Riga train depot who had given us the address of the hotel, came in, bowed deeply, and in a few words informed us that tomorrow at eleven o'clock at night a train was going to the Russian border and that we must absolutely, without fail, be prepared to leave Riga at the indicated hour. If not, he concluded, he would be forced to take us to the border in a convoy. He turned in a military fashion and left the room.

We didn't sleep the entire night. Each of us in his own mind speculated and analyzed what had happened here.

The next day, I rushed breathlessly to the Soviet representative to find out what had changed. He received me and I could read the answer on his face: We can do nothing more for you than what we've have done. "You know what, comrade," he told me before leaving, "try to go to the Department of the Interior and explain your situation yourself to them, perhaps you'll succeed in convincing them that you should travel on the train I have told you about that goes directly. In case nothing comes of your intervention— come straight back to me and I will see to tickets and other things that you will need on the way."

I stuck the address of the Interior Department in my pocket and a few minutes later I was already standing there waiting to be received. After two hours of my impatiently pacing back and forth, a sleepy official came out and said in a harsh, grating voice, "Denied!" They had refused; tonight at eleven o'clock, we had to take the train that went to the Soviet border.

On the way back to the hotel, I went in to see the Soviet consul. He gave me our passports and five tickets and we said a cheerless farewell. I went back to my friends with the sad tidings: "Denied." It was hopeless and we must do as we had been ordered.

We went to the train three hours ahead of time so that we could see to all the items that our kind-hearted friends had loaded under our name onto the ship in the New York harbor. Aside from small packages for close friends, we had twenty-six large boxes and one crate with two dozen typewriters that had been shipped with us from New York to support the Commissariat of Foreign Affairs in Moscow. The baggage ate up almost all of the few dollars that the five of us possessed between us.

All of the bags were on the platform of the train station, however, the stationmaster then let us know that since the inspector who had to review them hadn't arrived, we must travel empty-handed and our things would arrive at the border on a second train. I began talking to him, arguing "How is it possible that we would leave behind our things?"

He would not let me speak. "It's not allowed!" and that was that. Obviously, we didn't want to travel without our luggage, so as I spoke to him, I pulled from my pocket a five hundred lat[95] bill and pushing it into his hand, argued further that we couldn't leave without our things. The argument was effective as soon as the banknote lay in the stationmaster's hand (and in those days, it was a considerable sum) and he began with the worst of words that would turn even a Cossack red, to curse the absent inspector who hadn't fulfilled his duties.

A few minutes later a young man appeared with a brush, a pail of starch and labels and began gluing them onto the boxes. This cost another fifty lat, and a short while later our baggage was on the freight car of the train on which we later departed.

When we got off the train at the border station Zilupe, the same official from Riga who had informed us that we must go directly there, exited from another railroad car. On the platform he greeted us politely and told us to wait. A half hour later, he ordered us to come into the small, filthy depot and also ordered that our things that had been lying on the platform be dragged into the depot. He placed three soldiers with sharp bayonets on their rifles around us and around all our items. Then he informed us that we must wait there until a Soviet representative from the other side of the border came and took us over. He spoke severely, no longer with the same tone as in Riga, and like one who wanted to let you know his might. Then, without a by-your-leave, he disappeared.

With our luggage and with the three soldiers, we stood and waited. Hours passed, and we didn't see anyone arriving. I asked one of the soldiers whether we could go drink a glass of tea at the depot buffet, but he shook his head in the negative: it's not allowed.

We unpacked a small valise, pulling out a few cigarettes and some little boxes of American snacks that friends had given us to eat on the way. I noticed that the faces of the soldiers had become softer; the severe look was gone and their eyes continually glanced at us as we now and then took out some sweets.

---

95   Latvian currency until replaced by the euro in 2014

One of our female friends began offering the soldiers cigarettes and sweets—they became completely different people and regained their tongues. A half hour later, we were already free people and could move about the depot and the platform.

Night began to fall. The soldiers were replaced with new guards and it cost us a few more provisions to buy freedom of movement from them.

Suddenly the soldiers came to attention. An officer in the company of a civilian approached and the first one said in Russian to the second: "Here are your guests."

The officer with the soldiers left; the civilian man was the Political Border Commissar of Soviet Russia. He had vouched for us, he stated, and succeeded in us being allowed to wait freely. He needed only to arrange a few things, and in an hour he would bring us across the border in a train.

One hour went by and then two; the commissar was as if he now lay in the ground. At the depot there was not another living soul; a small propane lamp flickered in the middle of the gloomy waiting area. We had already begun to miss the faces of our three sentries, who had guarded us the entire day and now had abandoned us at night.

Spending the entire day freezing at the little depot brought on a heavy fatigue, and each one leaned against whatever was available—on a bundle, on a box—and sought to rest in an agitated nap. With each rustle, each step, our eyes would snap open and then soon close again, seeking rest. From time to time we exchanged a few words about the commissar who would bring us across the border to Russia.

Finally we heard sturdy footsteps. The door to the depot made a loud creak as a blizzard blew in with two men as they entered the depot. One of them was our commissar, and he brought with him a second man dressed in leather pants and a jacket completely covered with oil and soot. This was the train machinist.

The commissar, whose face at first glance gave the impression of being completely frozen—it was so very red—was good and drunk. One could tell this immediately from the first few words that he pronounced.

"So, come, we're leaving already, because by three o'clock we must be over the border."

Hearing this from the commissar's mouth, we stood up from our places. We asked him who would help us load our luggage into the railroad car.

"What do you mean, your luggage!" he said with a roar. "There's no time for this now. Your things will follow tomorrow on the regular train."

So I began explaining to him that we couldn't travel without our items; that we wouldn't leave the luggage here and must take it with us on the same train as we must present it personally to the people for whom it was intended, and therefore we were responsible for seeing this task through.

My categorical demand made the commissar hostile and with a changed tone and the bearing of a high authority, he shouted that he did not say things twice and that his word was a command, and if he ordered us to travel without our things, so it would be.

"Listen, comrade," I said to him, "it may be true that your word is indeed the law but we can't comply, even if it means that we must stay here and the Latvian government should arrest us. You see," I told him, "this large, heavily-built crate—it contains Soviet property. We have here the typewriters that we are bringing for the Commissariat of Foreign Affairs. In Moscow, we must hand them over to Comrade Gregori Vaynshteyn. [96] We must present these things to him personally."

Hearing this, our commissar did a turnabout and took on a completely different appearance; suddenly he became sober. He turned to the machinist and said, "We must look for someone who can carry these things into the railroad car, but let's make it quick."

I suggested to the commissar that we, the three men, would help and that the five of us could do it; meanwhile the two women could guard the boxes. He declined our help and stated that the luggage would be placed on the railroad car.

He left and fifteen minutes later returned with several porters who, aside from the little things that we carried ourselves, loaded our entire luggage into the railroad car. When it came to the big box with the typewriters that we had rescued, our commissar turned into an absolute general. Not taking his eyes off it, he kept giving advice on how to better transport it, shouting at every minute, "Careful, be careful, comrades!"

It was already well into the night when we heard the first whistle of the locomotive. The entire train consisted of the locomotive and two railroad cars,

---

96 Russian: Gregori Isaakovich Vaynshteyn (Weinstein), active in the revolutionary movement in the U.S. from 1915-1918 and in 1921, he went to Moscow to become head of the Department of Anglo-Roman countries of the Soviet Commissariat of Foreign Affairs (NKID).

on which was written in chalk: "48 people or 16 horses," meaning the number of creatures that could be carried.

In one railroad car they had packed our baggage and in the second, we occupied the place of the sixteen horses. The actual name of that railroad car was "Freight Car." It lacked only that inside it, it should be ... warm. In the middle of the railroad car stood a small iron stove in which a few sticks of wood burnt. On the wall hung a small kerosene lamp, of which the glass gave witness to the fact that since the fall of Kerensky,[97] the lamp had not been cleaned.

We sat down on the long bench and to the accompaniment of the noise from the metal wheels, began falling asleep.

THE FIRST KNOCK ON THE HEAD

The railroad cars gave a strong jolt, knocking one into the other. The locomotive made a loud whistle and came to a stop. Somewhere in the distance, a weak glow was seen from a tall gas lamp. We all pressed up against the small window but aside from the brightness of the gas lamp, we could see nothing else.

The door slid open and the commissar, with a lantern in his hand, came in. He was accompanied by someone in military dress, although it was from the Tsarist era. They greeted us politely and announced that we were now in Soviet territory and that we must show the military man our passports.

I handed him the entire bundle of passports for all five of our group. He looked through them and approved of their authenticity, and the train was underway again. We hadn't traveled for more than fifteen minutes when the same scene was repeated again: the train was halted and we showed our passports. Only here we were told that we were now at the first Soviet station. If we wanted, we could go stay inside the station until the baggage was inspected. If we wanted to stay in the car, that was also all right. They placed a Red Army soldier by the second car to protect the baggage.

We decided to go out into the station and have the first look at the land of so much hope. We went in the depot; everything around us was filthy and black. On the floor people were sleeping, cramped together and snoring. In

---

97   Alexander Kerensky: Russian lawyer and politician who served as the second Minister-Chairman of the Russian Provisional Government in 1917 but whose government was overthrown by the Lenin's Bolsheviks in October of that same year.

spite of the terrible cold—for the station was poorly heated—the air was so suffocating that we quickly changed our minds and returned to our car.

Before we climbed back into the railroad car, I exchanged a few words with the Red Army soldier and offered him a cigarette. He refused to take it while he was standing watch. I quickly put a few cigarettes into the pocket of his coat. He didn't protest and I was happy about this.

We all sat in the car and waited. The door was closed. Someone banged on the wide red door, stuck his head in and proposed to us that if we wanted to spend the night in town, which was not far from there, we could go there to rest.

We thanked him and declined. Sensing that we didn't have confidence in him and for that reason didn't take him up on his offer, he then suggested that if we would prefer, we could lie down to sleep in the patrol barracks by the station, where he would also be waiting. We thanked him again and excused ourselves that we must decline his hospitality. He wished us a good night and left.

We arranged ourselves on the bench huddled together in our light American clothes, and fell asleep from weariness.

When taking our things from the train, the official ordered that the large boxes not be carried into the depot because first of all, there was no room, and secondly, Comrade Polanski would soon come and inspect the baggage. He informed us that at eleven o'clock we would leave on the train to Moscow. We stood around our luggage, waiting for it to be "soon." The cold was piercing, at least thirty degrees, and we couldn't stay out in the cold for long. We divided it up so that each of us would stand fifteen minutes outside by the boxes while the others would be in the depot.

The "soon" lasted from seven o'clock until twelve. The train had already departed and Comrade Polanski, it was explained to us, was busy. Two young border guards came in his place and they began leading the inspection. Aside from us there was only one passenger, a woman traveling from Latvia to Moscow. As she had only one bundle, they began with her. Among the worthless rags that she had brought were two pairs of children's galoshes. The young commissar told her that one pair would be sent to the government administration warehouse, because one person was not permitted to bring in two pairs of boots. All the arguments the woman gave were useless, because the commissar maintained that the Revolution was already tired of speculators. He would not believe that she brought them for her two children. When I pointed out that the galoshes were after all, two different sizes, he ordered me not to mix in governmental affairs. I saw that with me, they would truly have difficulties.

When the inspectors turned to our items, I decided to take a firm position with the young officials.

"Comrades," I said, "do you intend to inspect everything here outside, in the cold? Let us take it inside." And speaking thus, I explained to them who we were, that we were traveling from America to Russia where our convictions had drawn us, that we were no speculators and that the items in the boxes were for the Soviet regime.

The boss of the two was a young Jewish man. On his face lay the total incompetence and vulgarity of a small town stable boy and the fact that he had little skill with the border regulations. I asked him if he had anything with which to write down the inspection of the documents and indeed, he did not. I took out a fountain pen that I brought from America and offered it to him. "Take it," I told him. "You'll have a memento from a friend."

He didn't haggle with me and stuck the pen in his pocket. I had guessed his weaknesses exactly and he said to me in Yiddish—which he spoke with more ease than Russian— that if we had something sweet, we should give it to the orl,[98] his friend, and everything would be in order.

Wanting to finally see the end to dragging our things around, we gave the young Russian a little box of sweets. Before we could even look around, he had disappeared with it.

"You see already," the chief inspector spoke up, "he's a bastard, a glutton." He quickly marked off our boxes, made a white cross and the inspection was finished.

We asked him when the train left and found out that it was tomorrow at twelve o'clock. So what do you do in the meantime, for twenty-four hours? After all, we couldn't stand there in the freezing cold. The commissar gave us a stockroom by the depot to lock up the things. We paid to have them brought into the room and were promised that they would be well guarded. He took us with him to the nearby town and brought us to a city club.

The club consisted of three rooms; in each was a table with benches,

---

98   Yiddish: pejorative word for non-Jew.

relatively clean. The manager of the club made us some tea, we later purchased black bread and sugar at the depot, and stayed at the club awaiting tomorrow's train.

The entire day no one came into the club; at night a few young people came in together and we had our first opportunity to see and hear the rhythm of the new life. One of the local party leaders spoke to those gathered about international events, and when he finished, his voice resounded through the club as he sang *The Internationale*.[99] Everybody joined in singing with great enthusiasm, but without the flair that I remembered from before the revolution. In that moment, it sounded like a chorus singing a well-practiced song.

We were given one of the rooms of the club in which to spend the night. The club watchman brought in some straw and we passed the night very comfortably.

Seven o'clock the next morning, we were already prepared and waiting for the twelve o'clock train. I went to the place where our baggage was being held. My heart had warned me that things might not go quite so smoothly and sure enough, I found out that without the command of the station commissar, they couldn't give us our things.

I didn't feel too much concern over this and went to find the commissar at his residence. I was told that it was still early and that he was sleeping. I spent the entire morning going to the commissar and him still being fast asleep. The clock already showed eleven o'clock and an hour later the train would leave. I became anxious and losing my patience, I dared to interrupt his sleep and knocked firmly on the door. For about five minutes we spoke through the wooden door, which was covered with straw. Finally he came out to me, still putting on his belt over his leather jacket.

I explained to him what the issue was, but he answered me calmly, "Never mind; in any case you can't travel to Moscow today."

"What do you mean," I said, turning towards him, "we must go, comrade. I want to send a telegram to Moscow."

He took a look at me and saw that I meant it seriously. He replied, "Well, then. Everything will soon be arranged."

---

99   French: *L'Internationale*, translated into Russian in 1902 and edited after the 1917 revolution, is one of the most recognizable and best-loved songs of socialist movements, often sung with the left hand raised in a clenched fist salute.

When we were already sitting on the train, the chaperone that had been sent with us let us know that we were not traveling to Moscow but to quarantine in Velikoluka. We were astounded: "What's that?"

"I don't know anything about it," the chaperone answered us. "That is what the commissar ordered. And you know, comrades, that he is the commissar of the station, the one in charge of the town, and the chairman of the Cheka."[100]

Our chaperone kept emphasizing that the commissar was the chief of the Cheka. I understood then, that he had sent us to Velikoluka only because I had not been submissive enough to such a "great" man as he.

For the few hours on the train, all my thoughts were occupied with the Cheka. I recalled how I had always defended the Cheka to everyone during discussions; how I would protest when an opponent would seek to discredit the Russian revolution by pointing out the terrible deeds of the Cheka. I would insist that in Russia, counter-revolutionaries had to be treated that way. I had now personally come in contact with the Cheka, and for my unacceptable conduct was being punished by being sent to a quarantine camp where they would examine our political purity.

Thousands of thoughts whirled in my mind. Foremost were the long months and years that I had spent in the Atlanta prison in the United States, aspiring to the time when the mighty would be overtaken by the worker class. Now I was being punished by a leader of the Soviet labor government for the audacity to request humane treatment.

I became very sad at heart, much sadder than in New York when Judge Clayton had sentenced me to twenty years imprisonment. When I had heard the sentence, I had made a joke and said to the judge that he would have to finish serving out my term, if he wanted to keep his word. I believed that the time would come when the entire world would be under the Soviet order and the judge would need to finish out the sentence to which he had just sentenced us.

The malevolent treatment by the chief of the Cheka created the first rupture in my deep beliefs. The pettiness of sending us to quarantine made my heart very heavy. I felt tears choking me.

---

100 The Cheka was the first Soviet state security organization, with hundreds of committees created in cities across Russian. They were brutal and ruthless, and many thousands of dissidents, deserters, or other people including women and children were arrested, tortured or executed by Cheka groups.

I was not afraid to go to quarantine and feared no punishment—not when I was young in Tsarist Russia and not in America during the political and economic struggle in which I took part. Every punishment in those years called forth even stronger feelings and the drive to do battle with the enemy who wanted to destroy us, and whom we would one day vanquish.

Yet why was it so hard now? Why did I want to cry, to cry silently so my friends didn't hear me, so that they wouldn't share with me these depressing thoughts? This was not because of the unpleasantness, but because of the feeling that my faith, my dreams, my certainty in the struggle and in a better world that the struggle would bring, had been shaken. It was not an obvious shock, but an enormous sense of anxious disquiet. It was the first time in my life that serious doubts entered my mind, where there had never been room for them before. I could not make peace with the thoughts and sought to expel them with different pretexts.

The train arrived at the Velikoluka station, which was a large terminal. The walls testified to the fact that gun battles had occurred there during the civil war and revolution. We went out onto the platform. In and around the terminal there was a great deal of activity, like a large beehive. The people who lay or sat on their baggage waited for the train with shouting and cursing. The wailing of children was heartbreaking, one climbing over another. People on all sides of the railroad cars were struggling to get in. The train workers unloaded our baggage. They took the luggage to the terminal warehouse and soon we were on our way to our temporary home where the Cheka border chief had sent us. After three-quarters of an hour trudging through deep snow and climbing over slippery footpaths laid over railroad tracks, we arrived at the quarantine that was set aside, as we later found out, for refugees and questionable persons.

The quarantine consisted of a large wooden barracks enclosed by barbed wire. On the perimeter circled several Red Army soldiers with rifles. At the gate, our chaperone told the sentry that he had brought Americans.

From the sentry box which still had the colors black and white in curved stripes like in Tsarist times, an official came out, took our passports from the chaperone, looked, searched, and was not able to read them (the passports were written in English); he could barely ascertain the names. He called each of us separately in a severe manner and when they responded, accompanying each with an indecent expression ordered him to go through the wire door.

I was the third person to be called and after his outpouring of vulgar speech, I remained standing. My Russian was not bad and asked him in an irritated voice, still feeling disconcerted after the mood of our several hours' journey to quarantine: "Why do you shout? Why do you treat people with such language and such arrogant behavior when you don't yet know who they are and you can't even read their documents? A little decency, comrade, the revolution has taught us that people should be decent to others as much as possible."

My officer, for whom it was something new that an American could speak Russian, stood still, dumbfounded and speechless. He no longer called out the names but told our group to come inside together. He came around in front of us and very quietly asked that we follow him.

We went into the large wooden barracks. Despite the cold, our breath was taken away by the foul air that filled the area, due to the density of people packed together who hadn't bathed for many weeks or even washed their faces.

We stood in a corner of the barracks for several minutes and didn't know how to begin this new, unforeseen episode of our hope-filled journey. The door opened and the same official came in. He ordered the people to slide together a little more and make room for us.

Wordlessly they began to slide across the wooden plank bed and there we rested. Before he left, the official said to me that he would soon be done with his work and that he wanted me to translate into Russian what was written in our documents.

AMERICAN BOURGEOISIE

The documents we had brought were not official government papers. None of us were American citizens and of our old Russian passports, not a trace remained. We traveled with documents that had been worked out by the attorney Charles Recht[101] who in America at that time had the role of representative for Soviet Russia.

After I explained to the military commissar of the quarantine that we had such documents because we were political prisoners in the United States, he

---

101 Charles Recht: attorney who represented the legal interests of Russia in the United States during Abrams' trial.

earnestly asked to be pardoned for the impolite reception we had received, and also made excuses for the Cheka official at the border who had sent us to Velikoluka.

We spoke of various things. The commissar unexpectedly proved to be a man with a bit of a past and with a certain political maturity. He asked us as many questions as possible about America, and everything about it interested him. The Russian revolution had inspired him and he emphasized many times as he spoke, "Let us just get through with the White[102] elements and liquidate the remnants of the Russian bourgeois traitor—we will be richer and happier than in America."

He spoke with so much faith and conviction that I began to think his earlier impudent conduct was really the result of his mistrust and fear of traitors. I had already pardoned him earlier on, especially after he had told us that at four o'clock tomorrow a train left for Moscow and assured us that everything would be made ready and that we would be able to travel in a special railroad car with a special person who would take us to the Commissariat of Foreign Affairs.

In the barracks it was cold—terribly cold. The little iron stove that stood in the middle only warmed the area around it within a few steps; any further and your very limbs would freeze. We somehow settled our female friends on the board plank, covered them with rags and tattered soldiers' coats that had been given to us, and we sat by the side and tried to doze. The cold pushed us towards the oven, but even standing by it, it was very cold and we passed the entire night without closing our eyes, talking about what we had heard from the commissar. His words had the effect of keeping us from falling into despair.

As soon as it became light, we began getting ourselves ready for the trip. Despite the fierce cold, we took off our things, brought water, washed and shaved. Our hair became covered with ice before it could dry. Our temporary neighbors in quarantine thought we were crazy for washing ourselves in such cold. One shouted out that we were American bourgeoisie who washed and primped. A young, well-built Christian asked if we would donate some soap and a razor to him; he knew that uncleanliness brought

---

102 The White movement and its military division the White Army, was a loose confederation of anti-communist forces that fought the Bolsheviks during the Russian Civil War of 1917–1923.

sickness and the cold didn't bother him, but he had no soap. We gave him these trifles and he was happy.

At about one o'clock, we were already at the Velikoluka terminal. The entire platform was full of people and baggage. The train was already at the station, but no one was allowed to board until a half hour before the train departed. The crowd, which was several times larger than the number able to board the train, stood glued to the railroad cars in order to board early, as soon as the doors opened.

We began looking for someone to help us load onto the railroad car the large foreign baggage that we had brought, and for which we had encountered so many difficulties along the way. The porters at the depot declared to us that the American bourgeoisie weren't sick and could do it themselves. I turned to the chief official of the station, asking that he give me a few carts and we would take care of it ourselves. The man, who the commissar had sent to be our chaperone, called the stationmaster over, whispered a secret in his ear, and the stationmaster gave us the required carts. We put ourselves to the task and placed the bundles and boxes in the specified railroad car.

When everything was taken care of, a pair of porters came up to us and excused themselves for not assisting us because they thought that we were American bourgeoisie. Now they knew that we were not such people and they didn't want to lose the tip. They asked that we give them something. I told them that someone had tricked them, that we really were bourgeoisie and that the bourgeoisie didn't give tips for doing nothing. The answer that my ironical remark received is best left out of the record.

Before the train's departure, the stationmaster came out and with a hidden smile, told us that we didn't need to stand in line—that there was a separate railroad car and if we wanted, we could board it. Naturally we obeyed him immediately and set out for the car.

The Red Army soldier that stood on the step of the railroad car took charge of us. He shouted to the crowd, "Make way!" and they moved aside for us. The five of us with our chaperone went into the railroad car.

The car was an old one; part of the window was covered with boards, but the interior was comparatively clean. All around the car stood many people and each one asked if they could come aboard. Our chaperone and the Red Army soldier answered them, "It's not permitted; it's for Americans."

From the first station, we traveled very comfortably. Our chaperone, a young man, spent the entire time singing Russian love songs and we had no opportunity to strike up a conversation about the new lifestyle in Russia. It seemed to me that he was singing intentionally to avoid entering into any exchanges.

We arrived at a second station and the train stopped for long time. The crush from the crowds of passengers waiting for the train was extraordinary. The only railroad car in which no passengers were allowed was ours, the "American railroad car." We saw a great wrong in this and felt guilty that we would commit this injustice. We traveled, including the chaperone, as six people in an entire railroad car and there stranded on the platform in the snow, day and night, were hundreds of people.

I began negotiating with our chaperone to let the passengers also come into our car. At first he didn't want it but then agreed, saying, "So be it, as you want so it will be, but you'll regret it later."

A few minutes later, our wagon was packed with people so tightly that you couldn't stick a pin between them. We slid together in a spot between two benches and this is how we traveled the fifteen hours that it took until we arrived in Moscow.

IN THE MOSCOW TSEDOM

Our train finally arrived at the place we had yearned for: Moscow. We were in good spirits and full of expectations. It was eleven o'clock in the morning, the tenth of December. The morning was wintry but a beautiful one. The sun irradiated the clean white snow. The weather was mild and snow dripped from the roofs. Of the friends to whom I had sent a telegram from Velikoluka, there was none waiting for us. The telegram, I later found out, was only delivered six days after our arrival in Moscow.

From the terminal to the Commissariat for Foreign Affairs where we needed to report according to the recommendations, we were told it was not more than a half hour by foot. We decided to walk there and in the meantime see a bit of Moscow. The chaperone agreed and went with us to the Commissariat. Here he bid us farewell and was off. We remained there to wait for Comrade Gregori Vaynshteyn, who I knew well from New York where he had been the editor of the Bolshevik newspaper *Novyi Mir* (*New World*).

Vaynshteyn now occupied a high position at the Foreign Commissariat. He was an old Bolshevist and a man with revolutionary experience. His position in Moscow no longer allowed him to be the bohemian that we knew him as in New York, where he would sit in the restaurant Zindorest bantering in a friendly way with everyone. The Bolshevism in New York during those years had the same weight as all the other "-isms" and no one would feel greater or less than in their accomplishments for the general good. Vaynshteyn was a good friend and friend to everyone, even to those that belonged to another facet of the Socialist movement.

After a long wait in the corridor, we were called to Gregori Vaynshteyn's office. The furniture and arrangement of the office were like those of the former Russian administrative offices, and the first impression demanded respect for a great person. Vaynshteyn received us in an oddly cold manner. He remained sitting in his chair when I greeted him, and I didn't even have the opportunity to shake hands. The first glance silenced me and I spoke no further. Our documents were lying before him on the table. He remained with his head bent over them and not lifting his eyes, asked how our trip had gone. He said it very impersonally and my answer had the same charm. With that ended our first meeting since five years ago in New York when a group of military sailors attacked the editorial office of his newspaper and I, along with the help of the industrial organization IWW,[103] saved his printing shop.

"So then, comrades," said Vaynshteyn in an official manner, "until you can get settled here, you'll be given a room at the Tsedom (Central House for Immigrants)."

To this I didn't answer at all, because after that tone I felt that there existed an abyss between us and the official bureaucracy. We waited for a few more minutes in the office but at a distance from the wide government desk and we spoke no more with Comrade Vaynshteyn. Here, coming back from America to the "free Russia," I felt as did a simple immigrant who was nothing more than a bundle with a tag hanging from his overcoat-button, waiting on the travel agent to be sent further along on his journey, per the designated itinerary.

The Tsedom of the Commissariat was a considerable distance away. After traveling for an entire night and half the day and then our walk from the train, we were already exhausted; we'd also had nothing in our mouths the entire time. We could scarcely drag our feet until we arrived at our residence.

---

103 Industrial Workers of the World: American international, radical labor union founded in 1905 with ties to both socialist and anarchist labor movements.

In the new Soviet dwelling, we were offered potato soup and a few pieces of sandy bread. Everything around us was poor and dingy. The room that they gave us had three beds, a small table and one small bench. The bedding was filthy and the black sheets spoke clearly of the many guests who had passed through the room since the Tsedom was opened. Despite everything, this first night we slept like the dead.

In the morning, we were called to the administrative offices to confiscate the unofficial documents, and each of us was given a booklet that took the place of a passport and affirmed that the owner had the right to work.

We went into the dining room and drank a few glasses of tea washed down with the same bread as yesterday, and then headed out to the street to see where exactly we were. However, the man who stood by the exit of the Tsedom advised us that we couldn't go out to the street until a representative of the Cheka came to inspect our baggage that had been brought from the station. The representative would be here at exactly eleven o'clock and we should please wait the two hours. To the question of where the baggage was, they answered that it was in the cellar, but we couldn't go down there until the official carried out the inspection and gave his consent.

I tried requesting that they let one of us go out in the city, as we had the addresses of friends from America and wanted to inform them of our arrival. The answer was given in a friendly tone, but continued to be negative. These were the instructions for all immigrants and we would not want, of course, for them to make an exception for us—so we were told.

We couldn't bear the injustice of being kept "under arrest", just as if we were contrabandists. We protested and argued, but nothing helped. We returned to our room and sat waiting for the hour when the political police commissar would come. With each minute that we waited, it became clearer that the people in America who had criticized the leadership of Soviet Russia were not completely wrong. Our friend Lipman, who considered himself a Bolshevik and had brought a document with him that certified his political commitment, sat with his head lowered and was ashamed to say a word as we conversed about the barriers that had been encountered at every turn.

I had not yet broken the habit I had from long years in the American prison of pacing my cell; here I also strode back and forth nervously across our room, from time to time coming up with a positive word or perhaps a justification, but the other friends bitterly rebuffed them.

The door to our room opened and in came the superintendent from the Tsedom together with the representative from the Cheka. Without a "good morning," he commenced asking us the preliminary questions about our coming to Soviet Russia.

Before the political commissar went down to the cellar with us to inspect our items, we had a brief but very sharp exchange of words. He asked how much gold had we brought. To this question, I answered him with a question: was he a political commissar or a criminal? The commissar became angry and the following dialogue took place between us:

He: "I actually don't need to tell you who I am, but I want you to know that I am the deputy for the chairman of the KRO[104] division of Cheka that fights the counter-revolutionaries abroad. You need to answer me, not ask questions."

I: "Yes, you're correct, but only when the questions are relevant to us. If you ask me questions as if I were a speculator from America; I must again answer you with questions."

He: "All Americans are the same."

I: "You think, Comrade Commissar, that the Americans are only one type of people? That in America there is no class division? We have come straight from an American prison after sitting there for years because of our struggle for the Soviet regime, and we have nothing to do with any gold."

He: "I've already heard the stories. We will keep an eye on you, and then we will see who you are and what you're all about."

With these last words, we went down to the cellar and they began inspecting the first box, which they opened. It contained canned products. The commissar broke open a tin can and said, "Not a bad thing, bourgeoisie customs; you were afraid that you would die of hunger with us." We didn't reply and they began with the second box, which held a few Yiddish and English books. He flipped through one book and then a second, and asked, "Do you also have Russian books here?"

We assured him that no, and—"If you don't believe us, take a look."

The third box— this was the piece of luggage that we had rescued at each station since we crossed the border. The commissar asked what we had brought in the large box, and I answered that I had the key but I couldn't open

---

104 The counter-intelligence division of Cheka.

it because I had been ordered to hand it over to the commissariat for Foreign Affairs. "If you want," I said to the commissar, "take it there to Comrade Vaynshteyn or Kantarovitsh, to whom this box was sent, and with their permission I'll open the box."

His gaze began wandering. I didn't know who he was looking at, but I sensed that he was now thinking that all these foolish questions would backfire on him.

He went up to me, clapped me on the shoulder in a friendly manner and asked me in an oddly mild tone," Do you already have your work booklets, comrades?"

We showed them to him. He quickly stamped them, writing on a piece of paper that the baggage was cleared, and going up from the cellar said, "When you've been here a little while, comrades, you'll understand why we sometimes can't recognize who is one of us and who is—a stranger."

IN RUSSIA YOU DON'T FEEL, JUST OBEY

When we came up from the cellar, it was already past noon. We all stood by the door of the Tsedom and didn't know what to do, where to begin. This was the first moment after many years that we could move freely without guards or chaperones. From prison they had taken us under watch to the Island of Tears,[105] then on a small boat to the ship Esthonia. We had been guarded the entire journey and now today, December 10, 1921, we were free, without guards or a chaperone; we could go wherever we wanted.

We were seized by a strange feeling. A friend, Ethel,[106] arrived, having learned that we were here. She came looking for her friend Lipman, from whom she had been separated for four years. She embraced her beloved man, stroking his head. We rejoiced with Ethel, who had already been in Russia for more than a year's time. We wanted to run and dance for joy that we were free. Wanting to laugh and cry, my heart was overflowing and the feelings were overwhelming.

We all went back to our room; Ethel accompanied us. There was much talk, laughing, telling about America, of our journey, one person interrupting

---

105   Yiddish: Trern-Inzl, Ellis Island
106   Ethel Bernstein, who was deported to Russia in 1919. She and Samuel Lipman married in 1924.

another—in such cheerfulness we spent more than an hour's time. Ethel was the most subdued of everyone, and I wondered about this. I knew her from New York as a carefree, merry young girl, who with her words and joyfulness always evoked laughter—yet here her words were now accompanied by a sigh and she held herself with such cold composure, one more suitable for a diplomat trying to lure his opponent into a trap.

Before we left the house, Ethel got in touch by telephone with our former friends from New York whom we had worked with together: Bernard, Perkus,[107] etc. They had come to Russia immediately after the revolution, whereas we had just arrived only because of the prison sentence.

We found out from the telephone call that the friends would come together to Ethel's house, not until nine o'clock that night because they were tired, Ethel told us. She also hinted to us that she had plenty of cigarettes because she had received her ration that day, but nothing else. She advised me that I should go see Bianki,[108] because he could provide good things. Bianki was my friend from New York. Born in Milan, Italy, to Russian parents, he had soaked in the idealism of a good-natured Russian and the temperament of an Italian. In America, from the first minute he was a sharp opponent of the proletariat dictatorship and we were political enemies.

"What does Bianki do here?" I asked Ethel in astonishment. "He is at liberty, and can get ahold of good things? What does this mean?"

Ethel smiled. "You see, Jack, here you can be the best of friends. He is now an ardent defender of the Soviet system and strictly observes the Bolshevik line; he is a commissar, and for what job?—in a military supplies warehouse. He has a lot of influence and will do anything for you; he'll bring you the entire warehouse of provisions. If we pick a quarrel with him during a discussion," Ethel continued, "he remembers you and he says that you had a far-reaching view of the Russian revolution, more than all the rest of us. But we're not in New York today and we seldom argue; we often keep silent more than our thoughts permit."

"You're mistaken, friend," I answered her. "I think that Bianki will be disappointed in me. I feel like we have changed places in how we view things

---

107 Nikifor (Hyman) Perkus, deported along with Bernstein

108 Peter Bianki, anarchist and secretary of the Union of Russian Workers in New York City, deported along with Bernstein.

and we'll be enemies again. Since we've set foot in this land for which I yearned for and dreamed of for so long, and for which I suffered—I've felt that something has gotten lost. Perhaps I'm wrong, but that's how I feel."

"In Russia you don't feel, you just obey!" Ethel told me calmly and firmly.

We couldn't wait until nine o'clock and went an hour and a half early to Comrade Perkus' house. Perkus held a position as manager of the Comintern[109] Cooperative, which served all the hotels under Comintern's jurisdiction and also the best private residences for the delegates of foreign lands. Perkus lived in one of those apartments. It had beautiful, well-lit rooms with a kitchen, central heating and in general all the comforts of a wealthy house.

In a large room stood a covered table shaped like the letter D. We soon filled up the table and were welcomed as guests. Comrade Dora, the owner of the house and a tiny, compactly-built woman with a brown complexion, sat opposite us. She had already been in Russia for more than a year, being one of the original 147 people who were deported from the United States to Russia after the revolution.[110] We knew her to be a good person by nature, but she always went around with a dissatisfied look on her face. She was very happy to see us and didn't know whom to hug first. After a few minutes of heartfelt greetings, she told us that we had surprised her by coming too early and that she still had much to do to prepare the supper. Our friends Mary and Molly[111] offered to help, but she refused to trouble them. Everybody kissed again and Dora went off to do her work.

After the long days of our difficult journey in the cold, of not having enough to eat and of anxiety, we felt comfortable here in the warm, clean house. In a lively manner, we shared our first impressions of the large, neglected town with the crooked streets and slippery, badly paved sidewalks that made up Moscow. We answered everything with the same argument: four years of war and three years of revolution.

Other longtime friends came, the first of them being Comrade Perkus, who entered with a reserved composure. His strong figure looked even more

---

109 Abbreviation for the Communist International (1919–1943), an organization that advocated global communism.

110 Deported along with Ethel Bernstein on the *Buford* in 1919.

111 Mary Abrams, Jacob Abrams' wife and Molly Steimer, who was arrested, convicted, and deported along with Abrams and their other two co-defendants.

powerful because of the bundles he was carrying. He squeezed our hands vigorously and said, "Who was right? You've all come here."

In our circle in New York, Perkus was thought of as the best speaker there, and he wielded a fiery pen for propaganda. He was an ordinary, sedate worker but also an expert in history and a specialist of the International Workers' movement, so much that our intelligentsia in New York couldn't compete with him.

Little by little all our friends came, and each carried a bundle under their coat. Each of them, as I later found out, carried with them their ration and after that had to spend the entire week running around trying to find something to quiet their hunger.

That evening there were all kinds of good things on the table, even caviar and wine. Perkus became animated and saying a few words, crowned all of us with the name "Our Family." We had in truth called ourselves this for a long time: we stayed together as a family, rejoiced and suffered together like one big family, and accepted each with all his defects and virtues.

That was an historical evening for us. We were outside the reach of the Moscow censor, and even those who subscribed to the communist party line spoke their heretical thoughts aloud. The only one who held firmly to the party line was Bianki, who during his entire time in New York had held a completely opposite opinion.

The night passed like a beautiful dream. When the blue of the morning filled the windows, Perkus opened up a new bottle and began a new ritual. He remembered something about a pact that everyone must then take a little more drink. He recalled that when they led us away from court after being sentenced to twenty years in prison, he had come to the patrol wagon we were sitting in and consoled us with these words: "Don't be despondent, friends. The Russian revolution produces fruit all over the world. It won't take long and with the same strength, the activists will open your prison. It might make a zigzag path to the victory of the universal proletariat, but the victory is near—you will not need to fulfill this sentence."

Remembering this, he spoke in a colorful manner. "We must make a toast for the first part being met, and also for the second part, that the zigzag be experienced peacefully and that the prophecy be completely fulfilled." Perkus finished his talk by turning to Comrade Bianki.

"What say you, Bianki? We're in Soviet Russia and to swallow our words is healthy for the revolution; is swallowing our words also healthy for us?"

It was already very late when everybody left. The good friend Dora began straightening the room. My head hurt from spending the entire night talking, drinking and being in such a happy, warm environment. I felt at home, just like someone who lived there; I went into the kitchen, lit the Primus[112] and in the true Russian way, put a small piece of sugar under my tongue and drank down a few glasses of tea.

COMINTERN SEEKS TO DISCREDIT DEBS

The American representatives in Comintern at that time were Israel Amter[113] and Carr.[114] They were the delegates from America to the Third International[115] and also the specialists in the American movement. When someone would come from America as a tourist or as a political emigrant, he had to interview with Amter and Carr and write down a report on his relationship to the Soviet regime and his plans in Soviet Russia.

Perkus, who worked for Comintern and was known as a friend of mine from New York, had been told that tomorrow evening I should report to the Hotel Lux[116] and Comrade Carr would talk with me. Perkus told me this, of course, and I was at the Lux at the appointed time.

When I entered the office of Comrade Carr, I found him not to be alone as I had expected. In addition to Carr, two other men dressed in leather suits were seated in the room and by a small table sat a young woman over a pad of paper, apparently a clerk. The room was half-lit. Carr stood up when I entered and presented me to the other comrades.

After speaking for a few minutes, the atmosphere became friendly. Carr, an American and non-Jew, spoke only English. Amter also spoke English;

---

112 The Primus, invented in 1892, was the first pressurized-burner kerosene stove.

113 Israel Amter: an American born to Jewish immigrant parents, he was a Marxist politician and founding member of the Communist Party USA (CPUSA).

114 John Carr: pseudonym used by Ludwig Erwin Katterfeld, an American socialist politician, founding member of the Communist Labor Party of America and later a Comintern functionary sent to Moscow in November 1921 as the representative of the Communist Party of America.

115 Another name for Comintern, referring to its formation after the three-way split in the socialist Second International over the issue of World War I.

116 A hotel in Moscow (now Hotel Tsentralnaya) that housed many exiled Communists during the early years of post-revolutionary Russia.

the other two men and the young women understood what was said, but couldn't speak much.

This was the time (the end of 1921) when the mission of the Bolsheviks was to destroy by any means possible—honest or dishonest—all the political parties and professional movements from other tenets that were in Russia. When someone wanted to become a member of the party, he would be offered a document to sign with these contents: "I am leaving such-and-such party because I have come to the conclusion that this party is misleading me and the worker-class and has betrayed the world proletariat. The only real party is the Bolshevik party; her leaders, Lenin and Trotsky, are the authentic and true proletariat leaders, and the Bolshevik line is the only one that will bring about the world revolution."

As I knew about this, I was not intending to join the party. At this time the political discussion between Carr and I truly began.

Carr knew that in America, I had led a huge struggle with my comrades and heatedly defended the Soviet regime. Everyone was talking about fanatics and traitors in the anarchist movement. Ethel's phrase that in Russia one doesn't feel, only obeys, was well engraved in my memory. I could see that I needed to be careful here, in this happy land.

The first one that Carr wanted to discredit was Emma Goldman,[117] the word-famous anarchist and revolutionary. He knew that we had been active together in the same movement for many years, and was very interested in hearing negative words against her. A sword fight began between us to attack and defend her. He attacked her shamelessly and brazenly, accusing Emma Goldman of living off the movement, that she was selfish and had bourgeois tendencies, etc.

I very cautiously defended her. Anyone who knew the tempestuous woman knew that she lived off her pen and had never exploited the movement. I admitted to him that there was selfishness, because to deny human selfishness is exactly like saying that a person can fight physically without hands or feet. It is chiefly among great people that selfishness develops, along with their greatness and the role that they are playing in the movement or society.

---

117 A Russian-born anarchist whose political activism, writing, and speeches were crucial in the development of early twentieth-century anarchist political philosophy in North America and Europe in the first half of the 20th century, she was deported back to Russia on the *Buford* in 1919.

As far as the bourgeois tendencies of which Carr had reproached Emma Goldman were concerned, with this he had given me a clean pot with a clean spoon, and I took advantage of the opportunity to reprimand him in a way that he had to swallow.

"Yes, Comrade Carr," I said, "perhaps Emma is not free of sin because she is a great intellect and as are all people with great intellects, she is also infected with bourgeois tendencies. Nonetheless, she is loyal to the movement and has sacrificed for it."

Carr himself belonged to the high intelligentsia of the movement, and after my double-edged argument on the subject of Emma Goldman, it was taken off the table.

I was afraid that as we continued speaking about the various people that we both knew, he would bring up the topic of Alexander Berkman.[118] This person was my teacher and I was a great admirer of his. I highly valued his insights and erudition and his love for people. In our movement, Berkman was a super-hero. He had served fourteen years in prison for his ideals and had emerged with a deepened resolve and even more conviction in his ideals. He was fearless in the struggle for justice. He never said a bad word against anyone, even against his bitterest enemies, and was always ready to give away to someone his last piece of bread that he had saved for himself.

I felt that speaking about Berkman, I wouldn't pass the examination given by the Comintern representative, the deputy of the order that must bring forth a new world, a free world, where each person would be entitled to his own opinion, even if it is thought not to be right.

Carr was politically adept enough and turning the conversation to a more antagonistic tone, began talking about the "half-Marxists"—the Mensheviks and Soviet deputies with whom I had been in prison in Atlanta, Georgia.

He mostly asked about the famous leader and teacher of the American Socialist Party—E. V. Debs,[119] who was then in the same prison for the fiery and determined position he had taken against the war. I saw what Carr was

---

118 Russian-born anarchist and leading member of the early twentieth-century anarchist movement, also lover of Emma Goldman, Berkman served 14 years in prison for his attempt to assassinate Homestead Steel businessman Henry Clay Frick for purposes of propaganda.

119 Eugene V. Debs: American union leader, founding member of the Industrial Workers of the World (IWW) and five-time presidential candidate of the Socialist Party of America; Debs was convicted under the Espionage Act of 1917 and sentenced to a term of 10 years; his sentence was commuted by President Harding in 1921.

trying to do with his question, and a shiver ran through me hearing it. Debs was liked and admired in America not only by his party, but by many of the American people.

Since 1919 when the Socialist party had fractured and one part had been converted into the Bolshevik Party of America, the Bolsheviks had done everything they could to win over this gem of a man to their side. This was because to win Debs meant to win the Socialists and the entire progressive might of America for the aims of the new movement. In turn, Debs was the kind of man who allowed himself to get carried away in the moment. Yet he possessed a deep sense of responsibility to his friends and above all, a deep and honest belief in socialist ideals. Debs had no sympathy for the split-off part of the Socialist party and they didn't win his trust.

Moreover, Debs was repelled by the slogan that was then in use: "the end justifies the means." Furthermore, he quite simply hated political tricks. The slogan that all types of ugliness were justified as long as the goal was reached—Debs hated this like a devout Jew hates pork. Therefore, the official Socialist party had no difficulty keeping Debs in their ranks. The Communists were bitterly angry with him.

However, this didn't stop the great and honest labor leader and also deep thinker from coming out publicly with a defense of the Russian revolution. His public appearances were indeed of great moral value and the Communists had hoped that with time, Debs would become a strong supporter.

America entered the war and Debs, along with others of his comrades, took a fiery stand against the war. The American government at that time considered his agitation too dangerous and for one of his brilliant speeches, he, the American Jean Jaurés,[120] the great champion who had railed against bloodshed, had been convicted and sentenced to ten years in prison. Eugene V. Debs was incarcerated in the Atlanta prison and it just so happened that I, together with several friends, had to serve out a sentence of twenty years in the same prison and for the same crime: agitation against the war.

Inasmuch as Carr knew that I had been in prison together with Debs, he wanted to extract from my descriptions of prison life something that would discredit the famous labor leader—something from which they could claim that the political prisoners could not bear Debs because of his non-Socialist

---

120 Jean Jaurés: French Socialist leader who became one of the first social democrats.

conduct, that he personally had acted meanly towards the comrades in prison, and that he was a bad, hostile type. He framed all his questions to elicit this kind of response.

Carr had yet another reason for trying to get information from me to compromise Eugene Debs. In 1920, during the American presidential elections, the American Communist Party wanted Debs to run on their ticket as the presidential candidate. The Communist leader Ben Gitlow[121] and several others had visited Debs in the Atlanta penitentiary and tried to persuade him that the Communist party was the real workers' party.

Debs was a man with a strong and honest soul and he lacked the toughness of a party politician. He could not humiliate people, especially those who had declared themselves ready to sacrifice themselves for their class, so he gave them a hedged promise. Immediately following this, the Socialist leaders, above all Morris Hillquit,[122] arrived. They presented facts proving that tens of hundreds of Socialists were in prisons in Soviet Russia and that there was no freedom to be found there. Then Debs, through an article published in the press, publicly refused to have anything to do with the Communist party and declared that he remained, as always, the presidential candidate for the official Socialist party.

Carr was aware of the uproar that surrounded Debs at that time and he wanted me to also say something compromising about Debs about this same issue. He kept asking me what Debs had said to us about the political struggle that was then taking place in the United States. He wanted to put words in my mouth, words saying that Debs sought his freedom and had made a deal that gave him promises of a better future after he was released, that Debs was a religious man, etc.

Carr put the questions in such a way that the answers themselves lay within them and that I should corroborate them.

I told Carr that Debs was not concerned with his own freedom, because when the prison wanted to send him to a farm near the prison, he had refused to go, adding that he would only go work there if all the political prisoners—fourteen in total—were sent to the same farm. Of the rumor that Debs was

---

121   Benjamin Gitlow: prominent U.S. socialist politician during the early twentieth-century, he was a founding member of the United States Communist Party.

122   Morris Hillquit: prominent New York City labor lawyer and founder and leader of the Socialist Party of America.

religious, I contradicted it with something of which I had just happened to learn. The prison chaplain had sometimes declared to a journalist that Debs was the only Christian in the prison. This originated from the fact that Debs, in conversation, would speak sympathetically about Christ—yet not as a "god," but as a man who in his time had given his life for his cause. The truth was that Debs would refuse to go to the prison church on Sundays and had led a fight for freeing all prisoners from having to attend church, although he had been threatened with losing his limited prison privileges.

The verbal battle between Carr, me, and the others who interjected comments from time to time, became a bitter one. When it came to the question of Debs' speaking out against the Communist Party of America, I got out of it with a justification that I knew Carr had to find acceptable: I explained that during that time I had actually been sent to isolation for three months for leading an underground mail post in prison. When I came out of isolation, I had lost the right to walk in the yard and therefore never had the opportunity to meet with Debs or hear what he had to say on the matter.

Carr saw that he would not be able to pry what he wanted from me, so he then tried a direct question to me personally: "What do you think about such a deed?"

"Me," I answered, "it's a little different with me. I strongly believe in the accomplishments of the Soviet regime. I believe that the tactics of the revolutionary government are the correct ones and lead to the general world liberation" (at that time I really believed this). "I, as a non-Marxist, knowing what an enormous task the Soviets have before them, would not have handled things as Debs did, had I been in his place."

My comrades at the Lux exchanged glances but found no material. The girl with the pad of paper in her hand, poor thing, sat without a stitch of work. Carr switched the conversation to the theme I desired—what I was considering to do there—and we began speaking about finding employment in Moscow.

A NON-PARTY MEMBER WITH A SOVIET LINING

In the Hotel Lux was a large restaurant that was once famous in Moscow for its delicious meals. The restaurant still remained in the hotel after the revolution, but without its former name. In the current Soviet reality the restaurant was still a luxury for everyone; it was the delegates from Comintern who dined there. An outsider could also eat lunch there, if he could manage the inflated prices demanded.

Carr, the American representative in Comintern who had conducted the interrogation with me, was an intelligent man. As quickly as he took off the official dress of the Comintern, he ceased to be an interrogator and became a kind person interested in a friend or acquaintance and was ready to help.

As soon as we stopped talking officially and the others, along with the clerk, began to leave, Carr suggested to me that I go with him to the restaurant for a glass of tea. We sat there until very late. From the glass of tea, things progressed to an entire supper and we chatted amiably. Carr tried to persuade me that the methods were not so important and that each person must contribute his share to the development and to ensure the security of the Soviet revolution, which was the sole solution for all the imperialistic-capitalistic problems. His arguments were sincere and came from one who was convinced of their truth. Carr listened good-naturedly to my objections against certain behaviors and justified them, saying to me that I did not speak as an enemy of the revolution itself, and this was something he valued very much.

I believed in the revolution just as he did; only I believed that the revolution must not become monopolized by one party. Rather, the revolution must belong to everyone, because it must liberate everyone. Here Carr tried to convince me that as soon as the revolution became everyone's, it became no one's. "Throw away your sentiments, Comrade Abrams; so what if there sit a few workers and socialists in prison." In addition, he quoted a phrase of Lenin's, that not all who work are workers; that workers are those who understand the worker's cause.

"You have the same opportunity as everyone else in Soviet Russia," he said, switching to speaking about me personally. "Don't look at it as that the revolution is forced to tear out its enemies by the roots; better to look at its great historical task. When you are here a bit longer and have gotten to know the hardships, you'll say the same as we do, even if you don't become a party member. We must have good activists, and oftentimes we unexpectedly have occasion to restrain party members for their deeds." Moreover, as an example he told me of several activities of my Italian-Russian friend Bianki, so much that I actually felt a chill (he was already an official in Cheka).

We began to talk about my working in Russia. I told him that my occupation was working in a printing shop, but there was no shortage of print shop workers in Russia. Therefore, I had a plan to work in another field, in an occupation that I learned in the Atlanta prison and of which I knew thoroughly. I would like to be given the opportunity to set up several large automatic laundries in Moscow. In the Atlanta prison we had kept four thousand prisoners clean, and for that had been set up a large laundry with all the latest technology; I was the steward there.

The idea appealed to Carr. "Here in Russia," he declared to me, "right now that is a very grievous problem. Something must be done in the area of hygiene and I believe that if you put yourself to it, indeed, with American gusto, you'll have done it the best of anyone. Let's pause this discussion; meet with me tomorrow and we'll discuss further how to accomplish this, how to obtain the needed machines, etc."

The next day, Carr discussed with me the particulars of the planned establishment of a large chemical laundry. Furthermore, he told me that in his next report that he wrote to the American party, he would share with them how it was that the revolutionaries deported from the American prisons threw themselves with all their energy into the Soviet economy. I had no objection.

Carr had written a letter to the economic manager of the Comintern (I don't remember her name) recommending that she assist me in carrying out my plan. He told me that I would work in the technical division of the Comintern and as this was the headquarters of the global revolution, he confessed with a smile, "We need to know who is sticking their foot in, and where." Bidding me farewell, Carr said to me, "Well, comrade, I believe that you will not embarrass me, and that you will do a good job."

An hour later, I was already at the commissariat of the technical facility of Comintern. It was not easy for me to meet with the leader of the department. There I handed over my letter, but it was only after spending several hours strolling through different bureaucratic offices that I was received by the manager.

The woman who occupied the position sat at a large desk on which were spread in a jumble many documents, papers, and notes. You would have to be a genius to have known what was happening on this desk. I noted that my letter lay open before her as I came in. She stood up, offered me her hand, and with a masculine voice greeted me in a completely self-assured manner. She was a woman of some forty years old with a sturdy build, masculine haircut, and was of average height. She spoke with certitude in a loud voice, and everyone knew she was in charge. She put questions to me about the plan while frequently heading back to the telephone in a small adjacent room. It turned out that the letter was not enough, and she asked about how different areas would be managed. She had probably also spoken with Carr, who had written the letter. The four-year revolution had taught people to be careful.

The manager battered me with a sea of words. She asked questions and then answered them herself, and I seldom got the opportunity to say a few words to her. She began speaking disdainfully of the American labor movement, of which she knew only what she'd been told by less than responsible people. When I tried to explain that there was indeed a growing movement in America, she roared out, "That is your misfortune; you were educated in a capitalistic democracy and when you come to us, we have nothing but problems from you. I want to hope that you will learn and forget about the excesses."

After believing that she had given me enough instruction, she stood up. I saw that her figure and her stance were in harmony with her voice and her firm convictions. She then told me, "Good, we will give you everything that you need for this new undertaking, only since there are only ten days left until the new year, you'll rest a while from your journey; after that you'll begin setting things up."

She called in one of her secretaries in order to tell him what I would require. A slim man came in, one who looked like Christ. His face was adorned with a small, attractive beard and the mild expressions on his face were pleasing. The entire soul and breadth of a Russian intellectual was visible in him. She said to him, "Here is one of your people" and gave him a paper with instructions written on it.

"What do you mean, 'one of my people'?" the secretary asked.

"A non-party member with a Soviet lining," she answered him.

The phrase appealed to me, and I was delighted that Carr had seen his way to recommending me.

In the few minutes that we remained in the Comintern manager's office, the secretary scarcely looked at me. He had not even told me his name, nor offered to shake hands when she introduced me and I gave him my name. Apparently it was not profitable for him to acknowledge me in the presence of his boss. Only when he invited me into his office did the mood change. He received me very amicably, told me who he was, and began to ask about America. He wanted to know if it was really true that since after the war, people in America were dying of hunger, that people there worked ten to twelve hours a day for a piece of dry bread, and that everyone there was waiting for the world revolution.

At first I wasn't sure what to say to him, because it was unclear to me what his role was. Yet his face didn't deceive me and we talked for a long time about America. He interrupted me several times, saying that he very much wanted to see this land of which the reports were so contradictory.

My new acquaintance was Alexander Utin. He was an engineer by occupation. Until the Bolshevik revolution he had been an Eserovets (member of the Socialist Revolution Party [SRP])[123] and afterwards when his party was obliterated along with several others, he became a "non-party member with a Soviet lining," as people such as him were called.

Speaking with Utin awakened in me old memories of the 1890s when we young people had great respect for the SRP and their revolutionary deeds and terror that they had inspired in the Tsarist rulers. I remember the fervor with which we would sing the SRP revolutionary songs. And sitting here before me was one of that movement who now, at the beginning of the revolution, was a servant of the victorious faction which had forced him to sew a "Soviet lining."

Alexander Utin spoke beautifully with a certain magic, and I felt reinvigorated from the conversation, as you do when you leave a suffocating place and feel the caress of a spring breeze. From then on I became friendly with him and our friendship lasted a long time; we became close friends. When he would say to me, "Comrade," he would stress, smiling, "'comrade' not in a bad way, as it is understood today."

Per the orders of the manager, he began issuing my documents and tickets. From a drawer he pulled out several blank forms with a ready-made letterhead from the Comintern printed on them, and began filling them out. One was for rations, the second—for the right to eat lunch at the Hotel Lux. On this, he remarked to me that I must have made a really good impression, because

---

123 Russian: Sotsialisty Revolyutsionery (SR or ESERY, hence Eserovets) an important political party in early twentieth-century Russia and a critical actor in the Russian Revolution.

eating lunch at the Lux was permitted only for the Comintern delegates or their coworkers, and this only if they were communists. A third paper he gave me to register with the military. In response to my question if he was truly serious that I would have to become a soldier at 37 years old, he explained to me that this was only so that the military authorities would know of me. Finally, he gave me a piece of paper supposed to support all the previous ones, saying that I was an employee of the Comintern in the technical division.

As I was now well-armed with all the necessary paperwork, we bid each other a friendly farewell and promised to see each other more often and talk again about America. I could see that America had been in Utin's mind longer than just today, and that to see America was his dream. If this was for political reasons or for something else, it was hard to tell; only that he was drawn to something about America. However, more than anything else, Utin had made an impression on me with his serious approach to things and the refined, intelligent manner with which he received them.

From the Comintern building, which was located on Mokhovaya Street, to the Tsedom was only a few minutes' walk. The day was a beautiful one, one of those days in the middle of winter when the freezing cold recedes, the sun shines, and from the rooftops beautiful crystals hang down which throw sparkling drops to the ground. On such a day no one rushes, rather one strolls, taking a breather from the harsh Moscow cold.

I went out to the street, my feet scarcely touching the ground. My thoughts were so busy with the construction plans for the new venture and with the impressions of the different people I had met these first few days that I didn't notice that I had gone farther than I needed to, and I now didn't know where I was. I hadn't yet learned the city and wandering around, I began looking for the street to the Tsedom. The passerby whom I stopped to ask the way to the Tsedom first looked me up and down, and then jokingly answered, "Two streets forward, three streets back, and then to the right." The people spoke with a Muscovite drawn-out accent and as I walked away, they looked back at me and wondered at my clothing made from such good foreign fabric. When I arrived at the Tsedom, it was already well past mid-day.

MY BELIEF CRUMBLES

When I arrived after being gone for so long, I was met by the worried faces of my friends. Our female friends, who were simply not enthusiastic about Soviet Russia, had by that time thought the worst. I put the blame on my packet of papers that had taken time to be put together, and we began sharing our experiences.

Our friend Lipman was ecstatic. He had reported as a communist and the party had sent him off to the famous Preobrazhensky,[124] who was now part of that world. Preobrazhensky had received him cordially and arranged an exam for him as an agronomist. As he knew no Russian, they told him that they would give him the exam in English.

"Comrade Abrams," he told me, "where in the world can you achieve this? It's already been arranged for me to receive a stipend of forty rubles a month. Now I'll be able to study calmly and finish as an agronomist. I won't need, as in the capitalist America, to work a full day in the fur factory and after that, exhausted with half-closed eyes, sit in the university class and oftentimes fall face down on the bench in the middle of the lesson. Jack, the revolution is ours!"

He expressed himself with so much enthusiasm that it would have been a crime to say something contrary to him and take away his feelings of hope. I gave him encouragement and justification, all the more so as in that time I had no doubt in the great possibilities for each person in Soviet Russia. The rest of our group had not yet determined what to do and in the meantime had to live off rations from the headquarters of the immigration house.

The ten days before the New Year that I had received as vacation before I began working were a great prize for me. With my documents as an employee of the Comintern I could go anywhere, and I saw many things and visited many interesting places and get-togethers.

By the end of 1921, the new NEP (New Economic Policy[125]) had begun

---

124 Yevgeni Preobrazhensky: a Russian revolutionary and economist, he was a member of the Bolshevik faction and then its successor, the All-Union Communist Party. Preobrazhensky was a leading spokesman for the rapid industrialization of Russia by concentrating on state-owned heavy industry.

125 The New Economic Policy (NEP): an economic policy of Soviet Russia proposed by Lenin, who referred to it as "state capitalism". It was a more capitalism-oriented economic policy designed to bolster the economy destroyed by the Russian civil war.

and people truly saw with their own eyes how the economic life flourished. Every day, people saw on the streets new small businesses that had opened overnight. Ninety percent of the businesses were private; a cooperative could be found only here and there. Moreover, the cooperatives rarely had anything for people to buy. Near the grocery stores stood scores of people repeating the names of the items arranged in the windows. On Tverskaya Street was a restaurant that was once well known in Moscow for its delicious knishes and coffee. One day, a display was placed in the window of several plates of knishes. Like half-savages, the hungry people stood reading the labels underneath the knishes and exclaiming with rapture, "Look, one with liver, one with cheese and also with cabbage!" This bore witness to the hunger during the years of War Communism.[126] Coffee houses began opening here and people had the freedom to buy tasty lunches made with meat. Food was available that people hadn't tasted in years—it was truly a holiday atmosphere.

Being that it was Christmas time, the anti-religious propaganda began an all-out campaign. The journal *The Godless*[127] led a fierce agitation against the churches and priests. In order to make the propaganda more effective, the Soviet government, along with the help of several priests, established a new "living church." Young people were organized and many demonstrations took place against the old church. In one such procession, a black coffin with a priest lying inside was carried while the crowds sang derisively the tune *Hospadi Pomilui*[128] as if at a funeral; that is, they were on their way to bury the priest. Next, a second group led a priest on a sleigh from the "living church"—a Soviet priest, a lively and happy priest, and people sang folksongs. People carried many signs with anti-religious slogans; on some of them it was written that the truly religious person was not persecuted, only the servants of capitalism and priests. On one sign, it was written that the Metropolitan Tikhon[129] sat in prison not because he was a priest, but because he had betrayed Soviet Russia to the enemy.

---

126 War Communism: the economic and political system that existed in Soviet Russia during the civil war to keep supplies of weapons and food available to towns and to the Red Army.

127 Russian: "Bezbozhnik," an anti-religion atheist newspaper published in Soviet Russia by the League of Militant Atheists that ridiculed all religious beliefs, particularly those of Christianity and Judaism.

128 Russian: "Lord have mercy."

129 Saint Tikhon of Moscow, born Vasily Ivanovich Bellavin, was the metropolitan archbishop of the Russian Orthodox Church during the early years of the Soviet Union.

During this same time the Soviet government issued a decree that all businesses must remain open during the days of the holidays. The explanation for the decree was that not all the population was religious, and that those who weren't religious shouldn't suffer because of those who were. To people who would close their businesses on Christmas Day, the decree threatened them with losing the right to reopen. As it turned out, on Christmas Day only the cooperatives were open and all of the private businesses were locked. The government was forced to back off their threat, because otherwise they would have had to punish half of Moscow and bring back the War Communism.

On the night of the holiday, the Moscow streets were very lively. The churches, which Moscow was full of, were packed with believers. Even on Tverskaya, where the Moscow officials stayed, was also the same distressing picture: the Russian Orthodox religious tremor dominated everything around it, and nowhere was it visible that it was already four years since the revolution that had undertook to abolish capitalism and religion. I felt disappointed in another hope. I couldn't grasp the rupture between the propaganda and the reality. Must they then spread such false thoughts abroad, about life in Russia? To feed the world with lies? Who would then demand, that the new order should accomplish miracles in such a short time? We didn't know back then, that it takes long years to rebuild the old way into the new, until the people are educated and entrenched injustices are rooted out.

When I was still sitting in prison in Atlanta, Olgin[130] had returned from a trip to Soviet Russia. He then published an article about it, and how the revolution had abolished prostitution. In our circles in America, the article was hotly debated. Many didn't believe that this societal injustice could be wiped out so quickly, and even more under the conditions of a civil war. I, on the contrary, believed his every word—this was how blindly I was in love with the Russian revolution.

To my great disappointment, in Russia I encountered a completely different picture than the one Olgin had painted. On the main street of Moscow, in front of the Hotel Lux where they cooked for the delegates of the entire international movement, I saw just exactly the opposite:

Young girls, badly dressed with greedy eyes, strutting up and down and

---

130 Moissaye Joseph Olgin: a Russian-born socialist writer, journalist, and translator in the United States during the early years of the twentieth century.

stopping everyone who passed by with whom there might be the possibility of quieting their hunger and cold for a moment. They would prance off with the officials of the Red Army, who would come with small packages in their hands containing a bit of food—this was the price they paid for sating their sexual hunger.

This contrast between talk and reality evoked a heavy heart. It made you dizzy—everything that people had read in the last few years about the wonders of the revolution, and now the previous convictions in those wonders was cut short. I lost my grip on many things in which I had until then believed in abstractly; the more I became acquainted with the real life, the more I felt my deep conviction in the revolution crumbling and breaking. Aside from the deep marks of hunger that lay on the faces of most people and that they went around in rags, I had not noticed any difference in the system, in the order itself. I remembered well the Russia of my childhood, and I found the same practices everywhere.

The only exception was the speech that was used. The spoken and written word was directed towards working people, and the pledges about their future happiness were prodigious; people delighted in them, hoping for a better era and an easier life that would soon come.

RED TAPE AND FAVORITISM—YEZHOV[131]

The sixth of January, the day on which it had been arranged to come and receive the full authorization for my work, I was at Comrade Utin's office early that morning. I had resolved within myself that everything I had seen in the last two weeks must not stop me from throwing myself into the task, and to use this project to forget about the bad impressions of life in this land that never ceased in promising so many good things and happiness for the Russian people, and for the entire world.

Comrade Utin brought me in to see the technical Chief Director from Comintern. The position was then occupied by Yezhov, and it was he who would provide me with the tools necessary for the work appointed to me per the recommendations of the American delegate Carr. Yezhov was a man of

---

131 Nikolai Ivanovich Yezhov: a Soviet secret police official under Stalin and head of the NKVD (the Soviet Union's security and intelligence agency) from 1936; in 1922 he was working in the Communist Party political system, primarily on various regional committees.

average height, still young, and with broad shoulders. His face, although it was smooth and slightly feminine, expressed resolve. After speaking for a few minutes, he gave me a short letter to the manager, Comrade Kivelevitsh, who would then give me all necessary materials and assist me in establishing the laundry. Additionally, he stressed to me that before I go to see Kivelevitsh, I should go visit Comrade Kavalyov, who would be the political commissar for the venture. "From him," he told me, "you must always be in agreement about each thing that you will need for your work."

Comrade Kavalyov was also my direct supervisor; he was a person who was an exception to all the other people I had met there. Koval, as I had later referred to him, was a very good-natured person. Were it not for his love of alcohol and that he would often get drunk, he would have been classified as a model of sincerity. The drinking had often, against his will, led him to improper acts for which he would have many regrets. He had, Koval, an extraordinarily strong shape, a physical giant with a lion's head, wide shoulders, and an Asian countenance. A few minutes after our introduction and explaining my charge to him, he switched over to speaking to me in a more familiar manner and I answered him in same. He himself had been a sailor since very young; his entire political baggage consisted of the fact that he had served the revolutionary movement during the imperial era as a courier for underground communications.

Koval received me as a coworker with delight. "We will work well together," he told me. "I know America, and I have been there many times. I am a shrewd commissar, but you, the Americans, know more than we do. You will do as is required and I will sign it. Just show what you can do and we'll make it go smoothly."

Speaking thus to me, he pulled out a flask from under a box. This sort of thing he was never without, although at that time the manufacture of alcohol was forbidden. Koval knew where to get home-brewed liquor. He poured a small glass for me also, saying, "Well, brother, take a drink; you'll warm up and I'll drive over together with you to the crafty manager Kivelevitsh." Here I had to help him out, because he had a hard time pronouncing the name. Like two old acquaintances, we set off to Kivelevitsh.

Kivelevitsh was a middle-aged man. The features of his face expressed intelligence and Jewish wisdom. He was also a "non-party member with a Soviet lining." Up until the revolution he was a prominent Social Democrat, a Menshevik, and therefore he did not enjoy too much confidence from the Bolsheviks. But since he was a good director and moreover, a completely honest man he was needed, and when there is a need, no excuses are accepted. He excelled in his post as manager for the Comintern and for this he was respected.

Comrade Kivelevitsh heard me out on my subject, and in a few short words explained to me what I was to do. At the same time, he confided in me that I should pay very close attention to my commissar, because he could waste more money on drink than the venture would bring in.

On one of the Moscow side streets not far from the Vindovski[132] stood a building that was an old factory. The imperial patriots had destroyed the factory during the anti-German war demonstrations, because it belonged to a German. It was a large glass factory and when the Russians were pounded by the Germans on the front, they beat up the Germans ... in Moscow.

Kivelevitsh suggested that we fix up the house belonging to the factory, making it into a living space for me and the commissar, then tackle setting up the automatic laundry. The space, he assured us, was very large and a shoe-making factory could also be added, for which there was already mechanized equipment at the factory. At the site, the house was full of broken furniture and benches and repairs needed to begin.

At my suggestion, Koval got a droshky and we went directly to the location of the factory where the tsarist Russians had avenged themselves against the Germans. When we arrived at the site, we met a Red Army soldier standing watch at the gate. The soldier had a small hut there and was charged with protecting the Soviet property—the remains of the demolished factory. The soldier was actually a guard in military dress with a rifle, and he would stand alert at the door when he saw someone approaching.

The factory was transferred to our authority and I began arranging the venture. When I talked about it with Vershagin, the engineer pointed out to me, to see what must be done, he stared at me: "And where will you find material? Where will you get it?" I answered him that I thought I would be able to obtain everything, or I would not have been given such a task.

Meanwhile, I called upon the labor exchange and I was sent a few dozen unskilled laborers. We began setting up the factory yard and the engineer

---

132   Per a 1922 version of *Hearst International* (Volume 41), a railway depot in Moscow.

Vershagin started putting together a list of the materials that I would need to purchase. The sum of money needed to buy the materials must be given to us by the economic administration.

Thus began the hell of running around and going on quests. Here we lacked shovels and no one could get them; there they were waiting for wagons to take away the scraps that had been cleared away; then estimates—should they do this or not, can they make do with five kegs of nails instead of twelve, should or shouldn't the machines for the mechanical shoe manufacturing be brought, etc.

For each thing I needed scores of documents from different offices and commissars. This would result in standing for long hours at the door of every commissar and very often, leaving without getting to see anyone.

On the days that I would wear my elegant but not warm enough American coat, the person standing at the door would let me in first. However, on frigid days when the January cold in Moscow was intense, I would wear a pair of boots with a Russian fur coat. On such days, I would stand at doors and go home without accomplishing anything. I had no choice but to wear my bourgeois, thin overcoat in the worst freezing cold.

For three and a half bitter months I worked this way, running from one office to another and buying material at the cooperatives. On the first of May, the task was completed. Everything was ready and people could begin working.

The technical management of the Comintern gave me an award of a hundred rubles in gold for organizing the venture, and a compliment saying that I served the revolution as a loyal soldier. In the practice and conduct of that time, this meant that the work had been carried out quickly and effectively.

The first few months, I was completely consumed by the work. The shoe manufacturing in the same factory building was entrusted to a Communist arrival from England, and the automatic laundry and a carpentry shop that we set up were under my supervision. In those days, the hardest part of the job was making sure that the workers had food to eat. The money that was received as salary became worthless from one day to the next, and the main problem was to make provisions with products.

In the factory building a collective kitchen was established. Thanks to my acquaintanceship with friends from America who were managers in different positions, I received items for the kitchen faster than other areas, and it consequently worked better than the other factory departments.

Yet this didn't last long and I had the worst experience, one that brought so much loss to the new venture. This was the favoritism used to place one's own people in good jobs and which brought me to my first confrontation with my chief political commissar and technical supervisor, Yezhov, who became the chief of the GPU[133] after the execution of Yagoda.[134] In that time Yezhov was not yet very powerful, but it seemed that he already had the makings of a villain.

In the factories then, there were more clerks in the offices than there were workers in the factories. We initiated a different, more rational system and for forty-some workers there was only one clerk, and he managed the office alone. The position was held by a young Jewish man named Bayer, and he did a good job. He would also help unload bundles when a heavy wagon of wash was brought in. Comrade Utin and others in the Comintern would always say to me that this wouldn't last long, because from other ventures came reports that they must have scores of employees, although no one did anything. I kept to my own ways and didn't bring on anyone else.

One time a young girl of about sixteen or seventeen years old came to me with a request from Yezhov asking that she be given work. The girl, who was plastered with cheap make-up, looked like a cabaret dancer and not a worker in a laundry. To the question of whether she could do laundry work—although the work was being done with machines—she answered me that she could not. She tried flirting with me from the start, adding to the bargain that she was a good Jewish girl and after that, in a serious tone, she let me know that Comrade Yezhov had assured her that she would receive a position here as cashier. When I told her that we had no cashbox here, she skillfully said that she meant managing the accounts book.

We had no such position, and together with Comrade Bayer we took care of all necessary things; the greater part of the day was taken up with unskilled labor. The girl left without saying good-bye. A few hours later, Yezhov summoned me and let me know that I did not behave correctly towards him as my superior official. I stood my ground and tried to persuade him that to do things differently would cause the venture to suffer.

---

133 Russian acronym for the State Political Directorate, the former intelligence service and secret police of Soviet Russia.

134 Genrikh Grigoryevich Yagoda: Director of the NKVD from 1934–1936 and tried and executed for treason in 1937.

From then on, the troubles began to pour in on us. Whenever Yezhov could, he sabotaged the work. Kivelevitsh, our political commissar, was powerless and when I would demand that he do something, he would tell me: "You should have hired the Yezhov-grandmother." I complained to Utin and he took it to the Comintern manager. She admitted that I was right, but could do nothing against Yezhov's tricks.

The winter was approaching and a supply of wood was needed for the factory building: we needed to have two hundred sazshen[135] of wood, but Yezhov had already made sure that we not receive any. Meanwhile, always being around such filthy work—with each wagon of wash, two wagonloads of lice would shake out—I became infected with typhus and was bedridden.

We had no type of remedy whatsoever, and lived in a tiny room in which stood one small bed, a table and two benches. During the eight days that I lay in bed, my friend Mary slept sitting at the table. Our friends from the "Family" took care of providing doctors and other needed items. My friend Lipman was quite simply my savior. He threw off his studies and for the entire time of my illness never stepped away from my bed, helping me a great deal.

During this same time, Yezhov did not forget that I had wronged him and on a certain day when I was barely up and around again, he ordered that I must leave the room in the Comintern building. He also instructed the sentry that no one allow me to bring in any wood to heat the room during the time that I was still there.

One of the leaders of the Comintern then was Piatnitsky.[136] Working for him was a young Moscow Russian, Peganov. The young man was very envious of Americans, above all of the Jews who came from America. "These are a different people," he would say. He came to visit me several times during my illness and we struck up a friendship. When Yezhov put out the decree against me, I told him about my situation. To find a room back then was a very difficult thing.

But Peganov was a man with a wide Russian heart. Saying nothing to me, he went to Piatnitsky and told him the entire story. My situation soon

---

135 Obsolete Russian measurement equal to 2.13 m. (7 ft.).

136 Osip Aaronovitch Piatnitsky: born Iosif Aronovich Tarshis, he was a Russian revolutionary and served as head of the International Department of the Comintern during the 1920s and early 1930s.

changed for the better. First, my rations were improved: I received good butter, oil and meat—a sick person's rations. Then a small oven was sent to my room.

However, I had decided not to work any longer under the supervision of that individual, of Yezhov. To resign from a post was not an easy thing. Nonetheless, as soon as I became healthy, I talked it over with the people at the Comintern technical division and convinced them that the woman Kapitanova, who worked in the factory, could replace me. She had effectively mastered the flow of the venture, being one of those types of students who learns and can then do it better than their teacher can.

As the Comintern boss signed my discharge papers, she told me that she happened to speak with Comrade Kantarovitsh from Narkomindel (People's Commissariat for Foreign Affairs) [137] about my important work, and he wanted to set up such an automatic laundry for the Byurobin Bureau[138] that served the foreigners. She advised me that I should discuss it with him, and that same day I went to see him. It turned out that he also had been in America, and we immediately set to work.

Kantarovitsh was a young man of about 35 years of age, short of stature and with a strong build. He had beautiful features, was well dressed and possessed elegant manners. Having lived a considerable amount of time in America had made him more energetic and he was a very precise man; consequently he excelled at his job. He seemed like an American businessman, and his having a membership in the Socialist movement was only because it was then as necessary as a passport. He had an academic education, knew several languages, and was the perfect fit for his position at Narkomindel.

The Narkomindel functioned better than all the other commissariats because there new people were coming in all the time: representatives of the press, people from professional organizations, and officials from government institutes. A special department had been established in the commissariat, the Byurobin Bureau, which had under its supervision the best hotels and restaurants and the nicest houses, which were required for use with the government officials and foreign guests. Those employed in Byurobin had

---

137 NKID: Russian acronym for the People's Commissariat for Foreign Affairs, as it was known prior to 1946.
138 Russian acronym for the Bureau for Services for Foreigners.

been selected carefully so that they might satisfy the guests who came to trade with the Soviets.

Kantarovitsh was the chief of all divisions of Narkomindel, and was also the steward of the Foreign Commissariat proper. To that end, it was fortuitous for him that Lenin had then issued a decree abolishing the political commissars in the economic section and industries; each manager would be the boss and with the primary capital that they were given for an undertaking, they must make it a success. The decree also specified that they must attract non-party people in all domains. The Soviets in the factories were dismissed, the workers were no longer allowed to be involved in the leadership, and everything was given over to the managers.

Having been given through Lenin's decree as one could say, "free hands," Kantarovitsh quickly put me in contact with his technical employee L. A. Poliak, an engineer by occupation, and we very rapidly—completely contrary to the custom of the leadership at that time—made an estimate and ascertained that to set up the venture correctly would require thirty thousand rubles in gold. The money was deposited in the Soviet bank at my disposition as manager, and I soon began establishing a new automatic laundry.

Quarters had also been arranged for me at one of the Byurobin Bureau houses where the ambassadors from the Mongolian government also stayed. Because of this, it was already a beautiful residence with central heating, a bathtub, etc.

In just a very short time, the new automatic laundry was working at full capacity and was to earn praise for its good service. The laundry that was brought here was of another type because the laundry served the hotels and foreign guests. The work was much easier, and I didn't have to put so much of my life into it as with the Comintern laundry. There was a lot of work, but we worked in two shifts and had enough time for ourselves.

I began taking more of an interest in the political life of the country; my circle of acquaintances and friends became larger every day. I soon learned the Soviet art of listening more and speaking less. I seized on all the new Soviet jokes that were many times useful in one's activities. It was on jokes that the Soviet people lived, and they delighted in them. If you had to arrange some business and the official—of high rank or low—knew that you could tell jokes, you were a welcome guest. And jokes at the expense of the revolution and her leaders went around in the thousands.

BETWEEN GOOD AND BAD

In Moscow in the month of October, the Fifth Congress of the Comintern was held.[139] I was already connected in different circles, and it was easy for me to obtain an entrance ticket to the congress. This was a huge moment for me and with my heart pounding, I went to witness the deliberation of the "World Headquarters of the Social Revolution."

The congress took place in the Kremlin, in the halls of Ivan the Cruel. Lenin was then recovering from a difficult illness and the doctors had forbidden him to attend the congress. However, he fought with his doctors and they finally allowed him to come and give a speech of no longer than ten minutes.

I was one of the first to enter the hall, which was large and opulent. The walls were high, white, and made of a smooth marble, and on them were engraved the names of the powerful soldiers of imperial times. On the platform stood a long table covered with heavy red tablecloths, and on the wall over the platform hung a sign with the titles of the countries that the delegates represented; in the middle of the red background was placed an enormous Roman number five, which signified that this was the fifth congress of the Comintern.

In the hall were people from all parts of the world, and at the Presidium table sat the chief leaders of the Comintern. In the middle sat Zinoviev,[140] the chairman of the Comintern. Seated around him were Kamenev, Bukharin, Trotsky, Rikov, Radek, Kalinin and many other Bolshevik leaders. Stalin was then still far from the seat of power, and he was not found at the big table.

The first session was taken up with reports, which were authorized immediately. At a second session, people picked commissions. Aside from the Russian delegates, the chief role was played by the Germans, French and Czechoslovakians. Then the sessions were postponed for three days while the commissions prepared their materials for further work.

I waited with impatience for the fiery speeches and motions of the commissions that would come from the headquarters of the world revolution. To my disappointment, the next sessions were repeated the same as the first

---

139 Historical sources list this as the Fourth World Congress of Comintern, with the Fifth being held in June of 1924.

140 Grigory Yevseevich Zinoviev: born Ovsei-Gershon Aronovich Radomyslsky, he was one of the seven members of the first Politburo.

one. Radek read the motions of the Germans, and the translators translated them into several languages. The delegates didn't direct any discussions and everything was approved unanimously. Then the delegates told of the wonders that the movement had made in their countries and after each speech, an orchestra played *The Internationale*. Without any kind of attraction or special appearances, the congress was closed.

My entire dream and expectation of attending a congress of the Third International resulted in a bitter disappointment. I had the occasion to be at a congress of all the unions in New York where ninety percent of the delegates were conservatives. This was soon after Tom Mooney,[141] the famous labor martyr, was convicted by the American court. The well-known lawyer Cockran[142] who was Mooney's defense attorney, gave his report. The delegates led heated debates for three days. Resolutions were analyzed and ways were sought to improve them. And here is the headquarters of the world revolution that must decide the fate of the world, the administrative body that undertakes to bring socialism to the world, made up of a flock of sheep without will and without self-respect. All that the tribune says is agreed to, and everything seems like a cheap crowd scene in a theater: a few actors play roles and the rest are "extras" that sit at the table and nod their heads to everything.

I had the occasion to speak about this with friends and comrades, party members as well as non-party members. The majority of their opinions were that the revolution cannot happen without discussions. Who knows what kind of people the delegates are, and if they can be counted on with such important issues. A democracy cannot be brought to bear while Russia faces hundreds of dangers. As soon as the dangers are over, people will become democratic. Meanwhile, things will be done as they are done. And I would then think: Who knows? Maybe they are right.

The anniversary of the revolution approached, the seventh of November. Moscow began preparing for the celebration of the October revolution. The city got dressed up like a rich bride for her wedding. The graves of the

---

141 Thomas Joseph "Tom" Mooney: an American political activist and labor leader convicted of the 1916 San Francisco Preparedness Day Bombing; believed by many to have been convicted of a crime he did not commit.

142 W. Bourke Cockran: United States Representative from New York, noted political orator, and Tom Mooney chief defense lawyer.

heroes of the revolution located behind the wall of the Kremlin were each covered with new flowers. The firefighters spruced up the buildings of the Soviet capital with greenery and banners. Especially richly decorated were the official buildings like the Soyuzav (House of the Trade Unions),[143] the Moscow city hall, etc. In the Red Square, not one corner remained that hadn't been decorated for the revolutionary holiday. Around and around were hung flower chains, signs, red banners and slogans.

My entrance card to the Fifth Comintern Congress also helped me receive a ticket for the day of 7 November, and I was allowed to be among the numerous delegations from the country and abroad. On that day, the Red Square would be closed to the public and only the divisions of the Red Army and the guests would hear the fiery speeches of the leaders taking part in the central parade.

Moscow was already considerably cold in November. The days were still pretty and partly sunny, but the taste of freezing cold was already in the Moscow air. The seventh of November being spoke about here, was a cold but beautiful day. At the designated hour of the morning, everything in the Red Square was in full glory. The Moscow garrison of the Red Army was in full armament and dress uniforms. All the prepared seats around the square where the grandstand for the Council of the People's Commissars[144] was located were filled with representatives of the governments, delegates, guests and press representatives from the ends of the earth. When everything was ready, everyone waited impatiently for the arrival of the War Commissar. At that time, the position was held by Trotsky.

Rarely have I found myself in such heightened spirits as on that day. With my eyes I devoured the personalities chosen to be on the grandstand near where I stood among the other guests. A cheerful feeling came over me as I looked at the panorama of the Red Square, where only a short time ago it was the place of the imperial rulers. Now here stood the leaders of the revolution, delegates from revolutionary movements, a Red Army …

My heart danced with joy that everything that I saw was ours, our own; each soldier, although he might even come from peasant and worker stock, but was now a soldier for himself, for his own power from the workers and peasants, for whom he was ready to sacrifice his life.

---

143 Now called the House of the Unions.
144 Council of People's Commissars on War and Navy Affairs.

As I was looking at the celebration with dazzled eyes, I saw the greatness and beautifulness of the revolution and little by little, began to forget and would even forgive the first horrific crime of that stormy revolutionary time: the trial of the Esern (Socialist Revolutionary Party).[145]

In theory one could perhaps forgive, especially during ceremonial moments, but to forget was nevertheless not allowed. Then, precisely then, sitting here at the Red Square, I recalled the trial of the Esern which I was fated to witness in the great hall of the Soyuzav. At that trial—the first the new revolutionary powers dared to stage against a Russian revolutionary party—Gots and his comrades were tried.[146] Lenin was still alive then, and a representative of international socialism was permitted to defend the accused. This role was taken on by Vandervelde,[147] the famous Belgian socialist leader. In the middle of the trial he was forced to abandon his defense because Krylenko,[148] the plaintiff on the part of the government, had primed a group of young party members to disrupt Vandervelde during his speech. Krylenko took the disruptors under his protection, saying that this was how the fury of the Russian workers was expressed against those who wanted to betray the revolution.

One time when Vandervelde had been hindered from speaking, Krylenko added that in the coming week the defense attorney would see here scores of thousands of workers marching on the streets, demanding the death of the accused Esern.

Vandervelde, with his quick mind and sharp polemical skills, then answered Krylenko that he was prepared to stay however much time was necessary, only with the condition that the Soviet government hand over the authority to him for a few days and he would show the accused an even larger demonstration, at which the crowds would demand the heads of the current regime.

The large audience of over a thousand people listening to the events of the trial broke out with so much laughter that the judges could scarcely calm the laughing crowd, which was not there by accident because each of

---

145 Known as the "Moscow Trial of the Socialist Revolutionaries," it began on 8 June 1922, and was part of the Bolshevik strategy to eliminate opposition groups.
146 Avram Gots, who was tried along with thirty-three other SRP leaders.
147 Émile Vandervelde: a Belgian statesman and a well-known figure in European socialism.
148 Nikolai Vasilyevich Krylenko: a Russian Bolshevik revolutionary and Soviet politician.

them had a permit from their superiors to attend the trial. The resounding laughter showed that the Russian people were not what Krylenko tried to turn them into.

*   *   *

Sitting thus engrossed in my thoughts, I felt a hand on my shoulder. I turned around and right behind me sat Alexander Trachtenberg,[149] an acquaintance from New York whom I knew there as a total right-wing Menshevik. He was so far to the right that when I went to him once about helping us with the different trials that were spread across the country after America joined the war, he cursed the Bolsheviks for their stance against the war. With me he was especially angry; why, during my trial, had I defended a regime of "kidnappers and bandits," because he, Trachtenberg, then believed that the left Bolshevik government would destroy the Socialist movement. And here I was meeting him several years later in the Red Square.

Suddenly a ripple passed through everyone's body in the Red Square. All the faces turned to the side of the Vasily Blazhenny church: Trotsky was approaching from that direction, riding a horse. Like an eagle, he sprung down from his horse, came up to the Red Square and with firm steps, his hand on his cap greeting the military and escorted by his general staff, he marched in front of the front rows of the Red Army.

The enthusiasm in the Red Square with Trotsky's appearance was indescribable. The official part of the ceremony began. One speaker after another appeared on the special dais. People spoke in different languages about the exploits of the revolution. Trotsky was the final speaker. His lion's voice started to thunder and the slightest rustle could be heard in the Red Square. He turned to the Red Army and said to them that a colossal task awaited them; they were not permitted to forget that they were not only a Russian, but an international Red Army, and when an injustice occurred, they would need to take their rifles in their hands and go assist the helpless and maltreated.

In the middle of his speech he quickly gave a turn, lifted his right hand to the sun, gave a short pause, and then with all the power of his voice

---

149 Alexander Trachtenberg: Russian-born American publisher of radical political materials, longtime activist first in the Socialist Party of America and then in the Communist Party USA.

and with his renowned art of speaking in elaborate sentences, sent through the sun a curse on capitalism.

A wave of applause and a boisterous cheer from the Red soldiers lasted for many minutes after the speech. For many people in the grandstands, tears sparkled in their eyes from inspiration.

Naturally, for each person such an impressive act evoked a spirit full of hope. I remembered Maxim Gorky's saying about the great Russian writer Lev Tolstoy: "As long as this man lives, I am not an orphan on this earth." Ignited by the revolutionary ceremony, I said to myself, "As long as the Russian revolution lives, the world is no longer abandoned." I chased away my doubts and thought that with all its defects, the October-revolution must be defended. For the large crowds, many ceremonies were organized in other parts of the city, for of course not everyone [*sentence incomplete as published*].[150]

GPU AND NEP

The Moscow winter in 1922 was a very animated one. The VTsIK (All Russian Central Executive Committee)[151] had made public that the Cheka was being abolished and this gave everyone a feeling of happiness. In its place a new secret police was created, the GPU,[152] and it was announced that its function would be sharply limited. Absolutely no kind of administrative arrests would occur. Each person who was arrested and no evidence of his guilt was put forward in the period of three days must be released; if evidence was shown, he must be publicly tried and receive full rights to defend himself; the state must provide him with an attorney.

The public was reinvigorated by the decree. The first weeks people went around with beautiful dreams, but it quickly proved to be that the ordinances of the VTsIK remained on paper and the new political police did the same things as the old. It was known in Moscow that each Friday, somewhere in the dark, death sentences would be carried out and no one knew what became of the prisoners. However, for political persons it did indeed become easier.

---

150 Translator's Note: A suggested ending could be that not everyone could attend the ceremony at the Red Square.

151 All-Russian Central Executive Committee (Russian acronym VTsIK): the highest legislative, administrative, and revising body of the Russian Soviet Federative Socialist Republic.

152 State Political Directorate (Russian acronym GPU): the intelligence service and secret police of the early Soviet Union.

The main task of the GPU was to occupy itself with the NEP community, whose numbers increased with each day.

As if with a magic wand, new businesses opened everywhere, foodstuffs became dirt cheap and grocery stores such as I hadn't seen in New York were appearing on the Moscow main streets. Everything was available to buy, and for much cheaper prices than before NEP. Food, clothing, luxury articles, butter items, shoes adorned with silver and gold flowers, cosmetic items, foreign manufactures—you could find everything in the new businesses, whose magnificence gave them nothing to be ashamed of against Fifth Avenue and Broadway in New York.

Also permitted was an open exchange of currency and this was located at the Prombank.[153] There on the street people exchanged foreign currency: dollars to Russian ducats, Russian ducats to Soviet marks, to merchandise drafts, etc. The ducat became a stable foreign currency and went two for one dollar. As for the Soviet marks which lost value with each day, the workers suffered the most; come Saturday, their weekly earnings were already worth only half.

The GPU was then principally concerned with the economic institutions of the country and with the NEP community. The managers of the factories speculated even more than did the NEP people. They would obtain the money for a few days, then buy on the exchange twice as many Soviet marks and earn fifty percent more. Since in the GPU nothing was sacred, many GPU people from one side and the managers from another would come together and would make a profitable deal.

Moscow prepared itself for the New Year's holiday; all day long decrees and ordinances continued to appear. Lunatsharski, the Education Commissar,[154] put out a decree that all students would be released from their studies for the entire month of December so they could travel to their villages and see their parents. Dzerzhinsky,[155] who was not only head of the GPU but also commissar of the railway, had ordered thirty percent lower train ticket prices. The holiday was also felt in the deepest corners of the Communist party, even though it was wholly associated with the day of Christ's birth.

---

153 The National Industrial Bank.
154 Anatoli Lunatsharski: People's Commissar for Instruction and Education.
155 Felix Dzerzhinsky: head of GPU and also Commissar of Transport.

At the laundry, we were slammed with work and all of our clients that brought wash from the hotels and restaurants demanded that it be ready on the twenty-fourth of December, Christmas Eve. It was impossible to fulfill these orders with our normal work schedule. Moreover, among the clients were all the high-ranking people and official institutions. I came up with a novel idea of how to arrange this and satisfy the public. I called together all the personnel of the laundry and made them a proposal: since we still had three weeks until the first of January, we should get the work finished quickly by working overtime and with increased intensity, until the twenty-fourth. Then we would close the laundry for eight days, being paid for that time. The workers were pleased with the proposal, and the work went off at such a pace that by the twenty-second there was not even a thread left to be done.

I went up to see my general manager that day and told him what we had done. He was delighted with the plan. He gave me the sum required to pay the wages and the workers were immensely satisfied. We also made all our clients happy by delivering the completed work on time. It didn't occur to me that this could be used as an accusation against me in the future; meanwhile, the entire technical division was talking about the American's idea to have everything ready on time, each client receiving what was due them, and the workers should have off the entire eight days.

MY NAIVETÉ

During these same days the Narpit[156] congress took place. This was an abbreviation for Narodnaie Pitanie, the organization that administered the people's kitchens. Since the technical division of Byurobin was a member of the Narpit, I thought to serve as a delegate to the congress. As I was a non-party member and thus was considered a necessity for the congress, I became a delegate.

At the congress was a large hall of delegates, but they hardly spoke to one another. A chairman of the central administrative body of the soviet professional unions gave a report and declared that as the Soviet Union was already strong enough, beginning with the New Year the unions would conduct their work independently and not be dependent on the government and the Communist Party. Economic institutions were growing as much on

---

156 Narpit: Union of People's Food Service and Dormitory Workers

the government side as the private, and the workers must take their fate in their own hands and defend the positions they'd won, with all means possible. Speaking thus, he announced that today a new decree went into effect, a decree about the independence of the unions, but—and here he began accompanying his conclusions with "buts."

"But as we are not yet completely free of the Whites, each union must have a cell of the party"; "But since the Mensheviks and Eserns are still not completely destroyed, at each union there must be a representative of the government," etc. By the time he was finished with all the "buts," it was obvious that everything would remain as before and the unions would in no way become independent. The delegates looked at each other and smiled quietly.

From the presidium it was declared that before people came forward to vote for a new six-month board of directors, whoever wanted to could ask a question or say a word. I completely forgot where I was and called out, "I'd like a word!"

The entire audience of delegates turned in my direction, and from the presidium their eyes shot straight at me. It became quiet as a grave in the hall and for the five minutes that I spoke, you could hear the heartbeats of the listeners in the hall—by no means because of my beautiful speech, but because somebody had dared to speak up.

In a quite naïve manner, I utilized the five minutes to say that it was not necessary to "pour from one empty glass into another," to issue decrees and with a few "buts" nullify them. It would have been better to state that when the time came, the professional unions would be independent—meanwhile, this cannot be. As long as the managers must deduct union dues from the disbursement of funds from the government treasury, the worker would often not know who his representative was, or even where his union was located. I concluded with the remark that rather than coming up with such unnecessary machinations, it would be much better to reinforce the propaganda among the workers about the necessity of being organized in the soviets whose base were the unions, so that they would know the value and power of organizing.

Before I had quite finished, I sensed that I had stuck my foot in it. The chairman, who was an envoy of the upper echelons of the congress, directed himself at me and began shrieking, "We know you, the Mensheviks and Eserns, and we know your intention!" I began saying loudly that he was making a mistake, that I was—contrary to his expectations—a total anarchist, to which he replied with even greater fury, "That's even worse!" There was nothing more for me to do but be silent.

They went straight to the vote for twenty-four people whom we didn't know and hadn't heard their names, and they were passed unanimously. Later, we found out that all of them were party members. People started to disperse. When I had entered the congress no one knew me and I knew no one, but when leaving almost all the delegates sought me out to say a "good day" or at least give a nod of the head. I did not feel very good about my exploit, but what I had done wrong here, I didn't know and couldn't figure out. Going home, I ran my words through my mind again and came to the conclusion that I had defended the interests of the soviets. Why then, had the chairman become so infuriated?

That night, as always our "semyo,"—the family circle, as we called ourselves—met together and I told them what had happened at the congress. Several of them expressed the opinion that it was no big deal, simply that only those designated by the party cell were supposed to speak. "There's no such thing as just speaking when one wants," said Comrade Kostia, our good friend and a party member. He was a high official and he consoled me, seeing that I was not cheerful about the whole matter. "People know who you are and nothing will happen to you," he assured me, "and in case it does, we will lend a hand and make this disappear."

I got no rest that night. I kept shifting restlessly due to the chairman's threats, and I thought to myself, "More than anyone, my affairs are in order. I work with heart and soul, and I'm no less loyal to the government than the party communists. Is it that I'm not in the party? What had I done that was so wrong?"

Several days passed. The holiday nights from Christmas until after the New Year were very merry in Moscow and little by little, I began to forget about the entire incident.

WHEN THE CONSCIENCE IS STILL AWAKE

The days and nights of the New Year's holiday passed like a beautiful story. All differences between people became wiped away. All Moscow, religious and non-religious, rejoiced and made merry, only the joy was not with the birth of Christ but with the newborn Russia.

For the first time in five years, the sleighs of former times appeared. Small lanterns winked on the carriage shafts, and the horses were covered with beautiful fabrics and adorned with small bells. The sounds of laughing couples twined together and rang out in the streets. The white snow was dazzling, and the cold-weather air became warm with the breath of the people around it.

I roamed about for many hours on the night of December thirty-first, and contemplated the wonders about me. All the cafes and restaurants were bubbling with life and happiness. The people were, after all, good—as people feel good when they are free and celebrating the holiday time. Even the GPU people, who at the mention of their name the mother's milk dried on the lips of children, became different. They too sat at little tables with a drink and wished happiness to people whom tomorrow they would perhaps treat as enemies. Everything was under a blanket of happiness, and differences disappeared.

Later that night, I was invited to the private dwelling of the member of VTsIK: Kaganitski. He had a very rich revolutionary past himself and was a hero of the "October" and of the civil war. It was said that the holidays held little interest for him, only that tomorrow was a free day and people should get together for a glass of brandy and a bit of conversation.

At the table that had been prepared at Kaganitski's place, one could see the difference between soviet officials, depending on the post that they occupied—his position was a very high one. After a few hours of eating and drinking all that we wanted, Kaganitski himself proposed to tell episodes from his experiences in the revolution, but each person had to give his word that he would not speak publicly of what he heard until it was printed, which was supposed to happen soon.

He gave a short preface, saying that he would tell about one important episode that, although he considered it as a great service to the revolution, he nevertheless had oddly conflicted feelings about it. For this reason, he wanted to unburden his heart. Everyone present remained sitting like statues, without any kind of movement or uttering a sound. Kaganitski told us:

"This was in the eighteenth year,[157] when the imperial family had been brought to Yekaterinburg. I was there attached to a Red Army division. One day, a young commander named Belovrodov came to me at headquarters and informed me that since the Romanov family was at the train depot in a closed railroad car, he was requesting that we immediately find quarters for them. At the same time, he handed over to me the orders of the Council of the People's Commissars.

"I, along with Belovrodov, who also stayed until the end, had to make sure that the guards around the house in Yekaterinburg where we had taken the Romanovs would consist of proven revolutionaries. The many years of the imperial dynasty had created among the people a divine belief in the "tsar priest," and an anti-revolutionary act was feared. Moreover, Kolchak[158] was then with his forces in Siberia and we were afraid that they would attack Yekaterinburg and liberate the tsar and his family.

"Among the Red Army Guard that was with me were a group of Kronstadter sailors who had distinguished themselves in the October uprising. With them was also Zhelezniakov, who was one of the first to enter the imperial Winter Palace in Petrograd.[159] Appointing them as guard, Belovrodov and I assumed this charge.

"At first, we hardly slept at night. We knew that the Council of the People's Commissars was in negotiation with the English government about handing over the family to England for an enormous price, only we didn't know if they were in earnest or not. To this day, it's hard for me to say. We were surrounded then with enemies on all sides and the negotiations were necessary.

"The days and nights dragged on. Kolchak drew near to our positions. We had neglected the front because of the ever-present fear that something might happen to the tsar, thus impeding the high-level political negotiations. The situation became quite serious. A conspiracy had been launched from inside. Peasants would come from all around Yekaterinburg, and from a distance kneel down to plead for the souls of the Romanovs. As we had not kept it

---

157 The Romanovs were executed on July 17, 1918.

158 Alexander Vasilyevich Kolchak: a polar explorer and commander in the Imperial Russian Navy who established an anti-communist government in Siberia during the Russian Civil War.

159 Anatoli Zhelezniakov: young Russian anarchist sailor who led a contingent of sailors in the storming of the Winter Palace in Petrograd (Saint Petersburg) in 1917.

secret, it was known through the entire area that the tsar and his family were here under arrest, and we could possibly be attacked in order to free them.

"We consulted several times with the central command. We would be grudgingly answered and given instructions to protect them. We never received any type of answer to our last inquiry, and we assumed that it had been left in our hands. We had Voikov from the Yekaterinburg soviet with us and we deliberated about what to do. Because of the danger menacing each day both from the Kolchak army and from an assault, we decided to free ourselves of them that very night, and that we ourselves would carry out the sentence.

"When the decision was taken, it was a strange thing. All of us had spent the last years fighting on many battlefields and our rifles never left our hands. Yet when it came to carrying out a death sentence as a result of cold logic, we all sat mute and it turned out that we were not prepared either physically or morally to do this.

"At this moment I used my authority as commander and said to Zhelezniak, as we used to call him, that he must carry out the order. He did not refuse, because it was easier to do such things as an order than of one's free will. We also had to decide what to do with Professor Botkin, an old man of seventy years who was a great physician and the longtime doctor of the Romanov family.[160] We decided to send him off to Moscow; afterwards, the execution would be carried out.

"Late that night we informed the tsar's entire family that they should get ready because they would be taken to another place. A battle broke out; they read the hour of their death on our faces and would not go. They were taken with much force to the cellar of the house. The only one who went willingly and peacefully was Professor Botkin, who refused our kindness and let us know that he did not want to go to Moscow. He had served them all these years—he told us briefly—and he wanted to die with them.

"Zhelezniakov and a group of loyal soldiers carried out the execution. A half hour later, he came up from the cellar with wild eyes and as one bewildered. He threw himself down at the table, rested his head on his elbows, and howled like a wild animal. We tried to calm him as he shrieked, 'How

---

160 Yevgeny Sergeyevich Botkin: court physician for Tsar Nicholas II; he went into exile with the Romanovs following the 1917 Russian revolution and was murdered with the family at age 53.

long will we go on like this? The revolution has made us into executioners—it may be holy executioners, but executioners. No, I will not do this anymore, I can't do it again. To kill defenseless people—no, I can't do it again!'"

"It was a short time later," Kaganitski continued with his story, "that Zhelezniakov broke with the party. He went to Ukraine, participated in groups and was considered as operating outside the law. He was felled by a White bullet against whom he was fighting. I cannot forget him," Kaganitski concluded his tale. "When the history is written, he will certainly be reviled. Yet he was a man of the people, a folk hero with a great soul. Let us drink to his memory!"

He was the first to lift a full glass of vodka and like one very thirsty, drank it down. All around him also drank, but without desire.

THE INDIVIDUAL IS NOTHING

The second of January, 1923, I came to work a half hour early as usual. This time I met many of my comrades waiting. Everyone's spirits were very happy and people greeted me with a "good morning!"—friendlier than the entire time of our shared work.

As I would do each day, I went down to the basement to review the boilers and see that they were in order. A certain Zabolev worked there, who supervised the woodcutters and boilers. He was a retired soldier and always had something to share about the army. His dream was to become a military commissar. He came over to me, looking around him to make sure no one was listening, and in a quiet voice that was absolutely not his custom, said to me, "You know, Comrade Yakob Leontevitsh,[161] they are intending to press charges against you."

"Who?" I asked him, surprised.

"Now there, the devil knows who," he said. "I'm not allowed to say this to you, only since I know that you're innocent, I'm telling you that in Mestkam (the local party committee) they intend to accuse you." I understood that someone had it in for me, and I was prepared for anything.

A few days later in the early morning, I received a telephone message that I should come directly to Mestkam. I went there right away and arriving at the administrative office, the secretary said to me that there were three accusations against me. I stared at him in astonishment: "A total of three?"

---

161 Leontevitsh is the Russian version of "son of Leon."

"Yes. You're accused of hindering the professional movement, of consciously ignoring the statutes of the Moscow soviet and also, that you have a religious approach to the workers. You must therefore present a written declaration to the Mestkam secretariat within three days."

I told the secretary that the charges were a way to mock me, and if he demanded a written declaration, I wanted a written accusation. It was clear to me that this had to do with my taking a stand with the few words I gave at the Narpit congress.

Knowing that it would be hard for this to end well, I went off to Comrade Kantarovitsh and told him the whole story. He promised to be present when the official charges were brought against me. I also had a good friend, a party leader, Kotliar, who was then a member of the Control Commission. He was certain of my innocence and he pledged to me that he would teach some manners to the Mestkam society. Bagaploski, the chairman of the GPU and Narkomindel who had often worked with me in America in the professional movement, also promised to defend me against the unfounded accusations. However, my close friends were very worried because we knew that in the best of cases, people facing such charges could come out badly, being sent to Siberia for three years and it would be very questionable that they ever return.

The three days passed and everything was quiet. Meanwhile, our factory received a letter from the Special Workers and Peasants Commission that reviewed the progress of enterprises, stating that it had found everything in our system to be in the best of shape—from the technical to the hygienic to the financial. My management was praised in the letter and in such a difficult moment, this meant the world to me.

Several days later, I was summoned again to Mestkam. This time the entire staff of Mestkam was assembled, and a hearing began. The chairman of the meeting was a member of the Moscow soviet, Comrade Berenshteyn, who was a nephew of Leon Trotsky. Kantarovitsh, Bagaploski from the GPU and Kotliar, who I mentioned earlier, had already arrived.

I summoned up my courage and gave a wide and bold greeting to all; seeing my three friends, I felt more confident. The secretary read the threefold accusation against me: 1) Religious approach: regarding the holiday of Christ's birthday, on the preceding day I gave the workers a week off, 2) At the Narpit congress I spoke out against the professional unions and severely damaged their prestige, and 3) While the Moscow soviet ordered that factories should not be shut down during the holidays, I closed the enterprise for more than a week. [Sentence incomplete as published]¹⁶² in a counter-revolutionary act that could end with a visit to the GPU, so I merely responded to the charges.

To the first part of the accusation, I referred to Lunatsharski and Dzerzhinsky. The first had released the students for a month before the New Year, and the second had given them free opportunities to travel by train. If they, as high commissars had acted thusly, no one else could be accused either.

About not obeying the soviet decree, I turned to the representative in attendance from the Moscow soviet with a question: Did he think that a laundry was a factory or a plant? In my opinion, it was no more than an enterprise that served but did not produce. The interest of the venture was in making sure that all establishments that were under the supervision of Byurobin should be served on time and that all hotels and restaurants have clean laundry, and if I didn't do it this way, as we had done with the unanimity and satisfaction of the workers, we would still have work left over for the next year.

Listening to my defense, the soviet representative made a declaration that I didn't understand the point of the decree, but he admitted that the behavior in this case was a [*word unknown*¹⁶³], that is, I behaved like a manager who understands the interests of his business.

To the third accusation about impeding the professional movement, I had a little more trouble. Yet since the first two were unfounded, the third could also possibly be overturned. I explained that as an anarcho-syndicalist, I had very little interest in the political struggle and what interested me more was the professional movement. I was perhaps unjust in my critique, but I had not been in the country long and per my observations, the foundation in the unions was an unhealthy one. I cited an example from our venture, where the several dozen workers didn't know their union or its responsibilities and it fell to me, as their representative and manager simultaneously, to deduct their dues from their wages and take them to the union. It would be much better if they themselves were in contact with their union and had obligations

---

162 Translator's Note: words missing at beginning of this sentence. We may guess that Abrams (Eybrams) was tempted to explain his general outlook but knew that if he did so, he would be suspected of counter-revolution. Therefore he restricted himself merely to answering the charges.

163 Yiddish word possibly of Russian origin: *pozoistvene/pozaistvene*

to it. Perhaps it wasn't correct, I added, but I said it at a congress where the representatives were present so they could contemplate the modus operandi of their organizations. For this reason, it could not be construed that I wanted to damage the prestige of the professional movement.

After ending with this, I noticed that the chairman and his colleagues looked at each other, giving me the clear impression that they didn't find a reason to punish me. Several minutes later, the representative of the Moscow soviet turned to me with the following words:

"You can return to work, comrade, only I want to point out to you that we live in a land of collective life and you must consult with Mestkam for each action. For us in Soviet lands," he lectured me further, "disorder cannot rule. It is anti-socialist to do things without consulting the authorities; that is why they have been created. This is not capitalistic America, the land of individualism and economic despotism. The wheels of our lives are moved through the collective strength. The collective is the boss and the individual is his servant," he concluded.

I listened to his chastising speech, which had the characteristics of a dressing-down and let me know that here there was no room for other ideas and made it clear that the party knows all, not the individual. I thanked him for the remarks and quietly saying good-bye, left the hall of the meeting.

My spirits were very depressed. The hearing and even more, the insincere speech of the soviet representative made a crushing impression. I felt that they wanted to turn each person into a robot, a compliant and non-thinking creature.

The improvised trial against me that was so poorly sewn with basting stitches sobered me up from my former defense of all actions in the Soviet land. It was clear to me that those who had prepared the accusations didn't even believe them themselves; that this was only a means that had been brought to bear against many people to break anyone who manifests his own insight of things, and expresses a thought according to how his conscience dictates.

In the new Russia, this was already not tolerated. The slogan was that the individual is nothing, the collective is everything. This must lead to a people who have lost their individuality and become slaves to prescribed formulas.

For a person with a free nature, this was a difficult conclusion to accept, and the thought ripened in me that sometimes one must abandon this land of one's hopes. In the meantime, one must join in and go along with the flow until he is able to find himself on the other side of the border.

Walking around with such ideas, I didn't go to work the second half of the day. I hadn't told my friends the entire story, and sharing the experience with my closest friend, we came to the decision that the best thing would be to find employment outside of a soviet institution. Being independent of state obligations, I thought to myself, would also make it easy to leave when the time came.

WE'RE THROWN OUT OF OUR APARTMENT

There was a group of anarcho-syndicalists in Moscow under the name Golos Truda.[164] The group was founded back in New York and there published a Russian weekly newspaper under the same name. They led diverse activities among the Russian workers there and after the revolution, the activists of the group went off to Russia, taking with them the machines. In Petrograd, as the capital of Russia was then called, under the direction of Bill Shatov[165] they developed a committed activism and began publishing the *Golos Truda* daily.

It was the same revolutionary fervor: Bill Shatov and his entire group threw themselves with all their energy into the movement and became fascinated with the revolution. Bill Shatov was a man full of energy; he became a military commander and led the battle against the Whites with much devotion. The entire group of Golos Truda was at the front lines in battle. The printing shop fell apart, and the Petrograd soviet took away the linotypes.

Later, the members of the group (no longer any of them Americans), took up their work in Moscow. They had a promise from the soviet that they would be helped, because during the funeral of anarchy theorist Pyotr Alexeyevich Kropotkin,[166] in his speech at the side of the open grave Kamenev[167] had declared that in the name of the soviet, all works by Kropotkin and also by Mikhail Bakunin[168] would be published.

---

164 Russian: Voice of Labor.

165 William Shatov: Russian immigrant in New York City who returned to Russia after the 1917 revolution.

166 Pyotr Alexeyevich Kropotkin: Russian geographer, activist, evolutionary theorist, philosopher, writer, and prominent anarchist.

167 Lev Borisovich Kamenev: a Bolshevik revolutionary and prominent Soviet politician, he was one of the seven members of the first Politburo.

168 Mikhail Alexandrovich Bakunin: Russian revolutionary anarchist, and founder of collectivist anarchism.

When I arrived in Moscow, I became a member of the group and in my free time would help them at the Golos Truda, which had a book business.

When the group decided to bring the machines from Leningrad and to begin itself printing the books that we had planned, I took on the technical installation of this venture. It was arranged for several representatives of the group to see Kamenev and Kalinin[169] and through them receive the permit for the printing shop, relying on the fact that the printing shop was being founded to fulfill the promise Kamenev made at Kropotkin's grave. After the request was made to them, it turned out that first the group must go to the GPU and Guplit. If they were refused, then Kamenev and Kalinin would take the matter into their own hands.

Naturally, long weeks and months passed around the question of the permit. It was neither permitted nor denied. Meanwhile, I worked at the Byurobin. No one made any more problems for me and the laundry functioned quite well.

In the middle of May 1923, we received a communication from the Moscow soviet that we could open the printing shop without the permit from the GPU. The latter said that it was not at all against the shop, but didn't want to give it an official permit. If we wanted, we could work.

We started making all the preparations right away. I began looking for a way to be released from my position. I spoke with the manager from the Comintern and showed how the laundry was already running so smoothly that I had almost nothing to do, and requested that he release me from the work.

As soon as we received the permits, we began setting up the printing shop. Procuring the means for the project proved to be easier than we thought. We had people everywhere who sympathized with us, and they gladly helped us out. One of our friends was the director of Prombank and he lent us a sum of money, provided that once the printing shop was operational, we would pay him back with work in whatever the institution needed.

Yet I was not able to be discharged from my job. The printing shop was already set up and people working there, but the manager for Byurobin, Lee, complained that in Russia one doesn't quit a job on his own. If I wanted to do this, he told me, then I should know that I would lose my quarters. This was, in these days of a lack of housing, the worst of punishments.

---

169   Mikhail Ivanovich Kalinin: Bolshevik revolutionary and later Stalinist functionary who served as the nominal head of state of Russia.

My comrades at Golos Truda reproached me. I would come every day and help with the work, but this was not enough. There was no printer, they must have me there, and their demand was that I quit the job in the laundry and pay the price.

The fifteenth of May, I willingly abandoned my post and didn't work for two weeks. Meanwhile I didn't work at the printing shop either, so no blame would be tied to them. Lee sent for me and warned me, but I held my ground. I pointed out to him that after the two weeks of my absence everything was in even better order, and that no harm would be done because I switched to the printing shop. He paid me my wages for the two weeks and told me to look in advance for a place to live, because in a few days I would be evicted from the room.

This is indeed what happened. Two days later, two men from the militsiya[170] arrived with an order to evict us from the room and before we even managed to look around, our things were already lying in the corridor. I didn't react much to the malevolent treatment but it greatly upset my friend Mary, and she said loudly to the executors that even in the imperial times the gendarmes treated people civilly. They were taken aback a bit and gave the excuse that they weren't to blame, and that they must carry out the order to evict us from the apartment.

We pushed our few rags together in a corner of the corridor and began thinking what to do. Here with us was another victim, one who was himself the commandant of the house and also removed from his residence for a similar crime. He had a family with a small child; frightened by all the commotion, that night the child became feverish. We didn't close our eyes all night and felt enormous pity for the child, who shrieked and groaned. We forgot about our own trouble, and in the morning I went off to the agencies to find a home for the Shat family and their sick child. Wherever I went, no one would help me. I was told that I could speak only for myself and I shouldn't mix in someone else's affairs. Yet my worry for the child would not let me rest. I went to see Kantarovitsh and after talking with him for a long time, I convinced him that they should be allocated quarters. Several days later the Shat family was taken to an old, dilapidated house. Since he was an electro-

---

170 Russian (also militia): the official name of the civilian police in the former Soviet Union after 1917.

technician and a good architect, with hard work he repaired the old, damp walls and the floor, and settled in with his wife and child.

We "lived" for a short time in the corridor and then having persuaded the house commandant to keep an eye on our bundles, we ourselves moved into the room of our friend Perkus. They were already cramped without us, but one has to cope. Just in case this wasn't enough, at that moment my cousin from the States unexpectedly arrived with her husband as tourists. He was one of the many who from afar staunchly defended the Soviet system and arriving here, they could find no other place to stay in Moscow but with us. We brought them in to Perkus' room and at night it looked like a barracks. In a small room that served as kitchen, dining room and bedroom slept together a group of six, and every corner was full of hands and feet.

"Well, friend," I said to my cousin's husband, "When you go back to New York, will you return with news of how people live here?" He categorically answered me that he would in no circumstances do this, because it wasn't important; the only important thing was the ideas. It was good to hear him speak this way, because in a few weeks he would have to return to America. I understood him completely and thought that "happy is the believer, for who even bad things become transformed into good ones."

Thus went by the days and weeks. Getting a place to live was impossible. Coming from work, we would sit in the corridor by our things and think dark thoughts. One time as we sat in the corridor a neighbor arrived, Florenski. A former colonel in the imperial army, he now worked as ceremony master for the Foreign Commissariat. He lived in the same house in a three-room apartment with all the comforts and my room, which was next to his, had been given over to him.

Florenski was a tall, slim man, elegantly dressed with a military dignity, and he was perfectly suited for his job. I already knew him from earlier and when he entered the corridor, I asked him if it was proper that he should get a fourth room at the expense of two people who now languished in the corridor for long weeks. Why I said it to him I don't know myself, only that when the heart is bitter, it speaks the bitterness.

The ceremony master listened to my question and with complete courtesy, bringing his feet together in military posture, bowed and answered me: "Comrade, Moscow is crowded —people are going out to the village where there are places to live." When I explained to him that in the village I couldn't earn any money, he said, "To earn a living—for this each person must fend for himself." He turned around, snapped his heels together and went off to his spacious apartment, not wanting, apparently, to hear more of such talk.

It was impossible for me to start work, because I spent the entire day dragging myself around from one office to another to get a note with which one could receive a room. One of my acquaintances advised me that I should go complain to the procurator; they would put me back in my old room or order that I be given another. I went to see the procurator from the Moscow soviet tribunal and told him the entire story. He agreed with me that they were not permitted to evict me from my room. I filled out a sheet of paper, paid two rubles for the stamps it required, and left with the promise that a week later the thing would be taken care of.

After the week the procurator informed me that I needed to go to the housing agency where he had sent my request, and there it would be taken care of. When I arrived at the agency, there was a line of people so wide and long that if they were taking care of ten people per hour, I would be seen a few weeks later. I tried getting in line, realizing that it was a dream to receive quarters through the housing agency. It just so happened that an acquaintance of mine from New York passed by, Nikolai Hurvitsh, the son of Yitskhak-Ayzik Hurvitsh, who then occupied a high position in the GPU. We greeted each other as old friends, started talking, and he offered to help me in my efforts. A few minutes later, I was already in the office of the housing agency.

It happened that there was only one girl in the office and the manager was not there at all. The girl explained to me that I would need to wait because he was at a meeting; meanwhile, she would find my request. Barely an hour later the manager came, a young man with curly hair. He spoke Russian with a Lithuanian accent and began questioning me about what was going on. I explained to him and he started studying my papers, at the same time making the face of a "big shot." He got up to speed on the entire matter and went to speak by telephone with my previous manager. After long proceedings, he told me that he could do nothing for me. At the same time, he emphasized that he could do a lot, only not for me.

To my question why he couldn't do anything for me, he answered that he was not obligated to explain it to me. Yet he soon added, "You must know yourself that your membership in a movement that we think is detestable is enough that you shouldn't come to us for any help."

I replied to him that maybe this was his personal opinion because, as it is known, the people from our movement had brought not a little to the revolution and had suffered before and suffer now for it, in very many foreign lands.

"If that is so, comrade," he said to me, "why don't you join the party? That would eliminate all your difficulties." I explained to him that we didn't think that people can serve the revolution being in only one party; what people need is to understand the tasks of the revolution and serve it faithfully. A member-booklet from the party was far from being a diploma in revolutionary understanding.

With my statement, the head of the housing agency lost his patience and told me forcefully, "If you don't want to receive free room and board, you would do better to renounce the counter-revolutionary opinions while there's still time. You can go. We have no time to listen to the disciples of the capitalistic equality and anarchist liberty." He stood up from his chair and simply asked me to leave his office.

After the encounter with the official powers that were tasked with procuring apartments for the homeless, I no longer looked for help from them. The only thing left to me to do was raise several hundred rubles (ducats); with money you could obtain a room no matter whether you belonged to the party or not. I knew that on Kremlevskaya a house was being rebuilt and that you could get a space in the corridor to build a room. I went there, and the manager of the Kremlevskaya commune read my recommendations and told me to bring three hundred rubles.

I gathered together what was for me a huge sum, and got a room of twelve square arshin[171] per the established regulations for living space for two persons.

After almost six weeks being homeless in the corridor, getting our own corner effectively turned into a holiday. Our friends rejoiced with us like at a poor couple's wedding.

However, the trauma from the six weeks of being homeless in the corridor, the hunt for a room, the seeing and feeling how people are tossed about like a piece of useless furniture, the not knowing where to turn, listening to each narrow-minded clerk's threats and being called a counter-revolutionary for

---

171 Archaic Russian measurement: a Russian cubit, equal to exactly twenty-eight inches.

the slightest trifle—this brought me to the thought that for now people must pick out the best from the worst and that in the end, they will probably have to seek an opportunity to extricate themselves from the prison life that the bureaucracy has created in the country.

WITH AN AMERICAN PRESS COMMISSION IN NIZHNY NOVGOROD

Due to my cautiousness, I was not yet able to begin working at the printing shop of Golos Truda. The situation there became dismal. The provisional manager Gerosimchik was no expert, and although he had much devotion, he could not control the enterprise.

Gerosimchik had claim to me and demanded that I come to work. However, he also saw that this could bring me harm, because he understood better than I did the circumstances of those days. He was a Petrograd Russian, an active revolutionary who had fought for the revolution for long years with a machine gun in his hand, and had a bitter hatred for the GPU and their methods. Being a man who knew no fear, he would curse out each GPU agent in the famous Russian folk language.

Finally, our group in Moscow decided to let the summer pass and then bring me in to the work. Then I could no longer be reproached for usurping a position against the will of the authorities. Until then, I began coming in from time to time and helping out in the printing shop.

Meanwhile, it was hard to go several months without work and I looked for something to do. I would often come into the Foreign Commissariat where I had many friends and acquaintances—and also to show that I was not working somewhere else. One day as I came into the Byurobin administrative offices, the manager Lee greeted me with a broad "good morning" and asked if I would like to travel to Nizhny Novgorod as translator with an American press commission that was here. "You'll be well paid for this," he emphasized.

I seized on the offer with both hands, first because the trip was in itself interesting. Second, I would indeed also earn some money; and third, to see for my first time an important Russian city that had a name for its large markets and fairs.

The press commission consisted of three people: Paul Blanshard,[172] the

---

172   Paul Beecher Blanshard: American author and assistant editor of *The Nation* magazine who was an attorney and socialist.

later commissioner of New York City during the LaGuardia administration; his wife, who was also a correspondent; and the third was a representative of the "Amalgamated Union"[173] (tailors) in America. Lee immediately contacted the manager of the Hotel Savoy where they were staying and told him that he was sending me over there to the commission, with whom I would need to get in contact about the journey to Nizhny Novgorod.

When I entered the hotel administrative offices, in addition to the manager I met a man whose face immediately gave away who he was. Before the manager even told me to sit down, the GPU representative was already asking me from where I knew the commission. I calmly answered him that I didn't know them and didn't even know who they were, to tell the truth. "If so, what is your interest in traveling with foreign people?" I, being already used to how every Soviet person is investigated at each step, answered that my interest was no more than what I would earn as a translator as had been proposed to me by Comrade Lee, who knew that I was fluent in English.

The questioning began: from where did I know English, and if I came from America, why didn't I know such important people who had been sent in a commission, etc. Wanting to convince himself that I really did know English, the guy turned to me with questions asked in a mutilated English that were hard for me to understand. I avenged myself on him by starting to speak very quickly in English: my young man quickly switched back to Russian. After a long enough investigation, he explained openly that the reason for this was that if someone knew the foreigners, he would not be allowed to be with them, because due to familiarity and trust he could say something that it would have been better not to.

Afterwards the hotel manager took me in to the head of the commission and introduced me as the person who would accompany them to Nizhny Novgorod.

Blanshard was the kind of American who was very comfortable with people and quickly becomes good brothers. He was a talented correspondent and feared not even the devil himself. We conversed together easily. It turned out that he was a socialist and that we had mutual acquaintances. If my earlier interrogator had known this, he would not have allowed me to be

---

173 The Amalgamated Clothing Workers of America (ACWA) was a labor union formed in the United States in 1914.

their translator and travel together with them. Blanshard said that he would have preferred to travel alone and without an escort except that he trusted me, because he remembered well the story of my trial in America. We quickly became friends and the same day we had already dined together. I experienced the taste of eating what an American is served who brings a few dollars, and to whom must be given the impression that here flows milk and honey.

The second day we went off to the train that travels to Nizhny. It was nine o'clock at night; we were traveling in the international railroad car. The distribution of the railroad cars was not as before—first, second and third class—just Hard and Soft,[174] and the first car was called the International. Besides us, there were only two or three people in the car, among them a Jew and an Armenian. The facilities were completely modern and clean. Before the train moved from its spot, a young man came in. He was elegantly dressed and from his appearance, was an Anglo-Saxon. He was however, a Russian and an official. He laid the small valise he carried on the shelf and seated himself opposite it, stretching his legs out on another bench. He took a small book from his pocket and began reading.

The train began traveling and each of us occupied ourselves. No one noticed how someone pushed a curved wire in through the window, hooked the valise, and pulled it out. However the owner did suddenly see it at the last moment and quick as lightening, he dashed from the compartment and began running after the person who had dragged out the valise. The fellow jumped down from the railroad car. A commotion broke out; someone hit the brake and the train came to a standstill. We went out on the platform and a while later we saw being led a boy with the valise, with such a battered face that it looked more like a piece of bloody meat than a face.

We went back inside the railroad car and everyone was upset at the act of "lynch-justice." Yet no one knew whom they were dealing with and therefore all were silent. The only one who couldn't tolerate the crime of beating a boy, was Paul Blanchard. He protested in English against the inhumane treatment. The man who was responsible for the beating answered sharply also in English, and a quarrel broke out between them. I got in between them and knowing that the man with the valise was a government courier, I

---

174 The word "class" was avoided after the revolution: Hard was crowded with wooden benches; Soft was more akin to a first or second class fare.

explained to him that Blanshard was a member of a foreign press commission; that he came from America, etc. Hearing this, the man switched from being aggressive to being defensive; that if he lost the valise, it had important papers inside it and he would have personally suffered much. He asked me to make sure that the correspondents not make a mess of this. "The Americans don't understand this but you, as one of ours, know what this means," he said to me.

The courier left our railroad car after that and the other passengers were happy that he had received such a dressing-down from Blanshard. I then told Blanshard what kind of mission the man was on and that had he lost the valise, he would have had a bullet put in his head and for that reason he mustn't be blamed. At the same time I gave him to understand that he must not put me in a bad situation either and to not write a word about this, because this would bring me harm also. Blanshard gave a smile and said, "What a terrible state we're in with socialism."

Our neighbors in the car hadn't lifted their eyes from the Americans. I sensed that they longed to ask me something, but they were afraid. They spoke between themselves, saying that they must be great American people. The Jew in our compartment added a remark that he wished several score thousands of Americans would come, so that our officials would become more humane to the Russian people.

The train pulled in to Nizhny Novgorod the next morning. A commission of the local press was assembled on the platform to welcome the American guests. It was easy to spot us in the crowd because of the clothing the Americans were wearing (I also still had my American garments on); we looked like millionaires among beggars. People immediately surrounded us to welcome us. With the reception commission was also a certain man named Minkin, who was once in America and spoke English. He was now a chief agent for the GPU and supposedly had worked in Latin American countries. Finding out that the Americans had come with a translator from Moscow he pulled back, leaving the job of translating to me.

We were taken to the most beautiful hotel, which bore the name Soviet Hotel. Blanshard, being himself a shrewd newspaperman, said to me as soon as we were across the threshold of the hotel that people would certainly come for a press interview; I must now say that today the Americans wouldn't be taking any interviews because they were tired from traveling and wanted to rest. So it went indeed. A half hour later, a representative of the Nizhny

Novgorod *Pravda*[175] came to speak with the chief of the press commission and with the American guests. I explained to him that they were resting now and couldn't be seen.

The colleague from the *Pravda* was very insistent, and I went to Blanshard in his room to tell him. Both he and the other correspondents gave different excuses and avoided a press interview.

Yet the next day, a conversation with the Americans was published in the local *Pravda*, in which the writer said that the enthusiasm of the American correspondents for Russia was indescribable.

Around four o'clock that same day, a messenger arrived from Malishev, the president of the annual bazaar, with an invitation for the commission to visit the bazaar. We were soon off to see the bazaar that had been world-famous for many years, since under the Romanovs. The street that led to the bazaar was heavily guarded by militia who knew of our arrival. All of them gave us a military greeting, pulling up straight as arrows when we passed by. They believed that there was no greater honor than to give a military salute and never imagined that to radical journalists from America, it made a bad impression. Blanshard remarked to me that from his observations, Russia was one large barracks.

Malishev was a typical Great Russian,[176] with a long red beard cut in the authentic Russian manner, and his red cheeks flushed with blood. He received the commission with a smile, delighted that these Americans were coming to him to see the bazaar. We sat down and through my mediation as translator, the conversation began.

Blanshard's wife was a pretty woman with a bright and beaming face and Malishev, it seemed, was captivated by this fine and elegant lady. He greedily stared right in her face the entire time. We talked about the bazaar and about Russia, and he never took his eyes off her. She asked me to say to Malishev that something must be wrong with his eyes because they stayed in one spot and never moved ... but I pretended not to notice and didn't translate her remark.

At the end of the discussion Malishev, who didn't know what to say to

---

175 Russian: *Truth*.

176 Great Russia: obsolete name formerly applied to the land native to ethnic Russians that formed the core of the principality of Moscow and then later, Russia.

the political questions, said that at eight o'clock that evening a banquet was being held for the commission at the main pavilion of the bazaar and many representatives would be present: the city soviet, etc. We took our leave and went off to prepare for the evening's reception.

When we arrived at the hall all the guests, among them the cream of the crop of the party, were already assembled. Minkin was also there, and he sat at the main table where places had been prepared for the American commission.

When we walked in, we were welcomed with *The Internationale* being played by the orchestra and solemnly sung by everyone there, with earnest faces and with rapture. We also stopped and stood tall singing with them, and I felt that this made a strong impression on the guests.

The commission was presented as American friends of the revolution to all the important guests. After a half hour of informal greetings and handshaking, we sat down to the table that had been prepared with such splendor that even in wealthy America, it would have been thought of as excessive. They had prepared the finest dishes and wine; schnapps and champagne were made ready as if for a royal reception. Things quickly became friendly and pleasurable. The orchestra played and the crowd sang cheerfully. On the stage appeared a few dozen girls in gypsy dresses and with drums in their hands; in the genuine Russian tradition they danced and acted out old romances. It was a pleasure to see and hear how skillfully they danced.

Everyone, certainly including the Americans, was carried away with the mood. People drank and enjoyed themselves as only Russian people can. It was also noticeable who had been designated to provide the guests with intellectual food, because none of them were drinking. The Americans also drank very little, but they enjoyed everything immensely.

Minkin sat and his sharp eyes observed everything that happened. I didn't understand his conduct back then, but years later when I bumped into him in Mexico it had already become clear to me.

During the course of the festivities people brought different gifts to the table: fine things from handmade workmanship, spoons used by the aristocracy, cigarette cases, etc. Yet each time, the gifts disappeared quickly from the table. Nothing was received by the guests, who were the intended recipients.

The speeches and welcoming statements began. After each speech by a representative of the soviet I had the task of translating it into English, and the audience applauded as much for me as for the speakers. It was then

Malishev's turn, the chairman of the Nizhny Novgorod bazaar. The simple "Russki" delivered an illogical, irrelevant speech that stuck like a pea to a wall. He spent the entire time lashing out at the Comintern and equating it with all kinds of terrors: the Comintern will do away with everyone; the Comintern is a ... etc.

Among those assembled, it was Minkin who more than anyone else burned red-hot at the idiocy. The American commission glanced at each other and didn't understand what was going on. They didn't know Russian, but they heard the malevolence with which he repeated the word "Comintern" over and over, which was after all, an international term.

I made notes in accordance with the speech and decided to myself that I would not translate Malishev's speech and since he had kept on shouting "Comintern," I would use that word often, but in a different way. Minkin was running around the hall, not knowing what to do. Meanwhile, I got up to give the translation.

With my words I gave a completely different speech, saying to the commission that it must pass on through the press that the task of the Comintern was the preparation of a new order, that the Comintern would show the world how great the capability of the worker was when he received the industries in his hands, and that the proletariat, with help from the political authorities, was capable of building a better order than capitalism, that the Comintern was an intellectual apparatus to instruct humanity, that no one need fear the Comintern, and that they shouldn't listen when its enemies defame it as a destructive organism.

When I finished, Minkin sat next to me. His face was radiant and he asked me if I was a party member. When he heard that I was not, he expressed his regret. "But be that as it may," he said to me. "Comrade Abrams, you salvaged the situation and with your words, you also rescued Malishev. I will let it go this time, and your speech will be written to his account.

When Minkin let Malishev know what I did for him he embraced me enthusiastically, because he knew what Minkin could do to him. "When I go to America," Malishev said to me, "I will bring you as translator."

We profited greatly by my having saved the situation with my translation: the local authorities and the Nizhny Novgorod GPU already had confidence in us, and the rest of the time we could move about freely.

One time when traveling down the Volga on a yacht that the soviet had placed at our disposal, Blanshard called out: "We've already spent enough time by ourselves; it's time we see what is really happening in Russia. The banquets, gypsy choruses and yachts are not what interest us here." As we moved down the river, we saw in the distance a village on a hill overlooking the Volga. We asked the boat captain to take us in that direction, and we went up to the village.

For the first few minutes the impoverished Russian village gave the impression of being abandoned; no one was seen on the dirt road or at the small houses with thatched roofs. We walked up and back, looking for someone with whom to talk. Little by little the residents, noticing us through the small square windows, came out in front of their houses and watched the distinguished guests walking around the village. Peasant men and women with small children wearing short, filthy shirts that barely covered their little bodies, watched us in astonishment.

We stopped at one of the houses. An old peasant woman with a face full of wrinkles greeted us good-naturedly. We asked if we could be given a bit of water to drink. "This we still have here," she answered with drawn-out words, "thank God." She invited us into her little house. The "Amalgamated" representative was a woman to whom the Master of the Universe had not stinted in height and she, poor thing, had to stoop over to crawl in through the little door.

Blanshard told me to ask the peasant woman to make Russian tea. When I explained what the American aristocrat wanted, she answered that she had neither sugar nor tea, but she did have a samovar that was from former days. If we wanted boiling water she could make it, and they could buy the necessary things in the cooperative. The hut was perfectly clean and tidy inside; the floor was smeared with brown clay, the window panes pasted over with green sheets, and the wooden bench that served for all requirements was covered with a sack that had many holes.

The peasant woman told one of her grandchildren to set up the samovar, and sat herself down opposite us. Her dress was ample and coarse. We struck up a conversation with her, but the years of the dictatorship-system had taught even such peasants to be diplomatic. To a hundred questions she answered one, and it was also not always to what was asked.

Only to the question of which tsar was better: the former Nikolai or the current Kalinin, did she smile, and pleased that she was asked this, said,

"Certainly the current one. That one, he came by our region and only the noblemen were able to see him, but the Kalinin, the new tsar, came to us some time back when there was a great hunger and he went barefoot out in the fields with the peasants ..."

Certainly he is better than Nikolai, I said to her, and the peasant woman answered, "Yes, better, but you can't put him in the oven; you can't bake bread from him ..."

Not waiting for the tea we looked for an excuse to go, gave the woman several rubles in addition to those we had given earlier to buy sugar and tea at the cooperative, and left the hut. The peasant woman accompanied us with a thousand blessings on her lips, crossed herself and gave thanks.

When we began going down the hill to our boat, the entire village stood on the hill and watched us go. Blanshard said that this "banquet" was more important to him than the earlier one, and he would not forget it. "I will keep in mind," he said, "that we overseas must now help the part of Russian that has no sugar and no tea; not that part with gypsy choruses and banquets."

WHEN PEOPLE WORK WITHOUT BUREAUCRACY

The short journey as translator for the American commission came to an end. I delivered the Americans back to Byurobin in Moscow, and with that my task in the soviet position was fulfilled.

Immediately afterwards I was off to the Golos Truda printing shop—and reported for work. My friends there received me with open arms. The management briefed me that the printing shop unfortunately had no work. They had printed several books in the meantime, but there was nothing with which to pay wages.

Everyone who worked at the Golos Truda printing shop and book business was Russian, our own people. For me it was not hard to put together an improved work system because I was after all called an American, and in such cases this was a big advantage. In many government institutions there were Americans in important positions, and this gave me the prospect of getting in touch with them easily and talking with them.

I received a great deal of help from the Prombank in Moscow that was well run by a certain Krasnoshtshokov, who was called Tobins in America and whom I knew well. Krasnoshtshokov was a good fellow and he joined the party only after coming to Russia. He hadn't forgotten that we had often worked together for the same cause, and he could see that our enterprise had the best of intentions. A man with much talent and energy, he had organized the Prombank on the same basis as the banks functioned in America and he had remained as director of the bank, which supplied credit to many ventures.

Familiarizing himself with the goals of Golos Truda and hearing out my plan to improve the work, he first ordered everyone that the printing work for the Prombank should be sent over to us, with the condition that we would do it for twenty percent cheaper than the Moscow "Printing Shop No. 27." Yet even with this the price was very good for us, because the bureaucratic machine of the "Printing Shop No. 27" gobbled capital and the work could be done for 550 percent cheaper. Krasnoshtshokov also gave us an advance of five thousand chervonets[177] rubles to be paid off in several months, as the work of the printing shop amounted to between five and seven thousand rubles monthly. We were able to set about the work immediately, and we established several agreements with offices where all the work was entrusted to us.

The workers at Golos Truda were owed several weeks wages, and they were indifferent to their work. I promised them that Saturday everyone would be paid what they were owed, but it appeared that they didn't believe it. Gerosimchik, my friend and director of the printing shop, looked at me in surprise when I advised him that on Saturdays everyone would work only until one o'clock. He, the Muscovite, couldn't understand how it could be that people would work fewer hours and do more work. Nonetheless, as I had by that time had several successes over the last few days, he went along with me.

The first Saturday arrived. We called together all the workers at two o'clock, and first paid everyone what they were owed. Moreover, we didn't pay them in Soviet "sovznaks"[178] that had meager worth on the market, but in chervonets. Then we proposed that people begin doubling the production and this would lead to us being able to double our wages. Everyone listened and with joyful faces expressed their consent. "Good," answered one worker, Lavrushik, in everyone's name. "We have learned, truthfully, to not believe in the promises made to us, but he is an American, we know, and a new broom sweeps clean ..."

---

177 Russian currency in both paper and coin form that was backed by the gold standard.
178 Sovznaks: promissory notes issued in Soviet Russia in 1919 and used during War Communism.

We did everything we could to win the trust of all the employees, some fifty men in the printing shop. Across the street was a Greek restaurant where they charged seventy-five kopecks for a meal. We made an agreement with the restaurateur that all our printers paid only sixty kopecks and we guaranteed him the money. Moreover, everybody received coupons from Golos Truda for the food portions and six portions a month were free, paid for by the proceeds of the enterprise. This in itself was already an increase in wages.

The workers saw that it was no bluff that the work and profits could be improved, and in several weeks the entire situation was changed. In place of the old Russian "Let's have a smoke"—the workers getting together and lighting up, letting the machines remain idle to the extent that they were doing half the work that a machine could produce, people began giving the full measure to the work and sometimes even more.

Golos Truda quickly got a reputation in Moscow as a place where the workers earned twice as much, worked fewer hours (we worked a half-day on Saturdays) and that the printing shop charged cheaper prices for the work. There were no miracles here, only that we succeeded in abolishing the bureaucratic system and to truly work as if for ourselves. In a very short time, we worked two full shifts.

The book publishing began doing good business and because of the revenue we could publish up to six books a month; publishing books was the objective of the entire venture. Yet it was very hard to sell the books, because there was no free market. We had made an agreement with Gosizdat[179] (its director was Stoyanov, who had long been in that sphere) and through his assistance with the distribution, we began procuring revenues from books.

The enormous difficulty, however, came from a completely different source. The censor was very powerful and many books, famous works, were not allowed to be printed. Much time would be needed to struggle with getting a permit and when the GPU finally provided one, the amount of books allowed to be printed was such a small number that it was impossible to publish. Books such as Professor Mechnikov's *Civilization and Great Rivers*,[180] a famous social-revolutionary work of several hundred pages that

---

179 The Soviet publishing house.

180 *La civilisation et les grands fleuves historiques (Civilization and Great Historical Rivers)* by Ilya Ilyich Mechnikov (also Elie Metchnikoff): a Russian zoologist best known by the epithet "father of natural immunity" for his pioneering research into the immune system.

was banned by the imperial government; now the GPU would permit no more than five hundred copies of it to be produced. Naturally, of course, with such books we were forced to commit "crimes" and print with one more zero: instead of 500: 5,000.

Additionally, as was typical, it didn't please the GPU that they had no control of Golos Truda and we were often searched. From August 1923 until Lenin's death in January 1924, the GPU searched us perhaps a hundred times, and although they never found anything undue, each time they would let us know that the printing shop would be closed. Each time we would have to go to Kamenev and he would rescue us.

I BECOME A HOUSE MANAGER

In the new quarters that I bought for three hundred rubles, I lived with a completely high class of people. The house was once the palace of a Moscow merchant. The house had been divided into two parts: the foremost side, which once had fifteen rooms, had been made into forty and upstairs, where the employees and servants of the merchant had lived, it was also reordered, into thirty-two rooms.

In the first wing lived exclusively party activists, the majority of whom were placed at the Kremlin. The house was located on Kremlevskaya Naberezhnaya 9, and it was very convenient for the officials of the Kremlin and from the VTsIK, which was also close by. In the upper part generally lived the mere mortals, but by chance I ended up in the first wing.

In the house there remained only traces of its former wealth and luxury; for the most part, it looked like a stable. The general heating had been dismantled because the house commissar had declared that the bricks from the great oven could serve for building a few rooms. The neighbors had to find little ovens to heat each room, and in the quarters it became even more cramped and filthy from the heating materials that each person had to keep in some quantity in the house.

The chairman of the house, which was called the Kremlin Commune, was the druggist of the Kremlin, Tshelnitski. His position was high enough that he was the spokesman over everyone. I became friendly with him and he sometimes listened to a word from an American. Once I suggested to him that since there was a small bedroom between both corridors and a bathroom could be put there, perhaps there could be a plan that the neighbors could talk over for putting in a bath. "If you can do it, I'll allow you," he answered me.

The bath was installed and we paid twenty-five kopecks a month for the collective heating. The neighbors were extremely pleased. We talked for a long time about making improvements in the house, until the point where Tshelnitski suggested to me that I become the commandant and do as I saw fit for the house. I accepted the position and became the house commandant. Receiving such epaulets, I began putting into effect plans to make small improvements in the house. The women helped out a great deal with this, and in a few months we all had many conveniences. We also created a sanitary commission and strenuously protected the cleanliness of all the rooms and around the house: it was forbidden to keep cats and dogs in the rooms, the floors were waxed, and everything took on another appearance. The neighbors would happily joke that they lived like the Americans.

The board of directors of the house would call for assemblies of the neighbors each month. In attendance would usually be more than a hundred people from the seventy-two households (the women would also come). I would very rarely attend the gatherings because I had already suffered once because of a residence and I thought to myself that here, in the land of the revolution, I should no longer be a public figure.

One evening in the month of December, three representatives of the board came into my room together with the chairman Tshelnitski and they let me know that at the neighborhood assembly that had just ended, I had been elected as the manager of the house with the same rights as the chairman. I could manage the house as I wanted, and Tshelnitski would be just the political director. He himself, the Kremlin druggist who was trusted to make the medicine for all the high-ranking community, was entrusting the position to me.

Put on the spot, I looked for an excuse to get out of the honor, but the delegation reasoned with me that the residents wanted it this way, and each must submit himself to the will of the collective. The individual had no right to refuse to fulfill a public duty. So I reminded myself that by refusing I had already one time spent six weeks languishing in the corridor, and it was better that I willingly agreed to accept the new post.

Had it not been for the "public duties" that I had to carry out for the position as if I were a police officer, the work would have been very gratifying.

As administrator, I instituted a policy that people shouldn't cook in the individual rooms, but rather in the large kitchen that I set up along with a comfortable bathroom and other conveniences that under the circumstances of that time, made life much easier. However, the second part—seeing to it that guests who came to visit the neighbors did not stay in the house, and to take their passports and send the courtyard supervisor to register them with the militsiya along with similar regulations of the bureaucratic type—this I did not care for.

It happened one time that one of our neighbors, Dr. Tsherbakov, a very distinguished communist and also one of the Kremlin physicians, received a guest. It was a man in his seventies, an old Bolshevik and professor of medicine at the University of Kharkov. The professor stayed a few days as a guest of Dr. Tsherbakov and out of respect for them, I didn't enforce the regulation to demand his passport. I understood that an elderly Bolshevik and professor should be treated as an honored guest.

A few days later I was called to the office of the party cell and was asked why I was not enforcing the law as was required for a house manager. I answered my interrogator with a joke that was then going around Russia about a house supervisor who stood outside in the morning in the pouring rain and sprayed the Moscow streets with water. A passer-by asked him, "What are you doing? It's raining so hard and you're standing here spraying the street."

The house inspector replied, "I have a decree to water the streets every morning, so I'm watering. A law is a law ..."

The cell leader laughed hearing the joke, and then I explained to him in earnest that I would do everything for the house commune, but I didn't want to become a police officer. It was pointed out to me that in this case it would allowed be overlooked and no fuss would be made, but I should remember in future that I was the one responsible for the house and must carry out all ordinances.

From this moment, I no longer wanted anything to do with the responsibility that had been put on me and I began looking for a way to get out of the position as quickly as possible.

REVOLUTIONARY VETERANS SPEAK TO ENGLISH LABOR LEADERS

The winter of 1923 in Moscow politically was a lively and interesting one. Lenin lay ill in Gorki Village near Moscow[181] and Stalin, who then occupied the position of Secretary of the Communist Party, saw an opportunity to seize a more powerful position for himself within the party. At that time it was known that there were twenty-eight thousand secretaries across the country and that all ate from Stalin's hand. The salary for a secretary was two hundred and seventy rubles, and with that sum one could live very well.

They served Stalin like slaves and were his flunkies. Stalin also ordered that the cells could send only the secretaries to congresses, and consequently each of his proposals would be passed by the congress one hundred percent.

The internal party conspiracy was carried out against Trotsky and his followers because they all knew that after Lenin, Trotsky was the man of the revolution and of the Soviet regime. Trotsky knew what was coming and since in addition to his position as War Commissar he also took a very active role in political life, he began a fight for democracy in the party. The public barely knew of Stalin; he began coming out to the forefront. On the contrary, Trotsky was wildly popular and this gave him the opportunity to carry the fight out in the public arena.

He commenced with an article in *The Pravda* under the heading, "Our Youth—the Thermometer of the Revolution." Like all his successful slogans and headlines, this too spread like a fire in a dry woods. Stalin began helping Kamenev, Zinoviev and others, and they put out a pamphlet against Trotsky.

A battle of pen and word began between the party and the government. In a book that Trotsky then published, *Lessons about the Labor Revolution*, he asserted that his opponents were cowards and that during October they—including Stalin—were for a coalition government.

In one day, the book sold forty thousand copies. The public masses were delighted; they were pleased by the war within the family.

On the second day, Stoyanov, the chairman of the Gosizdat, was arrested for publishing the book and the sale of it was halted. Trotsky wrote a letter of protest but *The Pravda*, whose editor was Steklov, refused to print it.

Everywhere in Moscow, in all the factories and clubs, heated debates were taking place. Things were lively and tempestuous. Each objective observer

---

181   Gorki Leninskiye: a work settlement lying 10 kilometers south of Moscow city limits.

felt that the great majority were on Trotsky's side. One morning, the news came out that Trotsky was sick and must depart for Crimea for treatment. Frunze[182] would become the provisional War Commissar.

Everyone knew that this was a diplomatic illness, but no one gave it much thought at the time. No one foresaw what would unfold from the internal quarrel.

* * *

At that time in Moscow there was a commission of the English Labor Party, headed by Ben Tillet. Among the commission was the leader of the clerks, John Turner,[183] who per his beliefs was an anarchist. Since Lipman, my friend from New York, was his official translator, he introduced me to Turner.

Turner was a man of more than sixty years old, strongly built, a true labor activist who had served the movement for over forty years. He wanted to see the unofficial side of the situation and while conversing, told me that he would like to meet with Vera Figner,[184] Morozov[185] and other old revolutionaries.

Vera Figner and a group of praiseworthy revolutionaries would often get together at the Kropotkin Museum.[186] In normal times, to meet them would be an easy thing; now it was a risky venture. The museum was under the supervision of our group, but we did know that we were merely managers. We advised Turner that he should approach the museum office and explain that as he was an anarchist, he wanted to see the Kropotkin Museum; we would make sure that during his visit, the people he wanted to meet would be there.

And so it was. A few days later, we were told that on Friday evening at six o'clock, the English guest Turner would visit the museum. In a few days we had prepared everything, and our friend Professor Borovoy took it on

---

182 Mikhail Vasilyevich Frunze: Bolshevik leader and a key Red Army commander during the Russian Civil War.

183 John Turner: an English-born anarcho-communist shop steward and organizer of British clerks who traveled to Russia after the revolution as part of the British Labor Delegation.

184 Vera Nikolayevna Figner: a Russian revolutionary whose memoirs, *Memoirs of a Revolutionist*, published after the revolution, is still considered one of the best examples of the Russian memoir genre.

185 Nikolai Alexandrovich Morozov: a Russian revolutionary who after spending twenty-five years in prison turned his abilities to scientific research and teaching.

186 A house museum in the city of Dmitrov, Moscow region of Russia, the home where anarchist Pyotr Alekseevich Kropotkin lived the last years of his life.

himself to arrange things so that nothing looked suspicious. At the appointed time, the old gang assembled at the Kropotkin Museum dressed in the nicest clothes that they could put together. The eighty-year old Vera Figner was dressed up in a black dress with white cuffs and aside from the wrinkles on her face, she looked the same as she did years ago as a student in Zurich.

Turner came alone; the authorities wanted to demonstrate to him that he could move about freely. However, the chauffeur of the automobile that brought him was Tomski, the son of the elder Tomski, who quietly served as a high official in the GPU. We knew, of course, why Tomski had been sent as the chauffeur of the car, but Turner had no idea of this. We were annoyed that not an unguarded word could be spoken, because Tomski also understood English.

The night was very cold. Before entering the museum premises with Turner, the chauffeur and GPU agent covered the motor with a large Russian fur coat so that it wouldn't freeze. When he came in, he sat down at the table without waiting to be invited and let it be known that he could not stay for more than an hour with Turner, because he must return.

During the ensuing conversation, the young Tomski often broke into the conversation and helped out with remarks. Of course it was difficult to speak about what Turner was interested in hearing from the people. We were afraid that the entire get-together would bring us problems later if Tomski interpreted it negatively.

We looked for a way that we could get the chauffeur away from the table for a little while. A good idea occurred to us: we went down to the street and pushed the fur coat down off the car motor, thinking that if the motor froze, Tomski would have a few hours work in front of him to get it running again; meanwhile in the museum above, Turner could talk without having an evil eye at his side.

Indeed this is how it went. The hour was over, and Tomski told Turner that he was going down to start the machine because it was already time to leave. When he had gone out, we let the group know that they could sit peacefully and chat—he would not be returning so quickly.

So during the time that the GPU official Tomski was scrambling trying to get the machine running—heating water, shaking the motor, etc.—the old revolutionaries who were sitting in the museum area with Turner began sharing their impressions about what was taking place in Russia, and what could be expected in the future.

The first one to speak was the old revolutionary, eighty-year old Vera Figner: the courageous woman who had spent more than twenty years in the notorious Shlisselburg fortress.[187] She not only spoke with disappointment; in her words it could be plainly felt that she had lost her faith in the revolution and quite simply regretted the lost years of the struggle. She concluded by saying that the man had not yet been born to implement in real life the changes that he created in his mind, that the processes of change were very long, and that it was a shame for the individual to sacrifice himself for it.

One of us stood by the door the entire time to make sure that Tomski didn't return. One person who had helped him in a front room to warm water for the radiator performed miracles: the longer the bucket stood in the oven and was heated, the colder the water became.

The last of the group to speak was the old revolutionary and Communard, Ashenbrener. He was about ninety years old at the time and was, it was thought, the last of the Communards[188] who had taken part in the battle at the barricades during the Paris Commune. He lived long enough to see the day that the revolution broke out in Russia and came here to the land where it was declared that after seventy years, the fight of the French Communards was not in vain.

The old Ashenbrener shared his feelings about the time when he was young and then told of how with a heart full of hope, he came from Genoa, Italy, to Russia after the October revolution. Yet immediately after the second and third week of the revolt, the annihilation of the revolutionary ideals began. He then turned to describing how nowadays, his students and friends were sitting in Siberia and in prisons. "The revolution has been liquidated long ago and in its place surprisingly, are committed the greatest crimes. Behold we sit here; we who have wasted away so many years in prisons; we never had a peaceful day and each night slept in a different bed, and now, in the land where the soil for the revolution was prepared by us, we have fewer rights than in the pre-revolutionary times."

The old Ashenbrener spoke the entire time with tears in his eyes, and he suddenly broke into tears and could speak no further. Everyone there fell into a

---

187 A medieval city located east of St. Petersburg that was turned into a fortress and for a time, a prison.
188 French: members and supporters of the Paris Commune, a reactionary provisional government that ruled Paris for several months in 1871.

very dark mood. Tears glittered in everyone's eyes and we were seized by a dead stillness. I stood in a corner between a table and a cupboard of books. Tears choked me, seeing the bizarre, tragic scene of how the veterans of the revolution sat and bewailed their accomplishment. I felt as if the hopes of generations were lying wrapped like a corpse on the table, stiff, dead, with their idealists mourning them. For a short while, all sat silent with theirs heads hanging down.

It was Sofia Kropotkina, the wife of the renowned thinker and revolutionary, who extricated us from this dark mood. She was the "youngest" of her museum circle friends, because she was then only seventy-some years old. With beautiful English (she and Kropotkin had lived many years in London), she turned to those present, chiefly to Turner: "Beloved children," Sofia said, "let us drink a Russian glass of tea. The tea is not yet debased and is authentically Russian."

The atmosphere became a cheerful one. Vera Figner helped her bring it in, and the old revolutionaries began setting up the table and serving tea. People began talking together and it became happier. Several began joking at the expense of Tomski, Turner's GPU escort, who would no doubt say that given how the communist order was being so strongly praised, he didn't want to interrupt and for that reason stayed longer, because it was important that the English guest be influenced by the old revolutionaries. It felt like in the good times when people would be exultant that a Russian gendarme had been successfully tricked, and thus did a melancholy evening and a sad meeting become a lively banquet.

LENIN'S DEATH

Beginning in January 1924, a great disquiet was felt in Moscow. It was said in all circles that Lenin was seriously ill, and the doctors were afraid that a catastrophe would happen.

It was no secret why there was a panic due to Lenin's sickness. His severe illness had also created panic even among his opponents. Somehow it was sensed that the death of Lenin would bring bad times.

In that time, the hand of Stalin was already beginning to be felt. Trotsky had been sent to be "cured" in Crimea under the pretext that he was sick. Stoyanov had been locked up in prison. Moshke Fishelev of the government printing shop that had published an appeal from the opposition had been, together with his friends from the printing shop, banished to the Szuralski

Monastery. From there, it was known, no living person ever returned. Trotsky's Secretary of Military Issues, Opeltshinski, committed suicide; in short, the air was charged with dynamite.

On 22 January, 1924, at about five o'clock in the evening at a session that was taking place at the Soyuzav in honor of the English commission, Kalinin got up and explained that he must halt the session for an undetermined time and announce something important. It became silent as a graveyard and Kalinin said that the news had arrived that Lenin had died. At first all remained seated as if paralyzed, and then little by little they began leaving the hall.

A half hour later, the sad news had spread over all of Moscow and the streets became overflowing with people. The day was a terribly cold one; the freezing weather had reached thirty-some degrees, but this didn't keep thousands of people from besieging the editorial offices of *Izvestiya*[189] awaiting the first printed bulletin. The streets were flooded with people until late at night. All the talk and comments revolved around what people could expect in Russia after Lenin's death.

The entire week that Lenin lay in an open catafalque in the Soyuzav, almost no one went to work. Everything and everyone was preparing for the funeral, of which there had never before been anything like it. To get into the Soyuzav during the day to view the dead Lenin was impossible. For dozens of blocks stretched innumerable rows of people, hundreds of thousands from Moscow and from different cities and villages; from the farthest corners of Russia they came to catch a last glimpse of the man of the greatest of revolutions.

My companion Mary and I determined that we would go at night to see Lenin for the last time. Before dawn, about three o'clock, it was extremely dark and very cold—when we arrived at the Soyuzav, we realized that we were not the only geniuses with this bright idea. Hundreds of people were standing in the queues, but it turned out that it was easier after all, to get up to the building.

Entering the hall, you got the sense that not just Lenin had died, but that something more was going to the grave with him. The people from his close circle, those who had worked with Lenin in exile and after that together had brought about the great transformation—they stood around the catafalque,

---

189 Russian: *News*; historically important Russian daily newspaper published in Moscow; it was the official national publication of the Soviet government until 1991.

despondent in mourning, and as if lost. During those days, Stalin did not appear in the light of day. There were many giant rallies during that time; all the leaders of the revolution made appearances, the exception being Stalin. People knew that he sought to usurp power and a rumor went around that he was supposed to have said before Lenin's death that there was nothing more to be heard from Lenin because he had not been in his right mind for a long time, and this Stalin was supposed to have said at a time when everywhere in Russia, Lenin's word was law.

On the day of the funeral, there was not a wheel turning anywhere in Russia. The streets in Moscow were full of troops and delegations from all corners of the land. All the unions and delegations had their places in the funeral procession.

Our group of anarchists in Moscow, although we hardly ever conducted any political activity, decided to take an official part in the funeral. The only question was what type of slogan we should inscribe on our banner. One of our Russian friends proposed that our banner should be red and black and the inscription read: "We honor the Lenin of 1917–1918."

The proposal was accepted. I confess that I was the only one in the group against it. I knew that for such a slogan, if we were allowed to come up to the Red Square, we would later be made to pay. Yet since the entire group was in agreement with the proposal, I abstained from voting. All our comrades maintained that never mind the consequences; as anarchists, we could not show up with any other slogan.

During the procession, our group along with our banner drew everyone's attention. On every street, people read the inscription and we saw how people commented on it. About three o'clock in the afternoon, we arrived at the Red Square and passed by the catafalque where the high members of the government and soviet stood as honor guards.

We tilted the banner before the casket. Above us, some of the honor guards read the inscription. From the daises above, they looked us over from head to toe. At that moment, I perceived that this would be the end of the group. If they did not use any type of retaliation, I thought to myself, they would just not let us publish any more books. At the same time, there was the satisfaction that there was a group of people who at such a moment found their courage and through one short slogan had separated Lenin the revolutionary and thinker, from Lenin the government man.

THE GROUP GOLOS TRUDA BECOMES LIQUIDATED

After Lenin's funeral, our group met together at the Kropotkin Museum, where we would always have our get-togethers. We discussed the question about what would result from carrying the banner with the inscription "the Lenin of 1917." We were all certain that they would not keep silent with us about it. We anticipated that they would pour out their wrath first on several members of the group, and then later would come the general blow.

We couldn't decide how to handle it in such a case. The only thing we could do was to be prepared for the retaliation that the GPU would bring to bear against us in the near future.

Aside from the printing shop that I mentioned in the earlier chapters, we also had a cooperative book business that helped us greatly to sell the books we would publish ourselves. In addition we had a permit to buy and sell old books, but this we had to do under the strict control of the GPU. For each book that we bought, we had to write down the title and also the name and address of the person from whom we bought the book. It was the same when people came to us to buy old books; they must also give us their names and addresses.

Therefore, we didn't care much for the business of old books. We were in the habit of whenever someone would come to sell or buy a book, we would explain to him the procedure that must be followed. If he agreed, we made a transaction with him. In the case that someone would show apprehension, we would inform him that he should go to another place, if such a one existed.

The business of old books was not a bad one. Among our best customers were the high Bolshevist leaders and officials. Even Kaminev and Lunatsharski would come to us looking for an old book, and they too had to comply with the demand from the GPU to write down what they bought. Every month a commission from the GPU would come to visit us and make a copy of the list of the transactions. They would also look over the books that stood on our shelves, and with every search they would confiscate several books. We would try to rescue the books from confiscation, but it would never succeed. We were able only to get them to give us a receipt for the confiscated books, as our friend Gerosimchik suspected that the agents sold the books somewhere else, then sent other agents there to confiscate our confiscated books, thus conducting themselves in accordance with the new line from NEP which was then popular.

Several weeks after our participation in the funeral with our group's banner and inscription, we noticed that the demand for old books had gotten stronger. Many unfamiliar people were coming in to buy books. They would select some, search and then not buy, not wanting to provide their names. As we suspected something, we didn't sell any books to the new customers who had unexpectedly shown up and not knowing what their motives were, we treated everyone equally with suspicion. We would answer as to what type of books we carried and would no longer advise the customer as we did earlier, that he would be required to provide his name and address.

Thus, for several weeks there would be many requests for books yet we would rarely sell one. It turned out that they were trying to catch us in a crime but due to our prudence, they didn't find anything. One day a wagon with GPU agents pulled up to our bookstore, placed themselves in every corner, and one of the agents asked for the manager. By chance I was in the bookstore and since Professor Borovoy, our manager, wasn't present, I replied that I managed the printing shop and also partially the bookstore. The chief agent courteously requested that I give him a complete list of all old books and with an agreeable "let's keep this friendly," ordered that the doors be shut and no customer be allowed in until they were finished with selecting books that had counter-revolutionary content. At the same time, he served me a decree signed by Dirbasov, one of Dzerzhinski's deputies, to confiscate all old books as he found necessary.

Among the books were old dictionaries and textbooks for which no permit was required and they could be freely bought and sold. Without sorting through them, the agents began carrying off all the books to the wagon. I protested and specifically pointed out that the dictionaries could not contain any sort of inappropriate material.

"These are old books?" the leader of the inspection asked me. "Yes? So then, why are you bothering me? In the decree it states that all the old books must be confiscated, that's the end of it." With that our conflict was ended, because I realized that they were not looking for counter-revolutionary items here; that was only a pretext.

In accordance with the receipt the books were diligently counted; they loaded them onto the wagon and shut it, leaving behind a written document stating that the books had been confiscated because of the counter-revolutionary content. Politely taking their leave, they told us that the right to further sell old books had not been taken from us ...

When our "comrades" from the GPU left, we looked at each other and exchanging a few words, came to the conclusion that this was the beginning of the end.

We decided to decline the privilege of buying old books and be spared all the difficulties. Yet to simply refuse was not an easy thing, because this could be interpreted as sabotage. We would do it this way: when people would come in with an old book, we would say that we had no money or that the cashier was not there.

During the next month, when the GPU came by to see how many books we had, they found nothing and the agents reported that Golos Truda did not buy any books. In the following days suspicious persons began coming with old books but we did not buy any of them, explaining to them that since we were not being able to sell any books because the majority of them had been confiscated, we didn't have any money.

A short time after that, when I arrived at the printing shop I was met with complete disarray, above all in the administrative office where everything had been upended. The only thing that lay untouched in its place was my briefcase, which had not even been opened. The laborers who worked during the night shift reported that a search was carried out in their presence and that the briefcase had not been opened because one of the investigators, seeing my name on the briefcase, ordered that the lock not be forced because he knew who the owner was and that there was nothing suspicious inside.

I immediately surmised who the inspectors were—that one of them was Bogopolski or Ondreytshin, both of them my close friends from America who knew of our work for Soviet Russia. It was also clear to me that we were answering for the inscription on our banner and that we had ruined all of our work.

It was soon apparent that a rigorous investigation had been done on our book business. They had also turned the scrutiny on a number of individual friends; among them my comrade Rubintshik who had been arrested on the charge of taking part in the Kronstadt rebellion[190] that had occurred several

---

190 An unsuccessful uprising against the Bolsheviks towards the end of the Russian Civil War that began at the Kronstadt naval fortress.

years earlier. At the Kropotkin museum, we were informed that each person who comes out of the museum would be photographed. The matter had taken on a serious tone; they had begun liquidating us as a group.

That evening I went to see one of my former friends, now a high GPU commissar. He received me with a wide smile and asked, "What kind of wind has brought you here? What distresses you?" From his words, I could tell that he knew of us being investigated and of Rubintshik's arrest. His wife, comrade Bushvik, a disheveled but good woman, brought in tea and without standing on ceremony, we got right to the point.

"Yakob," he said to me, "I know how you will look at this, but this is how it is. Your activity, such as it is, must stop. I can assure you that you will not be harmed and you will spare yourself a fuss. Be content they are not picking on you. My advice would be that you leave the printing shop and go visit somewhere for a few weeks until everything calms down, and perhaps then you'll be able to continue your work. For none of you in the printing shop are being considered as a counter-revolutionary."

"So why has Rubintshik been arrested?" I asked him.

"If he wants to go free, he needs to write a letter to the *Pravda* that he renounces his friends and former ideas and they will release him. Rubintshik is a man who can be very useful, and he is not allowed to be outside the party."

Rubintshik broke only after six months, and then he was released.

We were being squeezed from all sides and we could no longer work normally. For example, this is what happened to me: I happened to be in the professional unions building, where the Profintern[191] agency was also located. The building was enormous, and inside everything was buzzing like a beehive. The hallways were full of secretaries, delegations and clients. Doors opened and shut like eyelids blinking. A thousand people went through there every hour and were furnished with documents—or were refused to receive such. The place teemed with activity and people.

As I was going down one of the numerous staircases, a man stopped me and asked quietly if I knew where the Jewish anarchist Hersh could be found, who had returned from Siberia not long ago, from where he had allegedly escaped. I looked at the man who put such an odd question to none other than me, and replied that he could find out from Lozovski in the secretariat

---

191 The Red International of Labor Unions, also known as Profintern, was established by the Communist International with the aim of coordinating Communist activities within trade unions.

of the Profintern, because everyone who comes to Moscow reports there. He said that they didn't know either—he had already asked there—but it seemed to him that I did know ...

So I gave him no more answers and started back down the steps. When I came out of the building, I bumped into the fellow again and he began walking alongside me, turning to me with a question: "Have you been in Moscow long? Are you a foreigner, or born in Russia?"

By this point he had already annoyed me and I answered with a summary of my biography, at the end even adding that I had been in Moscow for several years, was a member of the soviet anarcho-syndicalist group Golos Truda and that I lived at Kremlevskaya Naberezhnaya 9.

The young man stopped speechless, hearing my third answer. He looked me up and down and didn't know what else to say. I gave him a cordial "See you later" and quickly left. When I turned back to see if he was still following me, I didn't see him but arriving at the house where I lived, I spotted him standing there leaning against the fence of a nearby house.

Of course this didn't add to my desire to work under such conditions.

A JOURNEY TO THE CITY OF MY CHILDHOOD

The entire time that I was in Russia, I had a strong yearning to revisit the city in which during my youth I had become connected to the political socialist movement.

For me, the city of Uman remained like a magical tale. It was the place where I first became socially aware and discovered that man is a world unto himself and must construct that world as his conscience dictates to him. It was in Uman that I first experienced the taste of prison, and I remembered that even though I was hungry, I was happy in Uman.

I often dreamed of being in Uman again, to look up my friends with whom I would meet in the Greek forest[192] in the Empress' Park, and with whom I worked at the underground printing shop of the orchardists who studied at the agronomy school.

In April 1924, my dream became a reality. One day that month, I departed from Moscow to my former kingdom, which with the happiness that I had known there was dearer to me than anywhere in America.

---

192 Many of the themes in the Empress' Park were based on Greek mythology.

I arrived at the railway more than an hour early—so great was my impatience. On the platform where the train stood, there was not yet anyone else there and I paced up and down, greatly preoccupied with the thought that I would soon travel to Uman. Crossing my mind were the sixteen long years, since 1908, that I had not been there. A series of images of those years, of my friends, of how the streets appeared and how I remembered them, bits and pieces of the past, were running through my mind.

My ticket was for soft (second) class. The compartment was for two people; my bag was a small one and when I entered the railroad car, I didn't even think it necessary to find my spot. With my small satchel and camera equipment, I remained standing by the first window in the train corridor. My only companion to the train station was my friend Mary, and through the window we chatted about the happy moment of traveling to see Uman.

The train finally moved. After a few minutes, Moscow with her buildings and suburbs disappeared from view. I went into the compartment. The other passenger in the compartment was a young woman. Her appearance was that of a soviet woman, but vestiges of the old regime were visible on her. She was a woman of approximately thirty years old. Entering the compartment, I greeted my neighbor as was the fashion, and she, the passenger, displayed scarcely any eagerness at all about my arrival. I occupied the second spot opposite my neighbor, made myself comfortable, opened a book, and we sat there opposite each other like an angry couple. The Russian trains are like the Russian people: they don't rush themselves; if not today, then tomorrow, one will eventually get there. Also, despite the fact that it was supposed to have been an express train, at every station and sub-station the train gave a heavy pant, let out a bit of steam with a huge racket, and came to a stop.

Night began falling. The conductor entered to check the tickets and let us know that at the next station, the train would stop for a half hour and people could get off and grab a snack. I was not even hungry, but getting off the train and eating at the buffet in the depot with the bustle and the many people was in itself enticing, and during all the years that I had been in Russia, I would never let such an opportunity pass by. As soon as the train came to a stop, I went down to the station for a bit of pleasure.

The small depot was brightly lit throughout. The tables were covered with white tablecloths, waiters were going around ready to serve, and the food that had been prepared was also available.

I hung around for a considerable time, bought something in the buffet and observed the public at the depot, noting that the majority of them were just officials and military personnel of different ranks.

My neighbor stayed in the car. When I came back to the compartment from the depot, she was sitting with a box of candy on her lap and was eating. This time she broke her silence and asked me if there was anything to eat at the buffet in the depot. To my reply of yes, she said, "Times change; you can't get something to eat like before." A word for a word—we stopped being strangers and became friendly.

More than anything else, my young lady was very excited to hear that I had been in America for many years. She kept asking me questions about America, and rapturously told me that she truly loved to hear about America and that she would offer half the years of her life to live there.

Inasmuch as she kept questioning me about America, I remained cautious and in contrast to her enthusiasm, displayed less delight with America. I didn't know who she was and I had seen that it never hurt to be cautious.

The young lady could see why I was speaking in such a way; nonetheless she kept on pulling information from me about America. The entire railroad car was already asleep and we were still talking about everything with America and life there until I pointed to my watch and promised that tomorrow we would continue; meanwhile, it was time to get some rest.

With a coquettish smile, my neighbor told me to turn around to the wall so she could get ready for bed. After a few minutes, she let me know she was done. I turned off the lamp in the compartment and lay down but even so, for a long time while already lying on the bench she kept asking me questions and half-asleep, I had to answer her. Exhausted from a long day, it seems that I fell asleep while my young lady was still talking because the next morning when I woke up, she responded coldly to my "Good morning." She remained angry, and for the rest of the journey to Kiev we barely spoke.

The train arrived at Koziatyn on schedule, where I had to change trains for the one to Uman. At the station, I was informed that the train had left a half hour ago; from the depot they told me that the next train to Uman would depart in twenty-four hours. Such soviet wisdom I could not understand. Why the train from Koziatyn, a small station, would leave a half hour before the train from Kiev arrived and then you had to wait twenty-four hours for the next one—no one could explain this to me.

There were a few people at the depot and among them, my eye fell on a man with a beard who from his clothing appeared to be a Ukrainian peasant. As there was no buffet, I went up to the man to ask if he knew where one could get a glass of tea there.

He looked me up and down. My American clothes had intimidated him, but when he heard that I spoke Russian he felt more confident and answered that he could provide me with tea and also a bite to eat and a place to spend the night, as he himself had an inn nearby. Even though it wasn't for high-class guests, he told me, by chance this week he had done a yearly cleaning for the holiday and I would have a clean spot.

Since this was Passover time, I saw that I was dealing with a Jew. I acted as if I had no idea and put the question to him, "What kind of holiday is it for you here in Koziatyn?"

Whether the peasant Jew could tell from my question what my intention was or not, he answered me, "It is the Jewish holiday of Easter, do you understand?"

"I understand," I replied. "It's understood. I'm also a Jew," I told him in Yiddish.

Here I saw how a weight fell from his heart. "So," he said, "you are probably from America." I told the Jew that I was from Moscow, but he kept to his own conclusions. "One can see that you were in America; where would you see such a coat with us? Moreover your hat and an epaulet." As he spoke, he contemplated my attire from head to foot and then jumped as if startled. "Oy vey, how will you reach my inn without galoshes? Do you think this is Moscow? Here the mud is up to your knees."

"Perhaps," I said to the Jew, "there is a coachman here and we can ride over there."

"Thank God," he said. "There are a couple of coachmen who die three times a day from hunger."

He left and brought back a Jewish driver with a worn-out little horse. That one made the first move and requested a ruble for the short journey, adding, "It is indeed close, but kind sir, one is burdened with many children and needs bread for everyone."

The Jew's inn truly was clean, tidied up and with the smell of Passover. The mistress of the inn soon came in, set up the samovar and sat down at the table to have a word with the remarkable visitor, as her husband had whispered in her ear that this was an American.

"Sir," she said to me, "You will probably also want to eat something?"

"Of course," I said.

"Then what shall I do?" she said. "You'll probably want bread. I will slip out and bring some—but you no doubt know that today is Passover; perhaps you would like some Passover dishes. I have prepared the best of Passover food; in case you don't, I will make you something leavened." This woman, at the same time as she spoke the word for the prohibited leavened food, actually trembled that I might say that I wanted that and nothing else.

"You know what, my dear Auntie," I said to her, "you bring me what you've prepared. I like Passover food quite well and I haven't tasted it in Moscow for a long time."

"Naturally!" the innkeeper clapped his hands together and there were even tears in his eyes. "I knew right away that you were no commissar."

"How do you know," I asked, "that I am not, perhaps you guessed wrong?"

"My dear Jew," he said. "They are easy to recognize. They come here sometimes to spend the night, may no good Jew ever know them ..."

It turned out very well for me that I had done the Jewish woman a favor and tried her Passover treats. For the last several years that I had been in Russia, I had not yet seen such tasty dishes. The matzo balls melted in your mouth and they were both delighted that I enjoyed their food so much.

The bill that the Jew presented to me the next day before I left for the train was an inflated one: for the same money I could live in Moscow an entire week, but it was worth it. I paid him and on the Jew's advice, left for the train a few hours early so that I could get a better seat.

This morning, however, it was not necessary. No one had come to take the train because it was the second day of Passover and Koziatyn was a Jewish town.

I was almost the first one in the railroad car. I had paid for a second-class ticket from Moscow to Uman, but how would Moscow know that in Ukraine there was no second class? It was, after all, an independent republic. I climbed up to a top bench and made myself comfortable for the trip. At the subsequent stations there were indeed many passengers arriving from everywhere, and it turned into a large crowd. From my upper bench it was roomy; I stretched out and listened to the conversations among the passengers, keeping silent myself.

It was noisy the entire way. At one station where the train had stopped for thirty minutes, I got down to grab a glass of tea and coming back, I immediately saw signs that someone had tried to discover who was this strange person. The book that I had been reading and had left lying face down was now closed. It was an English book, and this had certainly aroused suspicion in the fellow travelers that I was a foreigner. I took my place again and the crowd, thinking that I didn't understand what they were saying, began speculating in Russian and Yiddish who I was. One of them said that I must be a delegate; a second, that I was probably a representative from another government. One, a young man with an impudent face and the appearance of a thief in a horse market, began cracking jokes with vulgar expressions at my expense. As everyone laughed, he began singing under his breath a prison song in which it was said that if it had been a few years ago, he would have yanked off the beautiful little overcoat from the big shot and thrown him out the window. Yet today is a different time, thieves have become respectable men—may they have such a year—and you're not supposed to …

I restrained myself from laughing, and everyone believed that I didn't know what he was singing and what was being said.

The train was finally approaching Uman. The crowd started heading towards the exit with their bundles; it became very congested on the train platform, even though the train was still moving. One of the passengers, feeling stronger than the rest, began pushing and shoving. My patience snapped and when he gave me a shove, I turned to him in Yiddish: "Reb Jew, why do you push like that? Everyone will get off the train when it comes to a stop."

The fellow stared at me with a pair of calves' eyes and everyone around was dumbfounded …

"What? You're a Jew? A wasted dream … And we thought that you were a mute or from a foreign land …"

Everyone already wanted to know who I was. They stopped pushing and began asking scores of questions. The train stopped. I didn't answer them and got out of the railroad car.

MY RETURN HOME

In Uman there once was a hotel that was called Hotel France. During my childhood, this hotel was an extraordinary place of enchantment. It was the most beautiful building in the city; the hallways of the hotel were adorned with flowers. Heavy red carpets lay on the steps and there was always a lot of coming and going. We, the little children, would stop to look into the corridor with curious eyes. The doorman would chase us with sticks and because he chased us, it made our curiosity even greater ... In the Hotel, I remembered, would stay the richest of guests: military personnel, great merchants, etc. Next to it was a bakery and in the windows would be displayed beautiful pastries; this would drive our gang of small fry to sinful thoughts.

Sitting on the droshky in the early morning, I was recalling all this and it occurred to me that I should stay at the Hotel France if it still existed. The driver told me that now it was called The Sovetov. To my question if they took in guests there, he answered that if one could pay, they would take you in. I decided to go to The Sovetov.

When I went inside the hotel, I saw that of the former wallpaper, flowerpots and total splendor, not a trace remained. The hallways were dirty and shabby, so were the rooms. Tables were broken, the beds looked like they were kept in a smoky kitchen, and the sheets were black—my disappointment was huge. Nothing to be done, I thought to myself. My childish fantasies of the Hotel France had come to nothing, like so many other dreams.

Despite the fact that I was tired from having spent the last twenty-four hours on the train, I couldn't go to sleep. My impatience and eagerness to see old friends as soon as possible after so many years being away from Uman, filled me with nervousness and I stood by the window and looked out, waiting for the city to wake up and rub the nocturnal sleep from her eyes.

Facing the hotel stood the old, big city theater. It once was the place where all the intellectual life of Uman happened. Students and revolutionaries would gather there to express their protests against the imperial order; it was the center of public life.

The theater would also be used for the circuses, and in my youth I spent many nights there. I knew every corner and every rear door, and I was a good brother with the employees, for whom I would run errands and help them out when a circus would come. Therefore I had the run of the place and would swim like a fish in water, bringing friends into the circus, and they would be looking at me as if I were the director of the city theater.

When the sun had gotten high enough, I went down from The Sovetov and began to seek former acquaintances. My first acquaintance was the theater, and I went up to it to tell it hello. Coming closer, it was as if something tore at my heart. The building looked like a skeleton with empty eye sockets; everything was torn up, shattered, not a single unbroken window ... I stopped by the open door; from inside streamed a deadened cold—and I pitied the theater as an old friend that had once given me so much pleasure. For a few minutes I stood and contemplated the remains of the pride of the city that now looked like a ruin, and then left to further seek my youth.

Aside from the poverty brought on by the civil war, almost nothing about the city had changed. I walked down the main street and came to the house where I once learned my occupation. Everything was as I remembered it, except for now there was a small paper business. When I went inside, I met my old boss Kniazshanksi, whom I recognized. He asked me what I needed, and I requested a small pocket-notepad. He didn't have one but he suggested a notebook, so I bought a notebook.

He looked very outdated and his gaze was no longer so angry; his eyes looking with fear at this new person. Keeping my eyes on the notebook, I asked Kniazshanski if he knew Refoyl the tinsmith from the city, and the following dialogue took place between us:

"What is Refoyl to you?"

"He's my uncle."

"Well then, you do know that he is no longer a tinsmith?"

"No, what is he now?"

"Oh, he is the chairman of the unions. And who are you?"

"I've been away from Uman for a long time and wanted to see my Uncle Refoyl."

"And do you know me?"

He fixed his eyes on me, wrinkled his brow and tried to recall me, walked around me, but nothing. I told him that in 1902 I had apprenticed with him and after the first year, he had broken my bones and expelled me because I, along with a few friends, had pulled out the pickled apples from the cellar ...

"Yakob!" the old man shouted out. "Oh my goodness, my heart was telling me that I'd seen you before, that it is you ..."

It quickly became a hubbub; he called in his entire household and thrilled, stood in the middle of them asking them, "Go ahead, do you recognize who this is?"

His two girls, Genye and Manye, were already grown women for whom time and the hardships of the past years had added to their age. They called out several names of acquaintances and of relatives in America, but no one could guess who I was. Finally he revealed to them that it was none other than Yakob, the one who was an apprentice and who had not let anyone go down the street ...

Now that everyone knew who I was, they embraced me, looked at me from all sides, and received me like a rich uncle. They led me into the house, sat me down at the table for a bite to eat and chewing, got me up to date on my old friends, those who were still alive. With each one they added that he was now a big important man, a communist. Above all, they went on at length about my Christian friend Milovanov, whose father was the city mayor and now he, the son, was the chairman of the city soviet. They praised him highly for his kindness and friendliness towards the Jews, saying that he had a good soul, that the Jewish communists were anti-Semitics compared to him, and that he himself was the opposite of his father.

"Well, and you?" Kniazshanski asked me. "You are probably also one of their own? Weren't you a firebrand in those days?" He was beside himself to hear that I was not a party member. "You are doing wrong," he said to me. "Once people didn't really need all these things, but these days, you should be one of theirs ..."

Towards evening that same day, all my old friends already knew that I was in town. The first ones to come see me were my comrades from my old job. We agreed that in the evening we would all get together at the printing shop that was a unification of all five printing shops that Uman had possessed earlier, called the Uman Typographic Department. With a small exception, all my former friends met together. Among them was my former boss Torodosh, from whom I had endured not a little in my youth. Now everybody, the printing shop owners and their workers, found themselves in the same situation.

Also in attendance was Milovanov, the then-chairman of the Uman soviet. He was not in our trade, but he was one of the former social democrats and we were close friends.

The reception was a very solemn and sincere one. They were all members of the party, but had kept in the same job and lived in brotherhood. Each one had something to tell and to remember about the old times in the underground work, where I, as the youngest, had been greatly utilized.

Milovanov was the first to speak and each one after him who gave a few words had, like Milovanov, concluded with a curse against America, where the people die of hunger and yet there they didn't want to go over to a Bolshevik order. I sat among my old friends, exultant that after so many years I had found them healthy and courageous. Finally, I was enjoined to say something about the new order. I spoke a few brief words, sidestepping having to speak directly about my impressions of Russia. I made only a few light remarks and was careful with my words. In a few general terms I defended America, where the people were not so common but telling my group about my deportation, I ended with an attack on American capitalism.

This resounded strongly with my companions. They worked out a plan for the next several days: where to take me, who would bring me, and everything to go see. They passed a resolution that in a few days I should appear on stage at the former city theater and give a greeting from the American labor movement. At the same time, they also carried a motion that I was a Ukrainian and didn't need to belong to Moscow, but that I should move there to Uman and work with the former guard, become a party member, etc.

Each one wanted that I should stay with him; I told them that since I was already staying at The Sovetov I would remain there for the next few days and no one would feel slighted.

Very early the next morning, there was a knock on my hotel room door. A boy of about twelve years old told me that his father, Menasheh Valshteyn, one of my friends, had sent him to invite me to breakfast. Menasheh and his wife received me warmly and the meal was one-hundred percent Passover food. Putting food on the table, his wife said with laughter: "To the Bolsheviks what is the Bolsheviks' and to God what is God's ... but if you want leavened food I will give you some bread, there's no shortage. We are not strictly observant but given that Passover is, after all Passover, what is the harm ...?"

Thus began a series of Passover meals to which I was invited by my former friends and now Bolsheviks. Uman was a Jewish city, and in every house Passover was reflected in all its splendor. I was taken from one house to the next, and in my entire life I have never eaten so many Passover dishes as I did that week in Uman with my friend Bolsheviks ...

Among the friends I once had was one called Froyke, who was very active. Yet after the revolution he didn't choose a side and did not mix in politics. When I asked after him, I was told that he was a traitor, a NEP-man, and that the friends had absolutely no respect for him. However, for me he was my old friend Froyke, and I went to meet him in his small paint shop that he had near the market. From the "business" and his appearance, I could tell what kind of NEP-man he was; he didn't have to tell me that he was in difficulties.

When I went in, he warmly hugged and kissed me, standing speechless, and then after several minutes stammering: "Were you not even afraid to come see me?"

After a short conversation, I already knew about his unfortunate economic situation, his opinion about the system and the grievances that he had against it. We understood each other, although I didn't agree with certain of his objections.

Since we wanted to speak freely, I suggested to him that we go together to eat lunch. He invited me to his house but since I had already eaten my fill of Passover dishes, I preferred to go to a restaurant. Froyke invited me to Mendl's restaurant, which was a household name in Uman. He, Mendl, had long since died, but Mrs. Mendl still kept the restaurant in the same spot where it had been when I left the city in 1908.

We took a small table in a corner and ordered a non-Passover lunch. As we sat and talked, the proprietress arrived and went straight over to us. She called me by my old name and drew it out as my stepmother would do: "Y a n k e l e."

"Do you remember me?" She clasped me to her, radiant. The woman was very old-fashioned but I surmised that she must be Mendl's wife. I had never heard her name, because she was always called by her husband's. I answered her that of course I knew who she was, that I remembered her, and that she was Mendl's wife.

The restaurant owner began reminiscing with me about the past. She launched into a long winding conversation, as if from a mill:

"Do you still remember what you had to put up with from your stepmother? I remember this very well, how many days you hadn't eaten and nights you hadn't slept ... oy, how it makes me happy that you look so good. I rejoice with you as I would with my own child, because more than once I quarreled with your father about why he allowed your stepmother to torment you so much during your young years. And more than once I fought with him, and was cursed for taking you into the kitchen and giving you a meal. Oy, what a pleasure!" she exclaimed at the end, coming over to me and giving me a heartfelt, motherly kiss on my forehead ...

Mrs. Mendl wiped the tears from her eyes, tears that were also choking me in my throat. I wanted to thank her, to say something—but I couldn't. I knew that if I tried to say one word, I would break out in tears like a small child ...

A crushing silence enveloped us, for my friend Froyke had also been touched by Mrs. Mendl's words, and we could no longer continue our conversation there. So we said good-bye to the woman; I thanked her with all my heart and we went out for a walk. We both spoke a lot. Froyke was very bitter about the way his one-time friends treated him, although his economic situation was worse than theirs. His disappointment had forced him into doing what he was now engaged in. So I tried to suggest to him that I step in and see if I could improve their relationship. Froyke wouldn't hear of this. With a bitter smile on his face, he said to me that it was already too late for him to be reconciled. The friends had publicly insulted him many times.

I was despondent as I left my friend Froyke. This is how a man is crushed in the socialist fatherland, and how many more are here, just like him? I went into my hotel to prepare for my presentation and this time, being prepared was extremely important to me. My friends had spent much time reasoning with me about what I should say. It was not hard for me to attack America, because even in the best of circumstances there were things to criticize in the American order. But the conclusion which they demanded of me—that only Soviet Russia would liberate all nations from their slavery, I could not then bring myself to express. I was able to say it with deep conviction when I was in America, but for the three years that I had now been in Russia, I yearned for a free world that would liberate Russia also.

Thus I lay on the bed, stared at the ceiling and constructed my thoughts for the presentation. A knock on the door interrupted my deliberations. An old Jewish woman with a young girl came in, and the first one said, "You certainly don't remember me, but I knew your father well and I want to ask you a favor. You come from America and you certainly won't stay here; when you go back, perhaps you could please have a talk with my son, so that he won't forget about us."

I replied to the woman that I was not going back to America and was staying in Russia, but in response to this, she replied that she understood what I meant and asked me if I could at least take a letter with me for her son. At the same time, the girl handed me an envelope with an address. I promised, and intended to mail the letter just to get rid of her. This was only the beginning and all the rest of the time I was in Uman, people came to me to give me letters to America and I had to stick stamps on them and send them through the post. I couldn't persuade anyone that I wasn't going back. One Jew said to me quite simply: "I know that you have to say things this way in order to make it easier for you to leave, there's nothing wrong with that—with these fellows, it has to be that way …"

About eight o'clock that night, I left for the meeting at the theater. The audience was already assembled. There was weak lighting in the hall and among the activists sitting on the stage, almost all my former friends were there. There was a red tablecloth on the table and by each person lay paper to write on, giving the impression of a courtroom.

Before everyone was seated, I had time to observe the audience through the half-darkness and to put together my thoughts. I knew that I had to be careful and not let my words cause trouble for me later on. After a while, the meeting began.

The chair was taken by the chairman of the soviet, Milovanov. When he stood up, so did everyone on the stage and in the hall, and they all began singing *The Internationale*. The choral chant made an impression and I felt flush, a mix of joy and personal sorrow that it was so hard to be a fellow believer as were so many of the audience.

Milovanov gave a short speech, introduced me as a former revolutionary, and concluded with a mountain of invectives aimed at the counter-revolutionaries in the country and abroad. After him, several others spoke in the same spirit; their simple talk excited the crowd and they were warmly applauded. I was the last to speak. The chairman noted that since I didn't know how to speak Ukrainian, I could speak in either Russian or Yiddish.

Given that almost all in attendance were Jewish, I spoke in Yiddish. I vented what was in my heart against the then-American government, spoke about the political victims that were being held in the prisons, and on other similar issues. I said nothing about Russia and this was the best course of action. I closed with the conclusion that the world would be happy when capitalism became abolished everywhere. My friends were very pleased.

After the meeting, we got together in a private home and by a kerosene lamp we debated for many hours about the meeting, about politics, and on different questions. The debate went so far that they began talking about the opposition, and some of them defended the opposition point of view. I played the part of the foreigner who knew nothing about what was happening with and against the opposition. The words that the Jew had said to me as he gave me the letter—that I did well to be silent, so that I could get away easier—stayed in my mind.

NO LONGER CHAIRMAN

After the assembly, there was nothing left for me to do in Uman. For the few days that I still had left there, I had become redundant to my former friends. We did still meet and talk, but I had the feeling that they would be happy when I went back to where I came from. They were afraid that something might happen with me because of my "anti-Soviet" temperament. A couple of days later, accompanied by several friends, I left for the train station.

There were no uplifting thoughts in my mind as I traveled to Moscow. Dozens and dozens of coincidences had made clear to me the crooked way in which the revolution was being directed.

The same week that I returned to Moscow, someone from the Kremlin Commune informed me that Tshelnitski, the Kremlin druggist, had submitted a demand to the house committee that ten of the residents who lived in the house wing be evicted for counter-revolutionary deeds. Given that per the regulations of the house management, no one could be thrown out without the decision of the entire committee and endorsed by the chairman of the committee—so my informant told me—there would be an assembly today and this must be carried out and adopted, because "You well know, that when he wants something, he makes it happen."

I knew that Tshelnitski could get his way, but it was hard for me to understand why he wanted to do it. I knew that the story of the counter-revolution was but a pretext. Among the people who lived in our wing of the house there were also several workers and the others were indeed NEP-people. Their money had been taken and their quarters built; at the same time they were charged such prices that many more quarters were built with the money ...

Here at our house the element of people were far from counter-revolutionary activity; they thanked God that no one picked on them. Yet since Tshelnitski had already most likely promised someone quarters, he fabricated the story about counter-revolutionary activity and wanted to clear out ten apartments.

The housing issues in Moscow in those days had created many headaches for the population. The different bureaucrats would throw people out of their apartment into the street, and then rent them another for a lot of money. Then the Moscow soviet issued a regulation that when there was an accusation against a neighbor, it must first be dealt with through the entire house committee and if it was decided to evict him from the apartment, the chairman must endorse the verdict and then review it in court, which had the last word on putting the accused out of his apartment.

At our house committee session of which I was the chairman, it was a stormy confrontation. The author and discoverer of the "counter-revolutionary" activity threatened that if he was not given this "trifle," he would also throw out of there anyone who hindered him from cleaning out the counter-revolution, and he would be punished for helping the counter-revolution.

I utilized my rights as chairman of the house committee and requested one small thing—that before I would endorse this, I wanted each of the accused neighbors to be summoned separately and heard out. It could be that of the ten, one or two of them were not mixed up in such things, so why should the innocent suffer for the guilty? If someone brought butter from Siberia and sold it for an inflated prize, I didn't know if this was counter-revolution. Or if one of them who had founded a small cosmetics factory for which he had been given a permit by the Measurement and Finance Department, it seemed that this was also not counter-revolution, etc. Therefore, I requested that each one be summoned and his case treated separately. "Otherwise I will not sign," I stated, "even if everyone is in favor of it."

Tshelnitski saw that he could do nothing with me and to execute this plan that he still wanted, he attacked by shouting that he, as chairman of the communist party cell of the house, would call a general assembly and there he would demand that his claim be seen through and the ten tenants thrown out of their rooms. This message was meant for me as a warning, but my reply was that if an assembly of all the neighbors would thus decide it was hopeless, when I was called into court I would still state the same arguments, and clarify why I did not want to allow the eviction before the people could be heard.

I didn't know how, but all those who were being threatened with losing their quarters—and because of this they were very anxious—found out what happened in the house committee. They also knew who it was that stood up for them and didn't want them to be treated unjustly. One of these neighbors stopped me one day in the street and told me that they knew everything and didn't know how to thank me for how I acted—for them, it was a salvation. I told him that in my opinion, they should all come to the assembly of the party cell that would take place in a few days. They shouldn't be afraid or panic, and answer the accusations. It could be, I said, that the members would not decide in favor of the unjust Tshelnitski and they would allow the tenants to stay in the rooms.

The ten accused did as I suggested and came to the assembly. There was Tshelnitski, the one behind it all, as chairman of the party cell and he tore into the ten neighbors with everything he had. According to what he claimed was happening, the entire counter-revolution of the world was taking place in our house and men must save themselves or face dire consequences.

The assembly all sat mute, as if they were turned to stone. Those who had not been involved were terrified and decided it was better to remain silent; those who had been accused sat even more terrified, with sorrow and worry peering out from their eyes. It came to the moment when a vote was about to be taken and the thing would have been finished. I made a suggestion:

"Since those whom they want to evict from the apartments are here in the hall, let all of them state how they spend their time and what their occupations are. If after hearing them out the assembly recognizes that they are involved with the counter-revolution, we will decide to hand the matter over to the court, and the court will then decree that they must be removed from the rooms."

"Correct!" exclaimed a woman, who by chance wasn't a NEP-man but worked as a doctor in a government hospital. Her exclamation revived the assembly, and the whole course of the meeting changed. The audience of neighbors, even several party members, opened their mouths and began talking. One of them even stated that the assembly was counter-revolutionary because per the last decree of the Moscow soviet, the party cell had no right to interfere in the functions of the house committee. When it did come to the point that yes, the cell must intervene, a representative of the soviet must also be present and he must lead the session so that everything be carried out without personal vendettas, etc.

From all sides the neighbors began shouting that the assembly was not lawful and should be postponed, and that a new one would be called when it was with the unanimity of the soviet. Tshelnitski, against his will, closed the assembly and the neighbors were saved from being thrown out into the street.

Yet with me Tshelnitski would soon get even. One time before a general assembly of the house residents, a delegation came to me and informed me that since everyone knew that sooner or later I would return to America, the house assembly had decided that at the assembly they would choose another chairman. At the same time they asked me what my opinion was of Shtsherbakov, who they definitely wanted to put forth as chairman.

Before I had time to answer, they had already said for me that I had no objections and that they had made a good choice. Since I had not previously known how I came to be elected as chairman of the house committee, so now it was better for me not to know how I came to be removed as chairman. I assured the delegation that they need look no further than Shtsherbakov and as for me, whether I went away or not, the position of chairman was not suited to me.

I was satisfied that I was rid of the chairmanship, but on the other hand, it vexed me that this Tshelnitski, an insignificant official, could amuse himself with people as he pleased and then make it seem as if everything was done correctly and even ... democratically. I didn't go to the assembly and thought long and hard about the fact that for a second time, I had heard from other people that I would emigrate; perhaps it was truly better that way? The thought of leaving began ripening in my mind.

As I continued thinking about this, it became easier to pull back. The next day, many of the neighbors complained to me that I had not handled the situation well, that I should resign later, perhaps a few days before I would leave, but not now when I would certainly be there a while longer. My justification was that I had to resign early because I didn't know precisely when I would leave, and it was better that the new person should take over the administration of the house committee and familiarize himself with the work. Shtsherbakov was happy that I had excused myself and didn't tell how I had been persuaded to leave.

For me, this was in general a good thing. Since I was considered a useful element, no one paid any attention to what was happening with me in the house; they didn't look for any sins and everything was good. Yet as soon as suspicion would be thrown on someone—be he extremely loyal— his situation was not to be envied.

THEIR DISAPPOINTMENT AND MY REGRET

After I had been "retired" from the house committee, a group of tailor laborers arrived in Moscow from America. They had gathered together their few spare dollars and came here to become agricultural workers. They began establishing an agriculture cooperative, purchasing the necessary tools and also bought incubators; they even brought a specialist with them who could work with the modern poultry production.

Among the tailor agriculturalists were a couple that we knew in America and they had paid us a visit before starting up their cooperative. They also brought us presents from friends.

The cooperative had been entrusted with a lot of land in Pushkino, some thirty versts from Moscow, and it was there that the tailors had to set up their peasant economy. This entire time, we had yearned to take a vacation there.

So one day in September, we were off to pay a visit to our American tailor-farmers in Pushkino.

The tailor-farmers had already wrestled with great difficulties over one summer and they had long since came to the decision that if they could go back to America, they would do so. They simply could not adjust to the peasant lifestyle.

We came there in the afternoon and found the women at household management; the men were out in the field. Our friends from the cooperative were thrilled to see us. During the several months of their work at the farm, there had been no lack of quarrels because they had gone through a difficult stretch of time. They would often be visited by the district farm inspectors and all they would hear from them was that they were soft Americans. Each visit was accompanied by a consultation that would undo the decisions of the previous consultation and no matter what was done yesterday, it would have to be redone tomorrow.

The tailor-farmers rejoiced greatly at our visit and poured out to us all the bitterness in their hearts, complaints both just and unjust. Pretensions surfaced about the Russian way of life, which was far from what the American tailors had dreamt it to be. Dreams about the Russian steppes were pleasant when it was the peasant cultivating them, but as soon as they themselves had to take a shovel in hand and stand in a field sweating from early until late, the poetry disappeared and the salt from their sweat made their sweet dreams briny.

A young woman stood near us, a former friend who had dreamt of a life in a commune on Russia's free earth. She stood in a black silk dress and washed dishes and wept.

"Why are you crying, beloved friend?"

"What do you think, to be stuck with dishes from early until late at night, this is a commune?"

"What is a commune, then?" I asked her and she burst into tears again. She wanted to go back to America; she would no longer put up with it.

"So, is there also a commune life there?"

"I don't know," she answered. "'I want to go back to America."

Towards evening, the men returned from the field. They told us about their whole situation. Of the few thousand dollars, not a cent remained. With the money they had bought cattle and wagons, because they couldn't use the motorcar they had brought from America due to the lack of roads. There was no longer an incubator because the district had taken the specialist they had brought with them to the center to prepare specialists for the manmade poultry breeding, the incubator was ruined, and they'd eaten the remaining poultry.

For them, the situation had become very serious and one of the leaders expressed the opinion that whoever could do so, should return to America. They still had enough things that by selling them, enough money could be scraped together to cover expenses. Some of them, however, were not American citizens and consequently, returning to America was not a consideration for them.

Since they were unfamiliar with being in the city, they asked me to help them. Seeing the sorrow of these people and knowing that no matter what, they would accomplish nothing here, I promised to help. It was not hard to sell their things, and leaving was an easy matter for Americans like them because in those days, the dreamers were allowed to run back home.

However, nothing could be done in the next day or so and we stayed for a few days at the farm. The next morning, one of the tailor-farmers went to the other part of the farm to get milk. I got into his wagon and went with him so I could look over the farm. The man was not an American citizen and he could not go back. Sitting in the wagon, I tried to distract him a little, as sadness was written all over his face. He said to me: "What good are all the complaints? It's useless. I must remain here, but I can tell you that in the American tailor shop, I would dream of the Russian village. Now here I am in the Russian village and I'm dreaming of the American tailor shop ..."

We got down from the wagon and he went into the barn for the milk. Next to the building stood a Jew of about fifty years of age. His spine was bent, an inheritance from the American shops where he had sat bent over for years. He had a rifle and was keeping watch. We greeted each other and he recognized me, recalling that I had given out propaganda that people should leave America and go to Russia. The Jew mentioned this to me with reproach and when I asked him if that was bad, he answered that they not only should have thrown me out of America but if they'd never let me in, others would have had a lot fewer sorrows. Naturally he didn't mean me directly, but everyone that had agitated for Russia.

I pretended not to hear him and asked him why he was carrying a rifle. From his answer, I learned that he was the watchman for the commune, although he couldn't shoot. When you have to, he said, you can do it. "Better that you tell me," the Jew said to me, "how does someone go back to being a presser in a New York shop? After all, you shouted and agitated for going to Russia and setting up a commune; maybe you can shout the reverse. Go to America and make a life!"

This revealed to me even more the tragedy and disappointment of these ordinary working folk who toiled for so many years in the American shops and believed that in Russia, the revolution had created a Garden of Eden. Yet here no one paid any attention to them, no one had a good word for them, and no one explained to them what was happening here and what was going to happen.

I thought that the Jewish working man was right when he spoke with so much hate about those who went around in America persuading others to become farmers for Russia and who agitated for going there to work in a commune with people whose very age prohibited them from undergoing such a difficult experiment. I turned away from these thoughts, because I had no answer to his arguments.

GOLOS TRUDA IS DESTROYED

For me, no longer being the boss of the house was like a wish come true. The neighbors no longer came to me with their heavy hearts, and my life became more private. In the bargain, thanks to the rumor that we were going abroad and that we even had a permit already, it seemed that people found it easier to distance themselves from us. Moreover, Shtsherbakov was a man who hated the policeman's stick. All this made it possible to help our friends from the agriculture cooperative in their endeavors to go back to America.

They began bringing things to us to sell. Their items were not terribly valuable, but since no one could obtain them in Russia, the sale went smoothly: people paid the requested price. The residents of our house were well-situated and earned good salaries. However, the sellers needed to be careful that the neighbors did not find out that they were selling everything in order to leave the country.

Every night different friends from the cooperative spent the night with us. Such a thing was considered a crime because we couldn't register them—they would have to declare what their business was in Moscow. Also, each time we registered a new person, it would look suspicious and be very risky. The people were very nice to us, and we did everything possible to help them in their desperate situation.

With our help, five of the members of the cooperative along with their wives, gathered together enough for the expenses. They got their passports and satisfied, returned to America. The other members of the cooperative left for different corners of Russia and returned to being tailors. Thus did one more cooperative become liquidated, but this didn't harm the bulletins in America that spoke of their great successes and painted the work in the cooperatives in the most beautiful colors. In fact, the majority of them had the same end as the tailors' agriculture cooperative.

The thought of emigrating grew stronger in us with every day. The "don't do this, don't go here, don't stand here" in every aspect of our lives and the ever-present need to watch every word that came out of our mouths made our days intolerable. The only question was how to begin making it a reality and not fail in the process. Because, as people say, hand over your passport one time and not only do you never get it back again, but you're placed on a list of discontented people and in time this can result in free room and board in Siberia. We knew this well and were wary.

At that time there were a lot of people going abroad, but apolitical people, GPU people. They would pay a couple of hundred rubles for a passport and very often, it cost them just as much processing it through the different offices.

The attitude towards people like us was something completely different, and for that reason we decided to seek a suitable opportunity in which we could ask for a passport. Meanwhile, we began setting aside a few dollars.

My earnings were three hundred rubles a month, and in those days this was a considerable sum. For every two rubles, officially a person would receive a dollar from the bank. However, since a private person couldn't get this at the bank, they would pay three rubles for a dollar on the black market.

It was not hard for us to save fifty dollars for this purpose, but concealing it was very difficult. Actually, per a decree from the VTsIK, people could keep dollars but the authorities had to know about it. Thus, for example, I was sent twenty-five dollars from my family in America. When I received the money, I was asked if I wanted the money in dollars or in rubles. If I wanted dollars, I was told, I should be prepared to exchange it for rubles when the bank demanded it. I decided it was better to ask for rubles and thought that it was more sensible to have twenty-five dollars that the GPU didn't know about, than twenty-five dollars of which they were the masters.

When we had accumulated a few dollars, we began to feel the pressure of concealing them from two elements: from thieves and from the GPU. Necessity teaches and leads to evolution, as is well known—to that end we discovered a secure method. But we sweated blood every time when buying a five-dollar piece, and this often made it clear to me that it wasn't worth it and the plan to leave should be abandoned. However, on several more occasions we received various sums from America, and that part of the task was almost fulfilled.

To travel legally didn't require much money but the difficulties were colossal. In the administrative offices, mountains of paperwork were used up for each person and nevertheless it was not certain that one wouldn't be refused. To travel illegally was easier and of course, more expensive. Not able to decide what to do, in the meantime I worked full steam at printing four million questionnaires that the foreign commissariat had ordered from us. My friends from our group knew about my plan to emigrate and they had nothing against it. To the contrary, they promised me their assistance when I would need to act.

At the Foreign Commissariat we would receive money for the questionnaires every fifteen days. One day when I went there to pick up the money for the printing shop, I was told that we should submit a complete invoice, because the questionnaires were no longer needed. To the question of why they were no longer needed, they didn't know how to answer and I was ordered not to ask foolish questions. As to the hundred thousand questionnaires that were already printed, we were told that we could throw them away. So that there wouldn't be any repercussions, we were issued a written decision that we had permission to do whatever we wanted with them.

The work had been suddenly interrupted; our printing shop and publishing house stood in peril. It was easy to get other work, but only from private associations, not from the government. As soon as the GPU would find out that we no longer did government work, they would make problems for us as they had done before. Still, we had to go look for work, so we began to do so and quickly received many orders. Then the situation unfolded as we were afraid it would.

During the final days of August 1925, a GPU commission visited the printing shop of Golos Truda. After this, we got into a heated exchanged of words with them (I was with the earlier-mentioned Gerosimchik, who with such commissions could do no other than berate them) and they then carried out a rigorous search. They quarreled with every little piece of paper, looked for forbidden items, and ended the inspection late at night when the workers had already left.

As soon as Gerosimchik had hung the lock on the door, one of the agents asked him for the key, saying that tomorrow someone could come to the GPU for the key if we wanted, and if not, we could wait until they returned it to us themselves. Gerosimchik had to obey.

I could scarcely wait until the next morning. I went to the printing shop first. The house watchman informed me that he had received an order last night that he should not allow anyone to enter the courtyard and in the case that someone didn't obey him, he should report it to the GPU by telephone.

All the workers of the printing shop assembled together and we told them what had happened. Everyone received the news in silence, but the silence said more than could words.

Among the workers was one named Kniazev. He was once a comrade of Kalinin but since he had committed a sin by taking part in a political opposition, after a year in Siberia he had to work at a machine for three years in order to become a party member again. He worked in our printing shop. Now this Kniazev undertook to find someone to reopen the printing shop for us.

We all went to a tavern and had a long discussion about the situation, looking for ways to reopen the shop. At that time, there was an ongoing campaign to open artels[193] and cooperatives that would challenge the NEP-people. We decided that an appeal must be made to the GPU that they rent us the printing shop for a small fee and we would work as a cooperative. For that, we wanted only the right to print a book for Golos Truda from time to time, if the GPU would permit it.

The plan was put in motion and after a few weeks of hustling, the GPU agreed to open the printing shop, which was given a new name: "Quality Printing." It was under a contract stating that Golos Truda would receive a certain sum monthly if it was not possible to publish any books.

However, within several weeks' time it was clear that nothing would come of the matter. We finished the remaining jobs and the cooperative managers were not able to bring in any new work. No money was received, and the workers went off to better places where one could actually earn a few rubles.

One day Kniazev came with the news that the Serpukhov Executive Committee was looking for a printing shop to purchase. We sent a delegation to Serpukhov to present itself to the chairman of the Executive Committee. Our group determined that although the printing shop was worth more, we would sell the printing shop for no less than twenty thousand rubles. The printing shop employees who were still remaining agreed to this, and were happy that they would be paid the debt owed to them for the last month.

The delegation to the chairman of the Executive Committee consisted of Gerosimchik and me. We encountered a man with a lot of education and who was a true revolutionary. From his face you could tell he was Jewish; he had the appearance of a yeshiva[194] student, was near-sighted and had a comprehension of the sort of socialism that was in those days in Russia already a rarity, because everything and everyone had already become bureaucratized.

We told him who had sent us and what our business was. It turned out that he already knew all the details, as he had previously been informed by Kniazev. He even told us how this could be concluded, since the printing shop was not permitted to be sold. However, since the Executive Committee required the printing shop he would intervene, but with one condition: he would give us fifteen thousand rubles and we would receive the other ten

---

193 A general term for cooperative associations that existed before and after the revolution, traditionally concerning special producers' cooperatives.

194 Hebrew: a traditionally male Jewish religious educational institution that focuses on the study of the traditional religious texts, mainly Torah and Talmud study.

thousand rubles when the printing shop was set up in Serpukhov. At the same time he assured us that the Serpukhov party organization would protect us if the GPU wanted to pick a fight with us.

We agreed and the remaining step was that he, the chairman of the Serpukhov Executive Committee, would come to Moscow, look over the inventory, pay us fifteen thousand rubles, and we would immediately begin transferring the printing shop to him in the city. He also asked that no one speak of this, so that it would be easier to carry it out.

Satisfied with the successful deal we returned to Moscow, at the same time not understanding what sort of kind angels were amusing themselves with us.

At the appointed time, the chairman of the Executive Committee came to the printing shop, looked over the machines, and asked that he be shown the documents stating who owned the machinery. We showed him the papers we had from the Petrograd soviet giving us permission to transfer the printing shop to Moscow: in them was written they were the property of several American friends who had brought them to Russia for social purposes. That same day we received fifteen thousand rubles from him and per the deal, the keys were handed over to the buyer. We also received a note from him stating that when the machines were in Serpukhov, we would receive the remaining ten thousand rubles. Since I was an American, it was entrusted to me to be the one that turned the machines over to the new owners.

Meanwhile, we reviewed our accounts, paid the past wages owed, and also the royalties due to Sofia Kropotkina and Vera Figner for publishing their books. The chairman of the Executive Committee helped us with everything and gave advice on how to do things in accordance with soviet regulations.

Men came to disassemble the machines. I was the only member of the group Golos Truda in attendance, and with me was the buyer. We joked about how an anarchist group was lucky, to be able to conclude its publishing work in a normal manner.

Meanwhile, three fellows from the GPU arrived and began asking first of all, what was going on there.

"We're taking the machines," the chairman of the Serpukhov soviet replied to them. "We have purchased it," he said to their very harsh question. My young man took a paper out of his pocket and calmly handed it to the agents.

The document began migrating from one set of agent's hands to another and they started talking about it softly and calmly. After a long conversation, they invited him to go to the GPU so that the act of purchasing the printing shop could be recorded there.

I could tell that the buyer was a bigwig since he had no fear of the GPU agents; rather, they were afraid of him.

As they were leaving, the first of the agents turned to me and said that as the representative of Golos Truda I must also go with them to the GPU. Before I even had time to respond to the invitation, the chairman from Serpukhov explained in a decisive tone that I must remain at the printing shop and make sure that everything was carried out correctly. "I'll be responsible for him," he said. "I bought the machines and we must have them as soon as possible." As he spoke, he took the keys from his pocket and turned to me:

"Comrade, as soon as you are done here, please lock up the premises and then bring me the keys at the first The Sovetov."

He emphasized these last words. This signified that they weren't dealing with just anybody.

I worked with the mechanics until late at night taking apart the machines, then locked up the premises and went directly to the first The Sovetov to deliver the key.

I knocked on the door of his room, and found him sitting at a desk as if nothing had happened. He could tell that I was upset, and said to me with a smile that I could sleep peacefully and that everything would work out. He gave the impression of a decent, sincere revolutionary and before leaving, I asked him why he hadn't wanted me to also go to the GPU. The amiable man than candidly explained that besides being the chairman of the Serpukhov soviet, he was also the chairman of the GPU over there and he knew from experience that when the GPU takes somebody with them, they always want to be right and it is then very difficult to have somebody released from them. No matter how much it would be demonstrated that this or that person could be more useful when released than sitting inside the GPU, the agents would always find an offense in order to justify their actions. For that reason, he wanted me to remain in the printing shop.

We struck up a conversation about the Russian revolution. Despite that fact that he was the chairman of the Serpukhov GPU, I felt a remarkable confidence in him and quite freely gave my opinion as to what purpose the conduct of the revolution would lead.

The answer that I heard from him gave me a lot to think about. "People must stop dreaming," he said, "that socialism is an ideal in itself. It is an economic system and nothing more. To the men who have now come to power, history has put it in their hands to institute the new system. People shouldn't go around philosophizing and splitting hairs, but acting merely as ordinary mechanics, install the new system in place of capitalism."

"But how can one approach it with such dispassionate intentions?" I opined. "Even when people only want to adopt the new system, they can't do it mechanically. We are already seeing how the installation is often badly done, and the new engineers allow no one to even remark on it. A dozen years will go by, and they will look at the mass of the people as if they were their property. Instead of the socialist order serving the collective, it will become an instrument in the hands of a small group and the man of the masses will be their slave."

My interlocutor interrupted me and said, "You see, here lies the trouble with so many of you. Why on earth do you convince yourselves that you must be the custodians of the revolution and of proper socialism? We have, all of us, each in his own way, aspired to become the masters of the situation and we've achieved it. We must utilize it as much as is possible and not be worrying about all the future generations. If it doesn't turn out as it should, it is the job of the next generation to improve it."

"Why," I asked, "do you believe that history has not empowered us to be the guardians, and that history does indeed want that a single group be the ones that establish the new system?"

"Don't be blind," he said. "People do see, you know, that history has now chosen this very group, and that it has the power and the will to lead in this manner. Therefore we must all assist in the construction and what it will be later on—leave that for those who will come after us."

He spoke for much longer and gave forth on his viewpoint regarding the course of the Russian revolution. It had been eight years since it happened and although he unfolded his theories with cleverness, it was for the most part a cynical approach. Time had transformed many idealists such as him into cynics. He didn't want to be a victim anymore; rather, he wanted to be one of those who made a victim of someone else.

As we concluded this talk, the chairman of the GPU said that all that we had discussed there would be enough for a regiment of soldiers to be hung for it.

A couple of weeks later, the court determined that we should receive the remaining ten thousand rubles. With this concluded the episode of our group as book publishers and we were no longer printers. There was only one source of income left for the Golos Truda group: the stationery and book business. Yet the earnings had shrunk and not everyone could stay with it.

I began thinking more about emigrating from Russia. We had the means to do it, and only had to figure out how one obtains a permit without asking directly. It was necessary that it be done so that we were told to leave, rather than it being our desire.

Having such hopes, it was hard to take on another occupation, although through my acquaintances it would have been easy to find a position in some office. As I often met with acquaintances that were already high up on the bureaucratic ladder, they would ask me what I was doing and didn't I want to take on this or that post. The answer was that with time, I would probably go to America. In all such cases, even the most responsible commissars looked at me greedily, saying: "To America? Not bad."

Being that I had a lot of free time, each day I would go and help my comrades at the Golos Truda paper business, without reward for the work. With the sale of the printing shop and still more from the books and paper, we had saved a large amount of money in the publishing house, and we decided to use the money to publish all the works of Mikhail Bakunin.

Some of us, like Professor Borovoy and I, even thought that it would maybe be better to carry out our publishing abroad and there continue our work. However, the largest majority of our group was of the opinion that we would not be further persecuted here, because we were not involved in any political activity. The printing of a book would be done with the permission of the authorities. All that remained was that we make the preparations to publish Bakunin's work. We had already had a permit for quite some time and Professor Borovoy, who was an expert on Bakunin and had also been his student, sat himself down to prepare the material.

AN INTERROGATION IN LUBYANKA[195] AND A PASSPORT TO A FOREIGN LAND

It was the end of the summer in Moscow. For several weeks from September to October the days were still beautiful and warm, the silver stars lit up the dark skies at night and the weather was delicious—making people forget about everything. Even under a new regime where people had to be so pragmatic and must be cautious in all things—it brought joy to appreciate nature, who was not miserly to anyone and didn't select any one individual but distributed her splendor to everyone equally.

Yet even during those beautiful weeks in which the people were reinvigorated a little, none forgot that they must prepare themselves to meet the angry white-gray winter who was waiting on the threshold with his frozen heart. People were terrified of winter; they spoke of it with anxiety and each strove to use all possible means to weaken its bitter cold. Those who had only a couple of rubles would buy a cart of wood for themselves, a bit of coal, a sack of potatoes and other such things that could warm the body during the cold snowstorms.

In the previous years I had always prepared myself for the winter as did all the other soviet citizens, but with this fifth winter, I remained aloof and indifferent. My mind was occupied with returning to somewhere in America, and I was certain that before the winter had set in, I would already be on my way. To this day, I have no idea where this certainty came from. I had not submitted any request for a permit to leave the country because I knew that if I did so, I would make things worse. Those who had done so were refused, and such refusals would also lead to further troubles. Nonetheless, I would assure all my acquaintances that very soon I would be leaving the country.

My close friends who knew the truth and thought that I was going around with my head in the clouds, would often tease me about the large bouquet of flowers with which they would send me off. Yet my words were not wasted. I would tell about my plans to leave wherever I had the occasion to be, and spoke about it even to such people whose job it was to guard the political purity of the citizens. I also had these kinds of people among my acquaintances and when I would meet with them, the theme of the conversation would be my desire to go to America.

---

195 Russian: The infamous headquarters of the KGB with a prison on its ground floor, located on Lubyanka Square in Moscow.

One of these acquaintances of mine who was a good friend and had protected me more than once from an evil eye, was able to do what was necessary so I could leave. Yet when I would talk to him, his answer was that I should knock the idea out of my head and that when I stopped being an ass, I'd have no use for America.

This friend of mine—Bogopolski was his name—tried to set me on the "straight path." He would say, "The bourgeois democracy has penetrated your bones. One of these days, someone should take you by the neck and throw you down upon the mound of capitalistic filth and let you rejoice there with them." This gave me the opportunity to tell him that, on the contrary, I would like to see how he would do this. To my words he responded, now speaking seriously, that it would be done, and that even if I changed my mind afterward, nothing would avail me.

From the humorous talk, we switched over to a serious debate. I said to Bogopolski that he should understand how I felt; he knew what I had done in America and that I couldn't carry out any political activity here in Russia. If I could return to that part of the world, although not in the United States, I would be more useful than I could be in Russia.

Listening to what I was saying, Bogopolski became angry. "If you really mean that," he said furiously, "you will certainly remain here. Whether or not you will be able to do something here for us—we decline your offer to go elsewhere to do work." He was now speaking in the tone of one in an official position. "Would that your friends there in other countries would also do nothing, and that we had them here and could keep an eye on them."

After this conversation came the consequences. I noticed that from that point onward, the bookstore of Golos Truda was being more heavily watched. Before, we would close the bookshop when we wanted to, and often used the time when our doors were open to speak about our group's work. Yet now the street militiaman would not allow us to keep our doors open for even one minute after eight o'clock. Often, suspicious customers would sneak in and lend an ear to "what was being said in the shop." Moreover, I noted that the house where I lived was under close observation.

All of this was making me fearful and I began thinking that instead of my America, I would end up in Siberia. In those days, people were not put in prison but were ordered to pack up and leave Moscow, at the same time being pointed to a town in far-off Siberia where they must settle. The prospects were bitter, and my suspicion was not unfounded.

One day, on the eleventh of November, I received a card from the GPU that I must report tomorrow morning at Lubyanka 2. Now, this address was already well known at that time and would cause fear whenever mentioned.

I rejoiced very little at the invitation, but gradually I calmed myself. Had it been something serious, I thought, they wouldn't have sent me an invitation. Rather, without ceremony they would have simply come to me at night at my residence and told me to get dressed and go with them as required. So if I had been sent an invitation, it was probably not something that was very important. However, it was one thing to console myself and another to have a visit with the GPU looming. My heart was thudding and inside my head came the thought, "What do they have in store for me, and why have I been called in?"

In the evening, all of our group assembled together at a friend's house and the invitation card was considered from all angles. We went over all the possible hypotheses, but came to no definite conclusion. "They won't eat you up—and if it turns out to be something bad and you are detained, we will see what can be done." In any case, my friends told me to be cautious with what I said, and to keep in mind that the GPU were not the American secret police and that I should not cause my friends too much work.

The next morning we got up in silence, feeling perturbed. We ate breakfast and drank a little coffee without any comment. I avoided looking at the corner where my friend Mary sat. The feelings I had could only be known to those who had experienced the taste of a visit to the GPU.

From our house to Lubyanka 2, the corner of the holy shokhtim,[196] as it was called, was a twenty-minute walk. We walked pressed together, one to the other, but without words. As we approached the Lubyanka we felt ill at ease, wanting that the way there would last a lifetime.

No one would ever stand still at the courtyard of the Lubyanka; they would run by it as if it were a specter. We stopped opposite it. A few minutes remained before my appointment time.

"Well, behave yourself and be careful; this is no joke."

I remained silent and looking my friend straight in the eye, saw tears

---

196 Hebrew: (Judaism) ritual slaughterers of livestock and poultry.

sparkling in them, obscuring the gentleness that always looked out. I gathered my courage, at that moment summoning up hope, and said, "It will be fine, it's nothing. Wait for me until late at night and then go tell whoever is necessary, not earlier, because that can sometimes make it worse." We said goodbye without words, kissed, and I crossed the street to the Lubyanka.

At the door, before you could cross the threshold there was a small window where you had to report. I handed in my invitation card and was issued a permit. Going over the threshold, the Red Army soldier indicated with his eyes that the permit must be pushed down onto the rifle.

I went into the corridor. There I was shown that I must go up the steps to a second corridor where the administrative office of the Investigations judge, Rutkovski, was located. In the corridor were long benches and as it was very dark, for the first few minutes I couldn't make out the many people waiting. They sat on the benches and from time to time, an official came out and called a name. A body with feet quickly trailed after the voice.

The surrounding atmosphere was filled with terror, awakening in me a feeling of hate. I felt my fear vanish. Different thoughts flew through my mind about the repetition of a police regime that I saw here. And where were the dreams and the beliefs in liberty that the revolution should have brought?

As I sat there lost in my thoughts, a tall, slim man who had just arrived came up to me and calling me by name, greeted me and very courteously said, "I am Judge Rutkovski. Come with me, please." I stood up and went with him into his office.

"Have you been waiting long in the hall?" the judge asked as he took out a bundle of documents from a drawer.

I answered him: not long, maybe fifteen or twenty minutes. He told me to feel at ease, asked if I smoked, and offered a cigarette. We both lit cigarettes and my examining magistrate got down to business with me.

The first thing we'll do, he said, is take care of the official questions. You'll allow me to ask your name, your second[197] name, place of birth, how long you've been in Russia, etc. After a few minutes we were done with the questionnaire. Then he said to me that I was not compelled to answer any of the questions he would ask me. I knew that the process of the examination would always begin that way, but in the case that someone didn't answer as

---

197 Patronymic.

was required and how the interrogator wanted, it was too bad for them. I replied diplomatically that I had nothing to hide or to deny unless he asked me about something that I didn't know what it meant; then I would be candid and say that I didn't know. Actually, I didn't know what he would want to ask me and what I should answer.

I was taken aback as I heard Judge Rutkovski explain to me that he was the supervisor of interrogating those from the anarchist movement, and he wanted to know if I had read the series of nine articles that the famous anarchist leader Emma Goldman had published in the American press during that time.

I had not read the articles, with the exception of one that I had by chance seen in the Comintern library. When I had read through this one article in which she had attacked the Soviets in a dramatic way, I had written a letter to Emma Goldman privately on my own as a former ideological admirer, saying that with such articles she was doing harm to the labor movement and not being useful as she might have thought.

I explained to Judge Rutkovski how things were and it turned out that he … had read my letter before Emma Goldman had, and he was satisfied with me. It also pleased him that I told him frankly what had happened, and that it concurred with what he knew from my letter.

"Do you think," he said to me, "that this was a sufficient reaction to Emma's insolence?"

"I don't know," I answered, "how much of this was insolence, because I didn't read all the articles. I only know that people listen to Emma's words in America, and I felt it my duty to write her and say what I thought about it. This I did entirely in private, as for the last five years that I have been in Soviet Russia, I have not carried on any political correspondence with my acquaintances in America and have not had any opportunity to react to Emma's stand. Furthermore, I believe that in such cases, an answer is effective and desirable when it comes from people who live in that place. I am convinced that in America and other countries where there are anarchists, they will refute these articles, above all for the reasons that they were printed in the capitalistic press.

The judge showed a great interest in my explanation of the matter. We thoroughly discussed an array of points that were relevant to the issue. I took the opportunity to speak with him about our young friend Molly, who a little while earlier had been expelled from Russia and had gone to Germany. I knew her and had spoken with her many times. She was a passionate friend of the Soviet regime, yet for frankly criticizing those who did harm to it she had been expelled, which only provided material for a hostile press to use in making accusations against Soviet Russia.

Hearing my argument about the expulsion of our friend Molly, Rutkovski, the examining magistrate, like all of his type of officials, made a proposal to me in a polite way, one that I had heard before more than once. Coming across as a friend, he said, "You are correct. Such cases of expelling important and useful people ought not to happen, but why shouldn't you help us? If you would work with us and let us know who is who in your circles, we wouldn't make mistakes. In these cases, you must also help us out."

I already regretted that I had become entangled in such talk. I took another cigarette from the table and as I lit it, slowly thought about how to move past this without giving an answer to his proposal. However, Rutkovski drew me further into the same theme and hearing that I gave no concrete answer, then asked me if I knew of the anarchist paper "News," which was published in New York.

I had once seen a couple of issues of the newspaper before my deportation from America. What had happened to it later I didn't know because I hadn't seen it, and this I explained to my interrogator. He read several sentences from articles in one of the latest issues and at my request, let me take a look at the paper for myself. This was a gangster's political organ from some sort of group that was an enemy of the Soviet land, one that had assumed the former name of the newspaper for itself. I showed this to him and explained that the organ had no relevance to the anarchist movement.

Rutkovski admitted that I might be right, but why shouldn't I speak openly against such a group and write to my friends in New York, asking them to do the same? To this I answered him that I didn't know whether or not in America they were already speaking out against such filthy newspapers, but from here, to turn to friends there would obviously be considered as carrying on a political correspondence with foreigners and, "You know," I said pointedly, "with that type of thing, how it might end."

My examining magistrate pretended not to understand this, and switched over to the question of Molly's expulsion. "If you would offer us your help, we'd know who could be trusted in such cases. What do you say to my proposal?" I remained silent, and he wrote down some notes. After a long pause, he began speaking to me about something else:

"The printing shop of Golos Truda has ceased to exist; the business in your book shop is also not doing well—now tell me, comrade, what do you do there, and what type of an interest do you have there? With whom do you meet?"

I was well aware that such points must be answered clearly and I explained to him that I was still the chairman of Golos Truda and that the publishing house was still engaged in getting books published—books for which we had a permit. It was not a question of receiving my official salary; I received enough to get by, and the work was meaningful to me. As for "with whom did we meet": "You know it as well as I, and I wouldn't like to answer this sort of question. By no means because it is dangerous to do so or because the element is detrimental, but simply because it is outside of the revolutionary ethic to tell a third party the names of the people with whom you meet. However, since in this case nothing bad will happen, I will tell you. We meet with our American friends, with many party members with whom I am good friends, and aside from them, the members of Golos Truda also come; you must already be familiar with their names."

"I didn't mean that you should give me names," Rutkovski said. "You misunderstood me. I know myself who they are, your friends. I simply mean your work with us. You've already been here five years; you came in the time of NEP but have not become a NEP-man. I like this very much, but you are also not a party member and you work in a free institute, not in a soviet one. At the same time, you are friends with our friends. Our question is: what do you plan to do? We need to know not how you do it, but what you are planning to do and in general your opinion, to see if it is harmful to the revolutionary order."

Hearing the examining magistrate giving me such a speech, I could see that he wanted me to make a political declaration. I was not prepared to do this and decided it was better to tell him openly that I wanted to emigrate from Russia. He looked at me intently and listened to what I said:

"Comrade Judge, you've asked me a very serious question, and I will be candid and tell you what you want to know. The friends that know me, know that I don't walk around with any secrets; whatever I object to, I say so—but this is of little interest to the authorities. I don't carry out any anti-government agitation because I myself would consider such a thing to be a crime. I'm no NEP-man, as you yourself said, and I won't become one, but I also can't belong to the party because I have different viewpoints. For me there remains only one recourse: to get a passport to go abroad, where I will still be able to do something within the political area. I plan to go to the countries where I spent my younger years."

He bent over his chair, inhaled each time more firmly on his cigarette, listened to what I was saying, and let me speak. I forgot the difference between us and why I'd been summoned there, and talked about the American labor movement and in addition, truly meaning it, said that for me it would be much better to be abroad and defending the Soviet experiment, rather than living here unable to adapt.

"I like your concept," Judge Rutkovski told me. "So then, when we give you a passport, you will leave?"

"Yes!" I said emphatically.

"It is done; I will furnish you with this."

He called in the office girl and told her to bring in a questionnaire. When she had done this, he gave me the question sheet and said to fill it out. I filled it out and gave it to him. He looked through it and asked me what type of passport I wanted: a free one—that is, one without a fee; or was I prepared to pay a fee of twenty-two rubles for the passport. I chose the latter: to pay forty-four rubles for the two passports.

From his chair, Judge Rutkovski gave an exhale and said, "Well, it is late. Your matter will be taken care of. Take the photographs to the passport office and in three days, you can come pick up your passports to go abroad."

Coming out into the street, I breathed more freely. On the city clock, I saw that it was already past four. How quickly the five hours had gone, and what was so interesting, that a judge would devote five long hours to it? I could not come up with any insight into the conduct of the political apparatus and with quick steps, almost running, went home. I met Mary pacing nervously across the room. I briefly told her what had happened and above all, that we were getting passports and would be able to leave.

I didn't know when they would be giving us the passports but I thought that based on Rutkovski's instructions, I would be able to take care of everything in the offices. Several of my friends to whom I had told them my story that same day had doubts as to whether it would be that easy; Rutkovski had truly meant it, but what would be the word from above?

The chief of the Department of Control in such cases was Bogopolski, whom I already knew from America. Not thinking much about it, I set off to see him so we could discuss my matter. It was already evening and I found him and his wife, Rive—a good and sensible woman—at the supper table.

They received me as a welcome guest and invited me to eat. I told Bogopolski that I had been summoned to the GPU, and asked him if he knew anything about it. He began smiling and I realized that he knew all! "They didn't do anything bad to you there!" he said to me, smiling.

It turned out that he knew all about my visit there, and had indeed had a hand in it. He asked me if I was satisfied that I would be given a passport to leave. I answered him that yes, I was satisfied, but that I didn't know how it would turn out and because of this, if I would truly receive them. He assured me that it would be so, and told me a few days later to go pick up the passports. In the case that someone made problems for me, I should let him know.

Bogopolski knew that I wanted to leave and that I would not be able to adjust to life in Russia. He had thought about it, and came to the conclusion that it would be better for me to do so. On his own initiative, he had arranged it so that I would be summoned to the GPU and there offered a passport. It would be easier if it came to him as a proposal from another office, because he didn't want it to originate directly from him. He explained to me that in some of his past experiences, he had seen that when he had recommended that several acquaintances be given passports they had been refused, but when the GPU ordered it, it was taken care of and carried out.

I thanked Bogopolski for what he had done for me and shaking his hand, invited him to come see me before my departure. He promised me to come at night, when no one would be in my room.

When I returned from my visit, in our small quarters there was not even room to step inside it. All of our friends and comrades were there; they had found out that we were on the verge of leaving. Everyone rushed towards me and wanted to know if I had really received the passports. "In a few days—we will go," I told them. Several of them advised that we should wait another week, but one of my friends spoke up and said, "No, he is right! Go, as quickly as possible, they might have regrets!" And this friend of mine was actually a party member ...

It was decided that if I received the passports on Friday, Sunday night we would leave. However it came out, I began making preparations, and my friends began arranging a party on Saturday night so that we could say farewell with a bottle of 96-proof. Meanwhile, a bottle of brandy had appeared on the table, and a few friends rushed down and brought back something with which to wash it down. Thus after five years we, "our family," gathered together, with the exception of three friends who over time had gone home.

This was a remarkable little banquet. No one was pleased that one of the family was leaving. We who were supposed to leave were also not happy—and nevertheless we sat and talked until late at night and discussed our departure. All of the friends wished to themselves that when they would be able to leave, it would go as easily for them as it did for me.

Meanwhile, in complete certainty that we would be leaving in a few days, I went around to the offices where over the last five years I had made many friends and acquaintances, letting them know that I was leaving. Almost all of them simply expressed envy that I could go abroad. There were among them people who financially lived better than rich people in other countries did. Nevertheless, they wanted to throw away all their economic privileges and set off in the world to seek a new struggle. During those days I thought a great deal about this, and came to the conclusion that the maxim that economic welfare completely dominates man, is far from the absolute truth. Man needs something in addition to a full stomach and a warm house. Without freedom of thought, without freedom of movement, without freedom to follow one's conscience—economic prosperity may turn into poison.

THE FAREWELL WITH "BIG BILL"

Of all those to whom I said good-bye, talking with them more about their own situation than about my departing, there was one leave-taking that left an enormous impression on me: that was when I went up to the Hotel Lux to say good-bye to William Haywood, who was an American known by the name "Big Bill"—the big William.[198] He truly was big in every sense. Aside from being intellectually a towering man, he was also a physical giant.

---

198 William Haywood: popularly known as "Big Bill" Haywood, was a founding member and leader of the Industrial Workers of the World (IWW) and long-time member of the Socialist Party of America.

For years he was the recognized leader of the American revolutionary labor movement (IWW)[199]. After a trial during which he was sentenced to twenty years in prison, his friends had sent him to Russia.

For William, the first years of being in Russia were very interesting. He received support for all his activities on behalf of the new regime from all those who before the revolution had spent time in America. Among them were Bukharin, Trotsky, Gregori Vaynshteyn and other such prominent men from the new revolutionary order.

From his exile, "Big Bill" inspired his comrades, mainly the coalminers, with his propaganda for the new Russia. He called them to come help build the new world, and hundreds of faithful revolutionaries, coalminers all, came to Russia on their last dimes. They began working there with great fervor, but the results were the same as with all the rest that came with the best of intentions and would quickly become disillusioned. Their hands and feet were tied: they weren't permitted to think about their ideals, and at every turn they met with difficulties and restrictions. Bill's coalminers finally all went back to the capitalistic America with a curse on their lips for the Bolshevik land that they were formerly prepared to adopt as their own.

Bill suffered greatly because of this. He first tried to intervene for his "miners": he knocked on doors and went to the high windows, but couldn't bring about any action. A little later when those who had supported him were themselves cast down from glory and were subject to various hardships, Bill was left powerless and without anybody to turn to in a dark moment.

Previously, Bill had been surrounded with attention and had enjoyed many privileges. He would travel freely across the country visiting factories and new regions and the like, but now all that was forbidden to him. However, they couldn't just dismiss this man whose activity in America was such a big deal, where he was called "the king without a crown." He was allowed to live in the best hotel in Moscow and was given everything he needed for his physical existence. Yet for Bill, this was the same as a golden cage for a wild bird.

And now, here in his golden cage at the Hotel Lux, I went up to exchange a few words with Bill before I left. When I entered his room, I came across him lying outstretched on a leather divan, from which his hands and feet dangled like tassels of an elaborate bedcover. I introduced myself, saying who

---

199 Industrial Workers of the World

I was. He remembered me, asked me to sit, and went back to lying in his previous pose.

I told him that I had come to say good-bye because I was going away. The man fixed me with his penetrating gaze, and hearing that I was not in jest and that I would probably receive a passport in the next few days, he slid off the leather sofa and remained sitting on the floor.

We talked for a long time, and I found out that he was in much difficulty and suffering from emotional problems due to the arrangements that ate away at his revolutionary heart. "So now you also have come to say that you are leaving, as so many others have already done. And for me?" he said, as if to himself.

I didn't wish to rub salt in his wounds, and was silent. He got up, came over to me, lay his two great coalminer's hands on my shoulders and said, "It's good that you're leaving, comrade, very good. How many years have you been here? Five years—that's enough that you won't forget that you were here, and to remember Russia. And in case someone there asks you how I'm doing, how I live and what I'm doing to help build the new Russia—you tell them that I'm doing well, that everything is fine."

Bill then told me that he was feeling in poor health. Every day a new doctor came and treated him, but "if they'd let me go in a mine together with my fellow coalminers—oh, around them I'd be healthy again," he said. He shook my hand firmly and said that wherever I ended up, I should lend a hand to the IWW, which was his ideal. Before I left, he quietly asked me if anyone had seen me come into his room. When I told him that no one had, he said, "Go and leave quickly, before it gets hard for you to do so." We shook hands affectionately and I left his room.

For a long time afterwards, I could not get over my farewell to the one-time giant. I saw him now as a Samson with shorn hair. Once he was mighty and now he lay in a hotel, powerless, impotent, and afraid that some would come see him— and men played with him as if with a puppet. This was Big Bill, I thought, who in America men had shuddered to hear his name. He lies in the "Lux" in Moscow and is cut off from every activity? It upset me every time I thought about it.

In foreign lands across the world, different communist agents published Big Bill's opinions about Soviet Russia, where he was active and helping build the new world, etc. A few years later when I was already in Berlin, I read in the newspapers that Big Bill had died; it seems this was in 1927. I then thought that regardless of how he died or whatever he died from, it must have certainly been redemption for him because when we had said good-bye, I could see in his eyes that he very much wanted to leave Russia. But there was no other way for him to make that journey, except finishing out his life there. The day will come, I thought, when men will lay a wreath on the grave of the great Bill, who was consumed by suffering due to his ideals and deep convictions being desecrated.

I did not do any more visiting and I decided that until I had the passports I would not go see anyone, because from doing so I could be made to stay. The only thing that I had to take care of was with the management of the house where I was once the chairman. I had been promised that if I had to leave, of the three hundred rubles that I had paid for the room, they would refund me two hundred. That same evening, the management had arranged that tomorrow I would be paid the promised sum. This made the journey much easier for me.

MARY DANCES IN THE STREET FROM HAPPINESS

Punctually on the fourth day after the promise I'd been given, at ten o'clock in the morning we were off to the passport office. We weren't, Mary and I, actually walking but slowly strolling, as if we wanted to count our steps. We wanted to hold onto that beautiful illusion that we were going to get passports for a little longer. We spoke about everything in the world except that which in that moment interested us the most. The closer we got to the passport office, the slower we walked. A strange wariness gripped us about the whole business.

In front of the courtyard of the commissariat where they would give out passports stood a large crowd, divided into large and small groups. There were entire families there: men, women and children. This was during the time when in general, it was not hard for normal citizens to get passports to go abroad. Yet here also the categories reigned, and not everyone was treated equally. There were those who had paid only a little bit for a passport, and those who had needed to pay a great deal.

The largest number of people who stood in front of the gate waited for passports, for which they were prepared to give away everything they had. There were people from all corners of the enormity of Russia. The official story was that everyone could receive a passport in the republic from which they would be leaving, yet everyone still had to come to Moscow for a passport.

Among those who waited were Ukrainians, Uzbekistanis, White Russians and Georgians: people from the different republics of Soviet Russia. We could hear their conversations and understand what they were saying, not, heaven forbid, because they all knew Russian, but because they spoke Yiddish. The Ukrainians and Georgians, etc., almost all appeared to be Jewish.

From their conversations, we learned that the people had been waiting for months already for an answer about their passports. "When will they stop tormenting and torturing us?" was their complaint. "When will they stop postponing things until tomorrow? If only they could just one time say either 'yes, you can have one' or 'no, you can't,' but it's always the same answer: 'Your passport is not ready yet.' It's unbearable." Hearing what the crowds were saying among themselves, we looked at each other with hopeless glances.

We entered the administrative office. With a contrived self-confidence and steeling myself not to be disappointed by a refusal, I went up to the little window and asked if our passports were ready.

"When did you put in your application, citizen?" the clerk asked. I answered him that it was four days ago.

"What?" he said, astonished. "Four days ago and you are already here annoying us?"

"Pardon me, comrade," I said. "Take a look at what is going on with our passports, because I think that they must be ready."

He replied to me that it was not possible and I kept on asking him to take a look, until he consented. He got up, went over to a cabinet with many drawers and began looking in drawer "A." I saw that he pulled two passports out of the drawer.

His entire countenance changed. He came back to the window a different man, first of all switching from calling me "citizen" to "comrade." He held the passports firmly in his hand like a piece of treasure and looked severely at us and then at the pictures in the passports; he could not understand how they had been done so quickly.

Finally he said, "Yes, yes, your passports are here." He pushed a blank form through the little window and said to sign a receipt that we had received the passports. When I had done so, he kept on justifying why he had said that they weren't there, when the passports were actually ready. "You understand, comrade, I can't know, of course, who you are. Your case is an exception, and it's not written on someone's face who he is. Secondly, passports with such speed are usually issued in a special office. May the devil take it," he said good-naturedly. "You never know with whom you are speaking."

As he gave me our passports, he amicably offered his hand and wished me a pleasant trip. As we started to leave, I saw that he had stuck his head out of his window and was watching us go.

When we came to the exit, I thought with surprise that we might even start running. With quivering steps, we went out into the courtyard and here we began going faster. On the street we were almost running, as if we were carrying something stolen …

When we had gone a little ways, we took out the passports, looked at them from all angles, and only then started to believe that we actually had them. Mary started to dance with joy. "We are really leaving, is it true?" she kept repeating over and over. Dancing this way, she lost a boot. I saw it and pointed it out to her. She reached down and pulled off the other boot. "No more galoshes—we are leaving the Garden of Eden!"

Rejoicing over having received the passports, we decided not to waste any more time and to begin preparing right away for the journey. Who knows, anything could happen, they could still change their minds and tell us to stay at home, I thought to myself. Without delay, I set off for the offices to find out how one receives a visa and boat tickets.

It was then the policy that anyone traveling overseas must buy a boat ticket through the "Soviet Fleet," and this would take a long time while they made inquiries and determined this or that one might be leaving. I met a good acquaintance who was connected with the travel institution, and he gave me some advice on how to do this quickly through a foreign travel agency. This saved me many frustrations.

In a few hours' time, our room was not even recognizable. Our entire bit of poverty lay packed up in a large trunk and a few valises. That same day, we were already ready to leave.

APPROACHING THE END OF THE DREAMS

At night, we went off to see our best friend and before we were even over the doorstep, we began telling him of the good luck we'd had that day. Our good friend P. was an even-keeled person and nothing ever seemed to surprise him. Yet here he asked that we calmly explain to him the cause of our excitement.

We sat down and I told him precisely what had happened, concluding with the fact that we already had everything prepared for departure. For the first time, I saw on his face an expression of discontent. "Well," he said, "so this means you're tearing yourselves away from our "family"," as we called ourselves. This group of friends from America who are here in Russia really did cling to each other, be it in sunshine or in rain. P. heaved a heavy, deep sigh and concluded, "Are you really leaving? Perhaps it is better." And then, having already recovered his courage, he added, "Well, good. There's little time left here and we must have a good time with you, have a drink together, and say good-bye festively. Tomorrow, Saturday night, I'll bring the 'family' together here and we will live it up until the train departs."

P. advised me that I should go today to Bogopolski and say good-bye to him, because he had obviously taken care of everything so that we could leave.

I went straight to Bogopolski with my friend P., and we took him and his wife Rive Bushvik back with us to friend P.'s house. Rive was a remarkably sentimental person and she was sincerity itself. In her personal sloppiness lay her self-sacrificing devotion to others; she always sought to do good for others and would forget about herself. She was not fond of her husband's position and in order to justify it, at every possibility she would strive to keep him from doing something detrimental to someone else. People knew of her "weakness" in the party circles and when on the advice of her husband she tried to become a member of the party, she was refused therein due to hundreds of humane reasons.

We stayed enjoying each other's company until late at night, carrying on conversations and expressing opinions of a kind that for much milder ones, Bogopolski would have sent other people to Siberia forever. The mood between us was, however, an amiable one and in the course of our wrangling we came to the conclusion that in spite of everything, it would get better and not keep getting worse, and the soviet idea would emerge whole from all pitfalls.

Bogopolski was very pleased that he had made possible my trip back to America. "I remember well," he said to me, "how you defended the Soviet regime while not being a Bolshevik, and it will be better that you should continue doing it from afar, rather than stay here and be unhappy." He asked me that I not shame him after I left Russia. This I promised him and I kept my word for a long time, until the behavior of Stalin strayed from the well-known paths and in my little world, I could no longer maintain my amiable passivity.

We were thus together almost the entire night, and didn't notice how it flew by as we talked of the present and the future. At that time we all believed that we lived in a revolutionary epoch and knew that we would come to understand all the reasons why the new world order had not yet arrived, and that we were fully competent to eliminate these reasons and be the builders of a new world, a free world.

This line of thought of ours was much influenced by living five years in a country where no other opinion was permitted. The written word was so one-sided that unintentionally, people began to agree with it. Human thought became shaped by those who controlled the apparatus and held the power in their hands, and the strongest fell a victim to this.

*   *   *

We still had one day left before our departure. I had already gotten everything ready, so I took a walk to say good-bye to my first acquaintances in Soviet Russia, and with several friends whom I'd had the opportunity to meet through my work. Today they were all great functionaries and occupied important positions in the soviet economy.

It might perhaps seem strange, but it is a fact that all those whom I told that I was leaving Russia the next day not only didn't try to dissuade me, but—some said it openly and some with veiled words— were envious of the possibility to go abroad. Engineer Vershogin, for example, an old Bolshevik, bid me farewell with the words, "Go, brother. We will meet again somewhere over there." Comrade Utin said, "Write, but do it so it doesn't cause me problems. Write that it's bad there and that you regret leaving, and I'll figure out for myself what remains between the lines."

Other of our friends even said that they themselves would like to stay abroad if they had the chance, and to not be so closely tied to the apparatus. This was also said to me, as if he had a premonition, by the then-president of the Bread Trust and old revolutionary, Comrade Lurye[200] (he was shot in 1937—as a German spy).

Lurye had been abroad a few times, but always in an official capacity and couldn't remain there. That is, he could have, only as the old Bolshevik told me, "That would be called treason, and I'm too much of a socialist to do such a thing. If I could leave as you are, with the consent of the authorities and also with legal passports, I would do it."

Lurye was a thoughtful man and a pure idealist, and his high position had not consumed him. He suffered from the state of affairs that had risen around him and was very sad. I asked him how he saw the situation and the prospects moving forward, and with his keen vision, he told me:

"With each day we go downhill; it gets worse, comrade, I feel it at every turn. You should know that the two hundred thousand new Leninists that Stalin brought into the party, and as many again that he has recruited to assist him—they all are prepared for baseness. So now here in the bureau with me is a boy of some twenty years old; he has learned nothing and done nothing, and he goes around shouting at the top of his lungs that we don't need any Bonapartes. 'He should be expelled!' he yells about Trotsky. He is one of the two hundred thousand. They have been convinced that Lev Davidovich[201] wants to be a Bonaparte. Stalin does this, and who knows what it will lead to. If only Davidovich would become a Bonaparte for a little while; he would rescue much for me. However, he is against this and doesn't want a civil war in the party. Perhaps he is right, but at the same time we both know and we sense that the end to all of our dreams is drawing near, and the revolution stands to lose much of her holiness and objectives."

Lurye spoke these words with deep concern, from his heart, and sat lost in his thoughts.

WE SAY GOOD-BYE TO "OUR FAMILY"

Our beloved friend P. had seen to it that our farewell night be accompanied by a tasty bite to eat and a glass of liquor, and he had brought together our

---

200 Moissei Lurye, along with fifteen others, was tried and executed in August 1936 in the "Trial of the Sixteen," one of three Stalin show trials in this time period. Abrams gives the date as 1937.

201 Most likely referring to Leon Trotsky, who was born Lev Davidovich Bronstein.

entire "family." There were also many of our acquaintances and friends who were party members. The evening was unforgettable, filled with kindness, sincerity and devotion, and it became transformed into a discussion about Russia and about the world. Of the difficult present and the concealed future, we abandoned our everyday fears and with frankness everyone, as much the communist party as the non-party members, spoke their minds, words that to me would later on seem like prophecies.

I am incapable of communicating all the things that were said on what was for me an unforgettable Friday, November 16, 1926. With my words of farewell, I was the only optimist. Perhaps for that reason—I was about to leave—it was easier for me to talk that way, and perhaps a resentment had awoken in me that I was forsaking this interesting corner of the earth where with all the hardships, was after all a land full of new life and drive that people like us could find in no other land.

In truth, the pulse of life was a tempestuous one, full of electricity that kept us in suspense. In the hard days and often sleepless nights, in the atmosphere of uncertainty for tomorrow, of not knowing whether one would remain free or must rot in a prison for heresy—each of us yet felt that each day was different, that each week something was accomplished in this giant of a land, a type of thing that would take a long time to be evaluated.

Indeed, when I had to say good-bye I became uneasy. Some sort of new love for this land surfaced in me; I didn't want to believe that I was really saying farewell. It seemed to me that this was only some kind of bad dream. Therefore, in my words were found my guilt that I was abandoning this land. I blamed the fourteen years that I lived in America, the conveniences that I had there, the democratic freedom—all this had resulted in my not being able to endure the hardships that one must go through on the path to a new life.

In my words of leave-taking lay deep anguish. I wept with words and thoughts, why we were this way, and my friends, above all the Bolsheviks, were envious that I still had the deep conviction in a more beautiful tomorrow.

I didn't know then that my subsequent years would be taken up almost exclusively with the search for economic possibilities to ensure one's physical existence, to continue life for a few more years. I had rather thought that very soon I would be back on the path of an interesting fighter's life, that everywhere it would become better and more beautiful, and that I would soon go back to the land to which I was so strongly attached.

When our farewell concluded, it was already morning. Daylight forced its way through the windows. We turned off the electricity and sang songs in the dark. The mood was nostalgic and sentimental, and each person dusted off the old love affairs of his youth, the pessimism of Lermontov[202] and Andreyev.[203] Each song sung that early morning was soaked with the emotion of past experiences. The more people sang, the more they drank from the strong liquor that the "family" had assembled, and the more they drank, all the more they became sober. Sleep had deserted us. Scattered in different corners, by the light of the new dawning day, each person in a different pose—it gave the appearance of an artist's drawing, chiseled into bluish stone, and that somehow the artist had also succeeded in infusing his masterpiece with a soul, one that wept of the hard nights and sang with the hope of tomorrow.

The train to the Sekezsh border station was scheduled to depart at ten o'clock in the morning. Around nine o'clock, we were all already at the railway terminal; Lurye had also come. He called me off to the side and handed me a small package. "Give this to my daughter in Paris," he told me quietly, "and tell her for my sake, that here there are few such lucky people like yourself."

I looked at his face with astonishment and Lurye said to me, "Don't look so surprised. The entire time you were here, you were far from the Soviet reality and you can still be a romantic. We, the ones on duty, don't know who will be ground between the great millstones driven by the crude millers that now stand at the helm."

We shook hands firmly and I had a strange feeling, one that was hard for me to express, unsure if it was satisfaction or dissatisfaction. Accompanied by warm wishes from all our friends, we boarded the train.

WITH LOST HOPES, LEAVING THE GARDEN OF PARADISE

We arrived at the border late at night, the same border that five years ago I arrived at with so many visions and hopes. No matter how happy I was that I had left in time, a feeling of resentment also gnawed at me. This time the procedure at the border didn't interest me. We automatically followed all the demands of the inspectors, my mind occupied with reflections of the last five years.

---

202 Mikhail Yuryevich Lermontov: Russian Romantic writer, poet and painter.
203 Leonid Nikolaievich Andreyev: Russian playwright, novelist and short-story writer.

It was first here, at the same Sekezsh[204] station, how many hopes and beautiful dreams I had had—and today all was lost, broken, that conviction disappeared, those shining ideals. I entered the train and stuck myself in a corner. In my mind flew a jumble of the days and years spent in the new Russia that I had just now left—and the wheels of the train accompanied my thoughts: five years, five years ...

---

204 Spelled here as "Sekerzsh."

Portraits

The Rebel Berkman

I read in the news that the great Jewish anarchist Alexander Berkman committed suicide because of unbearable physical pain. How cruel these words sound in the daily press, and how lightly it is assessed. The reasons for the death of the great rebel, Berkman, the symbol of courage and struggle; the one that knew no fear; the one that—the more he suffered, all the more burned his courageous flame for the fight; the faithful soldier of the workers' army that with love conducted the fight for deliverance and for a better and more beautiful world. Behold, the great rebel is dead from a bullet put there by his own hand, not because of physical pain as is told in the colorless, cold press, but for much deeper reasons. Rather, this might have been the last protest from the courageous revolutionary against a world of violence.

Who is Alexander Berkman?

I worked together with him for a total of twelve years. I saw him at his home as a good, dear companion and a devoted friend. I saw him on the battlefield with his courageous gusto for the struggle, and with his unflinching spirit of enterprise. For us younger ones, Berkman was the symbol of the struggle and the strict general of honesty and courage.

Full of hope, in 1890 the young Russian revolutionary Berkman came to the land of the "free and the brave," to America.

Before he had even learned the national language very well, he threw himself with all his might into the movement. To him, the economic pressure in the States was even more pitiless than the political despotism in Russia.

In 1892, the famous Pennsylvania Steel Strike[205] breaks out. Frick, the director of the company, stops at nothing to break the strike. The area becomes inundated with thugs and hired police. A bloody struggle rages between both camps. Seven workers are murdered and scores of others injured. Berkman then goes to the battlefield and throws himself into the fight. He shoots the company director, Frick, who is guilty of the spilled blood of the workers. He is arrested and after a few days of a staged trial, is sentenced to twenty years in prison. For thirteen years and ten months, Berkman rots in the penal

---

205   Also known as the Homestead Steel Strike, taking place at the Homestead Steel Works in Pittsburgh, PA.

prison.[206] Yet the iron grates and stone walls are incapable of breaking his even more iron courage. In 1906, Berkman graduates from the University of Hard Knocks, coming out more courageous and stronger than ever. He writes a book of several hundred pages about his life in prison that is a literary masterpiece.[207] To date, the book has been translated into all the European languages and occupies a place among the classic works.

New paths and opportunities open for Berkman in the emerging country of America, but Berkman is not one to exploit them. Berkman again takes up his place among the working masses, participating in all the struggles of his class, and is once again arrested every Monday and Thursday.

In 1916, war hysteria breaks out in America. Berkman interjects himself with all his fervor into the war against war. An enormous patriotic war parade is held in San Francisco. Provocateurs' hands explode a bomb and the reactionary elements use the opportunity to get even with the faithful labor activists.[208] Five labor representatives are arrested: Tom Mooney, Billings, Regina Mooney, Nolan and Weinberg. [209] Billings is quickly sentenced to life imprisonment and accompanied by war hysteria, preparations begin for the Mooney trial. No one dares to oppose the gangsters of the San Francisco Chamber of Commerce. Berkman, forever unflinching, takes on the fight, visits all the professional unions and labor organizations, creates defense committees, and brings the crimes of the trade chamber to the arena of public opinion. The remaining three: Nolan, Weinberg and Regina Mooney, are freed and not tried. The dirty work becomes exposed and therefore revenge is sought against Berkman. At the suggestion of the lynch institute, Berkman is accused of no more and no less than tossing the bomb. Two agents and a district attorney come to New York to take Berkman to San Francisco. However, thanks to the powerful labor movement that convened a conference

---

206 Now the State Correctional Institution in Pittsburgh, historically known as the "Western Penitentiary."

207 *Prison Memoirs of an Anarchist*, Berkman's account of his experience in prison from 1892 to 1906, was first published by Emma Goldman's *Mother Earth* press in 1912 and is considered as a classic in autobiographical literature.

208 July 22, 1916: a suitcase bomb exploded during the pro-war San Francisco Preparedness Day Parade, killing ten people and wounding 40.

209 Charged with murder were Tom and Rena Mooney, Warren Billings, Israel Weinberg, and Ed Nolan (current records give Money's wife's name as Rena).

of seventy delegates who represent over a million organized workers, Governor Smith is convinced not to hand Berkman over into the hands of the San Francisco lynch mob. At the same time, American war planning is already well underway. Berkman is released and returns to the struggle against the war, for which he is arrested; the courageous rebel decides to use the courtroom as a platform against the war. He refuses an attorney and for the two weeks of his trial, the courtroom is transformed into a stage for propaganda against war. Berkman is sentenced to two years imprisonment and expulsion from the country.

Of the over thirty years that Berkman lived in the United States, some twenty of them were spent in prisons.

Berkman is expelled and a new chapter in his life begins. He arrives in Soviet Russia in 1920, during the bitter years of the civil war. The momentum of the revolution that demands so many innocent victims falls heavy on Berkman. The spirit of freedom in him cannot become accustomed to it, and he arrives in Germany. There, fascist winds are howling. Berkman is persecuted and settles in France. He becomes active, which is not to the taste of the French reactionary forces and he is told to leave the country. He secludes himself somewhere in a small corner of France and lives illegally. Then, every three months, the progressive world works to secure a permit for him to stay longer.

The great rebel becomes physically sick and broken down, although spiritually he is the same giant as before. Precisely because he is such, seeing that he has no choice but to remain sitting in hiding with his hands tied during that turbulent period of violence and fascism—he decides to commit suicide.

His cup had become overfull and when he was compelled to do it, he did it in his courageous way: better to die like a lion than live and be helpless.

We do not weep for those who die; great spirits live for us for eternity. For us, Berkman is not dead. He has left his body, but his intellectual courage is left for us as an inheritance.

(*The Times*,[210] Mexico, 11 July 1936)

---

210 Yiddish: *Di Tsayt*, the first Yiddish newspaper in Mexico.

Vera Figner

Such a wonderful person was this woman who had gone through so much: she spent a quarter of a century in the Shlisselburg fortress and was in exile for many years, yet she lived to see a long life. Vera Figner was ninety years old when she died, further confirming the true statement that great spirits place themselves in healthy bodies.

Vera Figner, the daughter of a wealthy Russian family, went to Switzerland as a young girl to complete her education. It was at a time when the absolutism in Russia was raging with an iron hand. It was also then that the Russian intelligentsia was strongly influenced by the French revolution of 1848, and by great writers and thinkers such as Gedtsen, Radishchev, Pisarev and still more men with ample souls and open hearts, who put their pens in service to the liberation of the Russian people. Vera Figner, the young and enthusiastic student, drinks from the great spring and becomes saturated with hate for imperial despotism, and with love for the tens of millions who are being tortured. She becomes an activist with the liberation movement known by the name "The Peoples' Will."[211] She returned to Russia and began working fervently for the liberation of the people; she fought, encouraged, suffered and paid with decades in prison. She spent twenty years just in the Shlisselburg fortress, and the memoirs that she wrote in her iron cell later became the classic work of revolutionary memoirs.[212]

Vera Figner cannot be ascribed to any one particular school of socialist thought. She was of that type of revolutionary spirit from the pioneering movement of the Russian revolution, that never selected any particular direction. To a certain degree she can be thought of as an adherent of the Lavrov movement,[213] social revolutionaries with whom the Russian intelligentsia became fascinated at the turn of the century. Vera Figner was a forerunner of the entire liberation movement.

---

211 Russian: Narodnaya Volya, a late 19th century Russian revolutionary left-wing organization that carried out the assassination of Tsar Alexander II.
212 *Memoirs of a Revolutionist.*
213 Movement founded by Pyotr Lavrovich Lavrov, a prominent Russian philosopher and sociologist.

The Grandmother Breshkovskaye[214] once said that her cold attitude towards the Bolshevist revolution came from the fact that she was never a socialist. I am, she said, a fighter for a free Russia and I have carried out my propaganda among the great peasant masses, wanting to liberate them from despotism and give them the possibility to choose for themselves the shape of their order, one that they should be able to freely develop, and lead a new life.

Vera Figner was also this kind of fighter: she took herself deep within the enslaved social classes and along with her father, taught them how to fight and how to create a new Russia.

If fighters for a free and socialist world lacked faith and conviction, they would not be able to carry on the struggle. Indeed, firm belief creates the willingness to make sacrifices and be martyred in the struggle for this very belief. When one is young and one's sense of justice develops, then each word, each call and each written tract—is sacred. The personalities that wrote it become transformed into divine figures, and the dream of a revolutionary is to become one of them. All the sufferings, iron chains, and difficult years in prison become a necessity and purification for those fighters worthy of bearing the name "revolutionary."

For many years, Vera Figner was a figure of inspiration for the young revolutionaries of Russia: not the dry political literature, but the living spirit of the Figners, Zasuliches, Breshkovskayes, Kalayevs, Sazonovs, etc.—they were the apostles of the great liberation school of thought. Following their example, thousands and thousands went singing to exile in far Siberia and filled the Russian prisons.

After October 1917, many of the great spirits and fighters who had endured the knouts of imperialism were already old and didn't have the physical capabilities to participate with those realizing the ideal of a free Russia. So it was also with Vera Figner, but she still maintained her rebellious and militant nature.

On the second anniversary of the death of the famous anarchist theorist Pyotr Kropotkin, I was present at an evening event in Moscow. One of the speakers was Vera Figner. It took place at the house where the great Kropotkin

---

214 Catherine Breshkovsky: a Russian socialist known as the Babushka (grandmother) of the Russian Revolution.

was born and after the revolution, the house was converted into a museum. The street also bore the name of the deceased theorist.

For me, it was one of my most beautiful experiences, and a great good fortune to be able to celebrate the anniversary of a teacher in such a place and among others who were the pure spirits for my generation during the visionary years, and to listen to the famous Vera Figner speak. It was a moment of sacred intellectual exaltation, an event that made one forget all the cold calculations and remember that only the Figners and Kropotkins and their like were capable of leading everyone's struggle, and to bear themselves the thorny wreath that the fight against violence and crime had placed on their heads.

There were five to six dozen people in the small hall, among them the old fighter Morozov who had spent more than two decades in the Shlisselburg fortress; the eighty-year old Ashenbrenner who had taken part in the French revolution of 1871; Leon Deutsch, the first translator of Marxism into Russian; and many other famous prisoners of the past generation.

Of all the speakers on that unforgettable evening, the one that interested me the most was Vera Figner. She was already a woman in her seventies, but her appearance brought back memories of the picture of her youth: a slim figure, a black dress with a white collar, hair combed smooth with a part—a dreamlike glance, but with wrinkles on her face. I looked at her for a long time, and a shudder ran through me hearing that in the course of the splendid years that she had experienced, something in her great soul had changed. She spoke very quietly. Her health was already deteriorating and her pronunciation wasn't completely clear, but in return her thoughts were lucid.

That which others dared not say, Vera Figner said. She stressed the hardships of the reality and with the same audacity as in her youth, made a reckoning of the journey thus far, sharply characterizing the events with which she was unhappy. She had not lost her courage and still expressed her deep conviction in tomorrow, but at the same time articulated her disappointment. Vera Figner emphasized that what she had fought for would not yet arrive so quickly; that man was still far from understanding that freedom was not a luxury, but a necessity; and that yesterday's ruler is today's slave and that the former slave becomes the same ruler as the latter: oftentimes out of fear of returning to slavery, he becomes a despot.

This was not an expression of disappointment but an allusion to reassess values, to point out that one must not be too sure of himself or of people, and to not think that from today to tomorrow, man can be changed.

In later years when Vera Figner was already approaching her eighties, there was news that despite her old age, she was alert and in good spirits, still protesting against injustice. She took a stand against persecution and having no possibility to advocate through the press, she took it directly to the lead personalities that were allowing themselves the pleasure of becoming modern despots. A few years later, it was heard that the old Vera Figner once more lived in the far-off, cold Siberia—but those who considered her struggle as holy nevertheless did not forget her and from time to time, she had the opportunity to bring her thoughts and opinions before the highest officials of the new order. Disappointed in human behavior or in the chance of a quicker release, she nevertheless had no patience for injustice and protested, being prepared to take on herself the greatest of punishments.

Vera Figner was a bearer of justice, and the expression and embodiment of protest. She was the Prometheus of the Russian revolutionary movement until the last minute of her physical existence.

Little is known of the last years of her long life; it is not known where and how she spent her last days, and whether she had had the opportunity to leave something written about her thoughts during the last quarter century. The report about her death did not clearly say where the place was that for eternity, she had closed her idealist's eyes.

With the death of Vera Figner, an epoch ended in the global revolutionary fight. She was one of the first that made contact with the broad population of Russian people, and awakened in them their consciousness, preparing the soil for the destruction of imperialism. She was one of those who plowed up the terrain of the hard Russian earth and thanks to her activity, new sprouts began growing on the vast fields and steppes of the immense Russia. She had contributed two-thirds of her gloriously rich life to the hundred-year struggle against despotism, and she was nearly the only one in its history with such a rich revolutionary balance sheet.

Vera Figner's spirit still remains alive; it will never be extinguished. The hundreds, thousands and millions that fight on the battlefields against fascism are not inspired by dreary politicians—rather, in them one finds the holy objective and freedom spirit of the Vera Figners. Moreover, when the great day of liberation comes, the Vera Figners will be honored as the great and true spirits of the new human race, as those who paved the way for a better world. Songs will be sung at the graves of the people that inspired the world and led humanity to freedom.

(*The Voice*, Mexico, 27 July 1942)

Otto and Alice Rühle

Otto and Alice Rühle [215] fought for all the years of their adult life so that no one, no matter who he is or in whose name and banner he speaks, has the right to hurt another; that no one has the right to allow someone else to go hungry or to cause suffering, not to mention taking away his life.

At the end of 1935, when I was traveling back to Mexico after a visit to Europe on the ship Meksik, I became acquainted with that great person, Professor Otto Rühle. Since then, and even later when his wife Alice also came here, we kept up a close friendship. I studied the humanitarian for more than seven years and no matter how many times we met, I never heard him complain about his personal situation—and his economic situation was very dire.

Otto Rühle devoted more than fifty years of his life to socialist thought and struggle. He fought for half a century so that the human race would become better, live better, and be happier. In 1914, he was the second one in the German Reichstag, together with Karl Liebknecht, to vote against the war budget, and from the platform of the parliament he carried on a fight against bloodshed and German militarism. Karl Liebknecht, Rosa Luxemburg and Otto Rühle were the founders of the Spartacus movement,[216] which had sought to create a different Germany some twenty years ago.

In 1920, Otto Rühle traveled to Russia to meet with his international friends from years ago, Lenin and Trotsky. At that time, he pointed out to Lenin the peril of dictatorship. Then, not like now, Lenin polemicized against Rühle in a pamphlet, accusing him of Leftism and of not wanting to understand the necessity of dictatorship. Yet Otto Rühle, with true vision realized that dictatorship must lead to domination by one person.

Otto Rühle came to Mexico as an invitee of the Education Department to prepare pedagogical norms for the socialist education in the schools. In this area of knowledge, he was known in Western Europe as an esteemed specialist, and he himself had created a library for children's education, having written thirty-four volumes on educational topics.

---

215 Otto Rühle: German Marxist active in opposition to both the First and Second World Wars, and a co-founder of the Spartacus League.

216 Spartacus League (German: *Spartakusbund*): a Marxist revolutionary movement organized in Germany during World War I, named after Spartacus, leader of the largest slave rebellion of ancient Rome.

Rühle's coming to Mexico was a great win for Mexico; his salary was very modest, but it gave him the chance to work peacefully here and in his free time, to write political works.

Just before this time, Trotsky had come to Mexico seeking asylum. Rühle had broken with Trotsky over his stance on dictatorship and oftentimes when he met with Trotsky here, would remind him that he was a victim of his own creation. Yet it is one thing to be political opponents and another to be political charlatans: the latter accused Trotsky, their former idol, of aiding the Nazis, of being a Gestapo agent, of sabotage and what else? Naturally Rühle, with his complete opposition to Trotsky's political position, could not tolerate such accusations and when a commission headed by the renowned Professor John Dewey[217] arrived from America to investigate whether these accusations against Lenin's former friend were based on any evidence, Otto Rühle agreed to be one of the judges. As is known, the commission ruled that the accusations were false and were merely a fraudulent means to take down an opponent. Otto Rühle signed the committee declaration with a clean conscience.

At that time the Education Ministry was influenced by the Mexican Stalinists and in a well-known manner, they consequently began intriguing against the old fighter and great pedagogue, Otto Rühle. It didn't take long before the pedagogue who had been invited in, was then pushed out of his position in the Education Ministry, and he lost his living.

It is true that this incident had a deep impact on Otto Rühle, but not because he had lost his daily bread; rather, what concerned him was that lies, dishonesty and base motives by human dregs were able to control the Education Department, which was itself dedicated for such noble tasks. The fact was, however, that in his old age, Otto Rühle had no means to earn a living. At the same time, he was of that proud nature that refuses to accept any help.

Rühle was endowed with a talent—painting. He began painting small pictures of the Mexican genre (Moyshe Rubenshteyn's book *Mexican Subjects* is decorated with them). Alice, his wife, who was also a well-known writer

---

217 March 1937: The Dewey Commission (*Commission of Inquiry into the Charges Made against Leon Trotsky in the Moscow Trials*) conducted hearings at Trotsky's home in Mexico, ultimately clearing him of all charges.

and together with her aging husband shared his life and pitfalls—she would go around with the paintings to the businesses and sell them for a few meager cents. Alice would also do translations and write articles for American journals; the pair of intellectuals could scarcely make ends meet.

The final years Otto Rühle felt desperate, as never before. He was already nearly seventy, physically weak and in addition, terribly disappointed in seeing what was going on in the world. The old fighter would speak with bitterness about how the so-called democrats must be the saviors of humanity and those that should have been the masters of the world, he would say, were so defrauded by their parties and governments that they no longer had any trust in anything; instead of becoming masters, they would remain as slaves.

It became hard for Otto Rühle to continue living. He was disappointed in everyone and everything, and his mental breakdown also left him physically crushed. His devoted life companion Alice had an interest in life just to the extent that she could help him, and fight along with him in his struggle.

We are myopic people. We didn't even notice how a great change had come over the two spirited fighters. We would meet, talk, learn from them how one should evaluate people and events, and at the same time we neglected the great couple toward whom we had such a duty. They were among those whose merit held up the world, and we overlooked them. They probably in silence sensed this and found it hard to bear. Nonetheless, they had no complaints against anyone because the matter concerned their personal welfare, and their personal pride was so great that they did not request even a sign of compassion.

Now, when these two people have left the world, we must consider that perhaps we bear a share of the guilt in having lost them at a time when we are in need of men of great spirit.

A few days before they both tragically perished, we spoke with the inseparable Rühles. Otto gave not even the smallest sign that he was so ill, that he was on the verge of dying; and Alice, that she was considering suicide. These two, now saints, concerned themselves with each individual person, and with the world situation. Otto Rühle burned with fury when he would speak about the Jewish suffering because of Nazism. He himself was a son of the German people, and he was greatly upset by the dishonor and shame that the Germans were guilty of in such a dismal tragedy. He had his complaints and original arguments for expressing fury against what is taking place in our time.

Otto Rühle had everyone and everything in mind, thought about everything, sought a remedy to all forms of malice—and suddenly died. No, it's hard to believe in his sudden death; rather it was a result of the death of a world that had become so hard for the old fighter that he had begun to be ashamed to be among the living.

(*The Voice*, Mexico, 3 July 1943)

Carlo Tresca

In Mexico Carlo Tresca is known only within the circles of the anarchist-syndicalist movement, but in America his figure and activities are famous.

Carlo came to America from Italy a few decades ago. He came from a well-to-do family, but in his convictions he was an extreme socialist. In America he was involved in the industrial labor movement that in those days was considered to be the idealistic movement. He possessed a sharp pen, and worked for the organization's publications. With his word and deed, he was of great benefit to the struggle against the appetites of the magnates to swallow up all the good of the world for themselves. He was one of those in charge of the defense of Sacco and Vanzetti—the two martyrs who were incinerated in the electric chair in 1927. He was arrested several times himself for his activities. During the First World War he stood against the bloodshed, and when thousands were arrested he worked tirelessly for their defense, finding a means for all without regard to their beliefs.

Carlo was a man with realistic expectations: he did not engage in political quibbles and had no use for hair-splitting theories. When fascism came to power in Italy, he correctly saw the danger for other countries as well, and dedicated himself to the fight against fascism, the significance of which others had not yet wanted to acknowledge. He was a person who held the ideals of freedom above all else, and was a fighter against every kind of dictatorship and also against communism. In later years after Hitler came to power and the shadow of war appeared, Tresca carried out a fight against Nazism with the same passion.

While the war of nerves went on and in America Roosevelt began speaking of perilous times approaching, Tresca was the first in the revolutionary camps who held the opinion that in the end, all the democratic countries would have to draw their swords.

Tresca was a man for whom the personal played no role, and he had many opponents who personally liked and respected him. His wife left him due to political differences of opinion, although there was a strong personal affection between them. Tresca, however, was not the kind of person who would give up his ideas for the sake of personal happiness. He remained alone in his later years, but nothing stopped him from continuing to carry out his struggle against wrongdoing and to preach a just and free order for the world.

Tresca had many enemies and it was hard to say by whom, or from what direction he was taken out. Tresca had opponents among the small groups of anti-war socialists, but deep in their hearts they certainly esteemed that he did his work so courageously. He was detested by the communists because he had once exposed the story behind Miss Poyntz, who supposedly was dragged away by Shachno Epstein for straying from the party line.[218] He then received epithets of the familiar lexicon. The matter, like many others, was with time and through diplomacy—of course forgotten, but certainly Tresca and his struggle for a decent life has not been forgotten. His worst enemies, however, were among the Nazis and fascists, who had lain in wait for him for years. They wrote him anonymous letters that they wanted to kill him, he was constantly threatened, and for a short time he carried around a revolver to defend himself against an attack. This became distasteful to him though and he stopped being so careful; his fight against injustice, he did not give up.

Now comes the news that someone, one of those who had threatened him, had carried out their threat—but who, no one knows, and who knows if it will ever be discovered. It was without a doubt a well-prepared political assassination.

With the death of Carlo Tresca, humanity's fight for freedom lost one of its sincerest friends and most courageous fighters, one whose tragic martyr's death will be long remembered. That which Carlo Tresca sowed in America, the cadre of fighters against every type of oppression and dictatorship will bear fruit and assist in creating something better in place of our intolerant and bloody world.

All honor to the memory of the great Tresca.

(*The Voice*, Mexico, 18 January 1943)

---

218 Juliet Stuart Poyntz: American communist and intelligence agent for the Soviet Union who disappeared in New York City in 1937 with the complicity of her former lover Shachno Epstein.

Clara Green

Clara and Walter Green, who swam up to the shores of Mexico, were nearly among the last who escaped the bloody regime of Hitler. Two young people still in their student years, they had already written down many glorious pages in the history of the courageous fight for a more just world.

Clara had a small build, dark skin and large, dark eyes. She had a face that at first glance immediately told the secret of the rich soul that lived in such a little body.

Clara grew up as a child of poor working parents in the large city of Vienna, where poverty had a place of honor in the labor circles. Yet being a child with extraordinary abilities, with the soul of a saint and the brains of a genius—Clara succeeded, despite her poverty, to finish a medical course. The arrival of Hitler's regime in Austria robbed her of the opportunity to receive her diploma, three months before she would have gotten it.

When Clara was not yet fourteen years old, she was already a member of the underground movement, fighting against the Nazi fascism. Throughout her student years she was part of the socialist military movement.

When Hitler entered Vienna, the tiny Clara became even more dynamic and militant. Her great spirit was the energy behind her fight against the bloody dog Hitler. She is arrested; by a miracle she escapes from Austria and goes to France, where with the same fervor she continues her fight against the Nazis. Thanks to her huge abilities and her love of study, she quickly masters the French language and becomes a child educator.

In 1940, Hitler seizes Paris. At that moment, Clara is at an OZE[219] school with a class of fifteen tiny babies. There is a great panic in France and a terrifying stampede begins. Clara, their educator, then becomes also the mother of the tiny children. She takes them under her protection, doesn't leave them alone for a minute, and marches with them from village to village looking for sanctuary for her little ones. With toil, suffering and tears, she finally finds a place for her small family. Only then does she begin looking for a way out for herself.

---

219 Russian acronym (Obschestvo zdravookhraneniia evreev): organization devoted to the promotion of health, hygiene, and childcare among Jews. OZE's founders wished to compensate for the social and legal discrimination against Jews, to address those health conditions and hereditary illnesses specifically affecting Jews, and to give proper consideration to Jewish religious and ethnic traditions. OZE, now based in Paris, is known as OSE (Oeuvre de Secours aux Enfants) World Union.

In the scant seven years of her being in Mexico, Clara (we called her Clarita) first learned the national language. She also learned English and greatly improved her Yiddish, which she had already been taught by her mother.

Like every new immigrant, Clara struggled mightily just to survive. Yet she never forgot that outside of her still lived a world that lay in the hands of political charlatans—a world that writhed in convulsions and in which no one was sure what tomorrow will bring. Clara maintains her traditions, fights, and dreams about an order in which each person enjoys from life whatever nature has intended for him. It wasn't long before Clara becomes the darling of everyone who comes in contact with her. To everyone she is a dear friend, and to all she demonstrates motherly feelings. All the refugees: German Jews, French, Spanish and Mexican—they all feel happy in Clarita's presence.

Clara has only one task: she always looks for whoever is in need. Thanks to her boundless, exuberant energy, she begins to earn a good living; however, she converts her earnings into packages that she sends to those who are destitute on the other side of the ocean, for whom she has only an address.

The dear Clarita works as an employee in a business; her evenings are spent at meetings. From France she brings a foreign child that comes from a family who during the dark days of Hitlerism, had rescued the children that Clara had brought to them. She puts the child in the best private school and becomes the child's friend and mother.

Later, a victim of Spanish fascism comes to Mexico— he is sick, paralyzed and cannot feed himself. Who else but Clara would commit to taking care of the invalid? She takes him in and is a sister to him for many months, until he can be put in a sanitarium.

Who could possibly undertake to list all that Clara was able to accomplish? Who then, is capable enough to write down the description of the life of the remarkable Clarita, about her rare noble character, about the indescribable sensitivity of her soul and about her limitless love for her fellow man?

The twenty-seventh of September, 1948, in the little town of Tuxpan, Veracruz, the big-hearted Clara died, giving up her life to save another. She jumped into a river to rescue someone who was drowning. She saved him, but she herself died of a heart attack. Clara died, as she lived.

(*Bulletin*, Mexico, November 1948)

Last Words and Thoughts

Abrams went through distressing days and nights when he found out that because of the serious illness of his throat, he was in danger of losing his ability to speak. There remains in the possession of Mary Abrams a series of pages containing the moods and feelings that Abrams expressed on paper, as if he wanted the pen to be converted into a tongue. Below follow some of his emotions, recorded by J. Abrams— as a conclusion to The J. Abrams Book.

* * *

Dusk. Quiet. Am I waiting for someone? No and Yes.

Later on, when the acquaintances will finish up with their businesses, several of them will, probably out of courtesy, drop by to look in on the friend to whom the doctors have ordered that he will end up a mute ...

A shiver goes through my entire body! A beautiful future? ...

... Today is an important day for me. Today the doctors will meet together for a consultation: the "four bigshots" will talk together and establish what should be done in the case of my wretched disease of the throat.

Their opinions, as I know from the doctors' visits, are varied: one believes that a complete operation must be done; that is, for me to return to health, I must lose my speech ...

You understand what that means? To lose my ability to speak. What else do I have? After all, this means to lose my entire mental being! What else do I have? Wealth? The fact is that I am struggling for a grip on life, and the entire meaning of life is to express my thoughts. If I can't even do this, then what reason is there to continue living?

I heard a remark that after all, I don't need to be an orator. It should have been a consolation, but it cut to the quick. I don't care about oratories, rather simply in the possibility to talk together with people, to express my thoughts and defend them—and the prospect is—not to be able to speak?!

—How will I not be able to speak—and live?!

A friend visits me at home, an intellectual. We talk about my situation and the calamity that has befallen me. I am pleased to speak with a cultured person and hear a word of encouragement. The conversation now turns to whether I will be able to speak after the operation on my throat—and I remark that there is a method to teach yourself to speak with the stomach.

My interlocutor doesn't restrain himself and laughs—he'd like to hear how I would be able to speak with my stomach, he says.

It is a painful moment for me. I'm looking for support and this guy speaks so lightly and jokingly. Inside, I'm irritated, and I don't talk anymore. When my guest speaks, goes on and on about his business and his plans in which I have no interest, Mary sees my situation and asks him, does he have any more important subjects for this conversation, which is such an ordeal for me.

My guest is embarrassed. He stays for another minute and then decides it's already time for him to go. — — —

... Today will be the consultation of the four doctors. It's already decided about the operation, but the physicians want to ascertain what the possibility is that I will still have my tongue or that I will be left mute, not being able to speak.

I have delayed the operation a couple of weeks, truly because of the terrifying prospect—not being able to speak! I wanted to hear another opinion and more advice, from ordinary people and from doctors. I was, like never before, agitated and unsure about tomorrow.

Several of them spoke with regret and couldn't give any advice. Others were completely carefree and even reproached me with a smile—why don't I let the doctors do as they see fit.

Well, today is the consultation. I met earlier with a couple of the doctors and wanted them to understand my viewpoint and realize what it means for a human being to be left totally mute. I entreated them to think it over carefully, and go ahead with the operation only as a last resort.

The lead doctor told me that based on the course of my illness, I could remain an invalid and be useless, or the operation could give me the possibility to be useful for many more years to my family and to society.

Whether I would be able to speak after the operation—the doctor didn't say. I was supposed to understand what that meant. I didn't answer; I felt as if I already no longer spoke.

... Alone, I sit pensively. My thoughts fly by, soaring in the air. Different episodes of my life rise from memory, evoking pleasant recollections. Now it becomes easier for me, and then now harder.

A great human tragedy is unveiled before me—the tragedy of the world-famous fighter for women's and human rights: Emma Goldman. In her turbulent life, the dynamic and enchanting Emma Goldman had experienced prisons and persecutions, yet she continued on with her fight with holy perseverance.

One time when Emma Goldman was appearing on stage for a lecture in Canada, in the middle of her speech she became paralyzed. Now the woman who had made a name for herself with her steely character, whose words had inspired the tens of thousands of people listening to them—she, Emma Goldman, was paralyzed!

I recall that Emma Goldman lay paralyzed for two years, and dark thoughts seize my brain. I use all my strength to pull myself together and console myself with the thought that in life there are many tragic events, and one must be able to control oneself and not give in to them.

How immense are the tragedies of those wounded in a war? The war is given a patriotic celebration, but millions of people perish and others return home mutilated, with shot-off limbs, blind, lame and also mute …

It occurs to me: a young soldier returns from the war, wounded in the throat; he is treated and discharged, but he can no longer speak. He is dumb. He comes home and great is the joy of his parents, friends and companions—he has come back home alive!

Everyone has forgotten the enormous tragedy of his muteness—or everyone acts as if he had. — — —

*   *   *

I sit alone in the house. The doctor has come and gone. He threw in a few words about the inevitability of the operation. I reflect on his words. I understand the situation, but it is hard for me to grasp what awaits me. I struggle to stay calm—and it seems—I am crying! But no; for whose misfortune should I weep? For mine, or for that of the many tragedies that play out for millions of people, tragedies that have already happened, and those that are yet to come?

I continue sitting and am ashamed of my thoughts.

Yes, I have a will to live! With all my senses, I now feel an intense desire for life.

Yet one should be able to live, create and fight—even when something physical is missing. — — —

J. Abrams during the last months of his life, while he was in the hospital

Cover over the grave of J. Abrams, which is often visited and covered with flowers by his eternally faithful Mary

The inscription on the headstone reads:
Jacob Abrams—born the 24th of January 1886—died the 10th of June 1953—
Fought passionately for human rights, tolerance, and freedom.

www.ingramcontent.com/pod-product-compliance
Lightning Source LLC
Chambersburg PA
CBHW021119300426
44113CB00006B/212